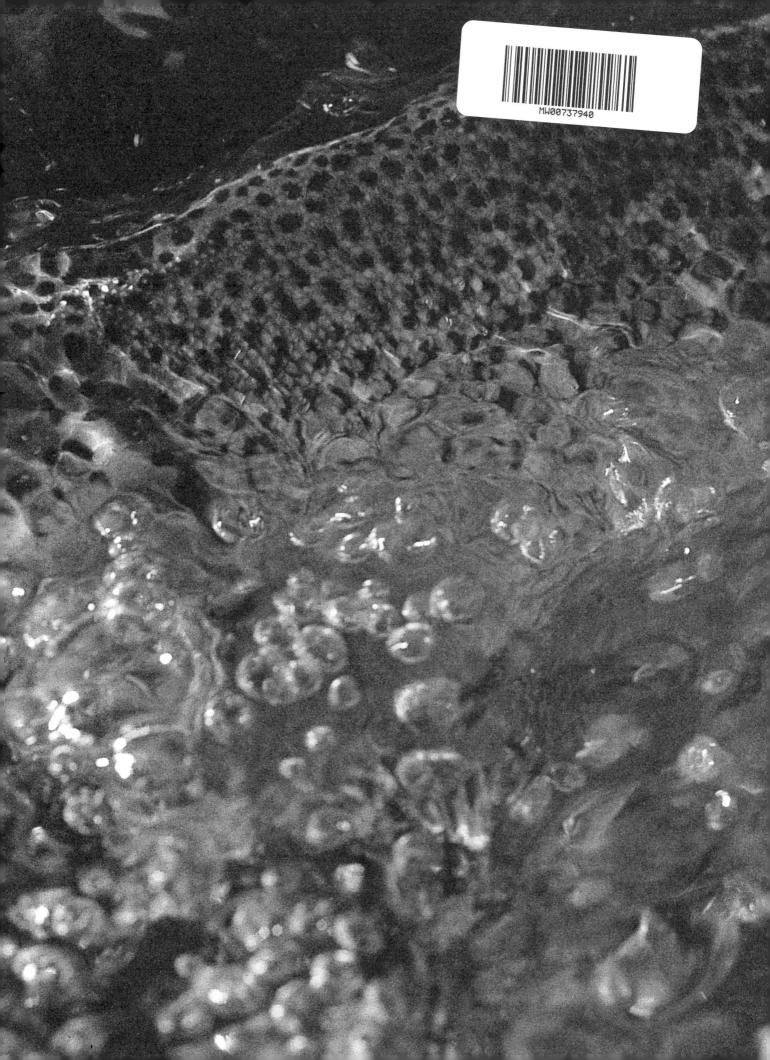

The South African
FLY✦FISHING
H A N D B O O K

The South African
FLY-FISHING
H A N D B O O K

DEDICATION

To my late father, John.

Author's note: In the interests of conservation and the promotion of trophy
fly-fishing in South Africa, all fish pictured within the pages of this book were released.

First published in 1998 by
New Holland Publishers (UK) Ltd
London • Cape Town • Sydney • Auckland

24 Nutford Place
London W1H 6DQ
United Kingdom

80 McKenzie Street
Cape Town 8001
South Africa

14 Aquatic Drive
Frenchs Forest, NSW 2086
Australia

Editor Sally D. Rutherford
Designer Peter Bosman
Cover design Peter Bosman
Illustrator Peter Stewart
Reproduction Hirt & Carter Cape (Pty) Ltd
Printing and binding Times Offset (M) Sdn Bhd

2 4 6 8 10 9 7 5 3 1

ISBN 1 85974 101 0

Front cover: *Dean Riphagen pictured with a double-figure rainbow from a lake near Underberg.*
Pages 18–19: *Dean Riphagen nymphing a slow run on the spectacular Boarman's Chase section of the upper Bell River.*
Pages 38–39: *Well-known Rhodes fly-fishing guide Fred Steynberg nymphs the Park Gate section of the Bell River above Rhodes.*
Pages 62–63: *Fred Steynberg battles a hefty rainbow on New Zealand's magnificent Clinton River.*
Pages 86–87: *A Mount Arthur rainbow, hooked by Mike Somerville on a Flashback Nymph, puts up a spirited battle.*
Pages 100–101: *Bill Sharp drifts a dry fly through a run on the upper reaches of the tiny Riflespruit in the north-eastern Cape.*
Pages 126–127: *Lessons learnt trout fishing in New Zealand are invaluable to all fly-fishers; here professional fly-fishing
guide Frank Schlosser and a client make their way carefully upstream on New Zealand's breathtaking Ahuriri River.*
Pages 144–145: *Dean Riphagen explores the upper reaches of a crystal-clear stream in the north-eastern Cape.*
Pages 172–173: *The lower Elandspad River in Du Toit's Kloof Pass offers interesting riffle and pocket-water angling.*

Acknowledgements

ANY BOOK ABOUT FLY-FISHING is, in some way or another, a team effort. This book is no exception. While many people have contributed to the finished product, certain individuals deserve special mention for their efforts in helping to turn my dream of publishing a fly-fishing handbook into a reality.

I am especially grateful to Tom Sutcliffe for the effort he devoted towards the completion of this book. In particular, I would like to thank Tom for the many hours he spent proofreading the original manuscript and subsequent drafts, as well as for writing the Foreword. Tom was always willing to give assistance on all aspects of the text, too numerous to mention here, and to him I will be eternally indebted.

I am also deeply grateful to Gerry Mulford of Whitecliffs Photographics in Randburg, Johannesburg, and to my very good friends, Roland Walker and Michael Somerville, who unselfishly gave up many hours of their valuable time to help with the photography of the step-by-step tying sequences. Only they can truly appreciate the many hours it took to obtain the correct lighting levels and to complete all the photographic sequences required. I also would like to thank Michael Somerville and Fanie Kriel for the use of the Nikon camera equipment which they very kindly made available to me for the photography of the tying sequences.

My sincerest thanks also to my very talented friend, Peter Stewart, who spent many hours of his time completing the superb line-drawings. As a part-time fly-fisherman, he was able to turn my ideas into the beautiful illustrations that grace the pages of this book.

Several other anglers, fly-tiers and entomologists also made valuable contributions with regard to fly patterns, fishing techniques and aspects of entomology, and I would like to extend my sincerest gratitude to all those who gave up their time to assist me in my research: Dr Ferdy de Moor and Helen James of the Albany Museum in Grahamstown for their assistance in acquiring much-needed information regarding certain Western Cape and KwaZulu-Natal mayflies, and Dr Tanza Clarke, the Curator of Invertebrates at the Durban Natural Science Museum for the many hours she devoted to proofreading the sections of this book related to aquatic entomology. She is a mine of information and was always ready to assist with all my queries.

Thank you to Neil Hodges who has the finest collection of aquatic insect photographs of any fly-fisherman I know in this country, and who without hesitation allowed me to use them for this book. Neil was always willing to assist with photographic aspects and his enthusiasm was a contributing factor in the final outcome of this book.

I would like to thank Tom Sutcliffe, Terry Andrews, Michael Somerville, Tom Lewin, Ed Herbst, Elwin Love and Chris Jones for the use of their fly-fishing photographs.

Thanks to Ed Herbst, South Africa's encyclopedia of fly-fishing, who spent many hours of his valuable spare time proofreading the draft. Thanks also to Dave Rorke, editor of *Flyfishing*, for his editing and proofreading expertise.

I would also like to thank my numerous angling friends, specifically Terry Andrews, Tom Lewin and Mike Somerville, whose companionship has provided me with many years of fishing pleasure. They, more than the fish themselves, have ensured that the time I have spent in the pursuit of trout has been worth every minute.

Finally, thank you to The Struik Publishing Group, and specifically to Linda de Villiers, Sally Rutherford and Peter Bosman, who turned seven years of work into reality.

Contents

Foreword

IN THIS PART OF THE WORLD we have been slow to embrace the great renaissance in fly-fishing which, as Dean Riphagen rightly points out, started overwhelmingly in the United States. It began, I guess, around the early 1960s and peaked in the mid-1980s, and lifted fly-fishing from a mysterious, almost occult art, into a largely scientific pursuit. Happily, the element of artistry has survived this transition and the modern sport is now a keen amalgam of the empirical and the philosophical.

In this country, Dean Riphagen's book is the first work from the new mould of fly-fishing. As far as I am aware, no local book of relevance has preceded it. Certainly, a few local anglers have become disciples of the modern school themselves and have thereby greatly increased their enjoyment of the sport, but for most ordinary mortals who love to catch trout, and particularly for beginners, little has been available to help them through the steep learning curve towards proficiency in modern fly-fishing. The thirst for knowledge exists – in fact, it's a universal trait among fly-fishermen – but appropriate literature on local conditions has, until now, been scarcer than snowballs in Kimberley.

Not that Riphagen sets out to answer all the questions people will ask. He does, in these pages, answer enough to increase the average angler's knowledge by a mile and, even more important, shows us just what waits beyond the doors of 'old-fashioned' fly-fishing for the angler happy to make the most of what is already a very good thing.

It was a steep hill that we climbed back in the 1960s with the likes of Biggs and Beams, Huntley and Hodges, in our search for knowledge and new horizons in fly-fishing. At the time a book like this would have been devoured, would overnight have become our Bible, because it answers most of the questions we were posing back then.

In those early days we were concerned not simply with catching more fish (happily, there are always more than enough user-friendly trout around), but with understanding why we were catching them at all. That, and the endless drive to refine all we were doing – to become super-competent – consumed us. The advent of a book like this in those dark times would have been to us then like the Second Coming of the Lord.

Some might regard Riphagen as too young for such an authoritative work. But his tender years and his boundless enthusiasm about anything even faintly allied to fishing should not be mistaken for inexperience. He is a serious and mature fly-fisherman, skilled beyond his years, long enough at the game to have been tempered by the odd fish that wins, and old enough to realise, I hope, that he is not the universal master he once thought he was. Having said all that, and now hovering close to the ominous prospect of an impending lawsuit, let me hastily add that in fly-fishing circles he is a giant among his peers – regardless of age. He has all the attributes needed to write about trout. In fact his fly-fishing CV is impeccable. But what makes an otherwise good writer a real discovery is the mix of skill, experience and – above all else – genuine enthusiasm.

Dean Riphagen celebrates in the sport of fly-fishing. He is perpetually heady on the twin opiates of rod and line and is knocked unconscious by fins, furs and speckled things. He is, give or take an inch, a mainline fly-fishing junkie, firmly in the league of others of similar ilk I know and fish with, men like Ed Herbst and Mario Cesare, who perpetually hover on the fringes of imminent certification. It's this kind of angler whose writing should make you sit up and take notice.

I'd suggest you read this book with care and with an open mind. If you don't learn from it you are either already professional material or braindead. You might, in terms of your own experience and wisdom, disagree with some of the theories he puts forward in these pages. That is as it should be. But you will be stimulated by his handling of this vast subject and, even more importantly, infected by his boundless enthusiasm to expand and refine the horizons of our sport.

Like the first tentative mayflies that herald the coming of a hatch and with it the promise of exciting fishing, I see in the preparation of this book the promise of great things to come for anglers in South Africa. *The South African Fly-Fishing Handbook* is a milestone in our angling literature and I welcome its appearance.

TOM SUTCLIFFE
1998

Introduction

I WAS INTRODUCED TO FLY-TYING almost 20 years ago when I enrolled in a series of classes at the Westville Hotel with well-known Durban-based fly-fisherman and fly-tier Jack Blackman. In the late 1970s and early 1980s, when I first began to tie my own flies, the only patterns commercially available to South African fly-fishers were traditional patterns such as the Invicta, Connemara Black and similarly styled flies, most of which originated in the United Kingdom. A smattering of local patterns existed, but most were based on patterns from other countries and many did not suit the changing fishing styles and techniques that were beginning to emerge in South Africa in the early 1980s. While the most interesting developments in fishing techniques and fly patterns were taking place in the United States, the flies originating there were designed for that country, particularly with respect to colour and size, and South African fly-fishers remained with a limited number of patterns designed for local conditions and situations.

However, local patterns started changing in the mid-1980s, as anglers switched to more refined fly-fishing methods. For many of them upstream nymphing with a floating line, for example, proved to be a more productive and enjoyable technique than quartering a sinking line downstream. This change in angling style required a corresponding change in fly-pattern choice, and consequently many new and effective flies began to emerge to mimic local aquatic and terrestrial insects.

One of the first publications showing the trend in local pattern development was Robin Fick's excellent work, published in Durban in August 1985 by the Fly Fishers' Association, entitled *A Simple Guide to the Aquatic Life of the Stillwaters of Natal and My Imitations Thereof*. It provided a wealth of information on local aquatic and terrestrial insects, gave the author's imitations of those insects and described the techniques required to fish them effectively. It set out to identify several insect species and recommend an imitation and fishing technique for each. Had this particular publication been available when I first began fly-tying and fly-fishing, it would have saved me endless hours of frustration, both at the tying bench and on the water. Subsequent to the publication of this simple guide, several South African fly-tiers have made their mark with innovative and effective patterns, but still the South African fly-fisher lacked a book describing these patterns. This, in essence, is why I began work on this handbook.

From the outset, I would like to make it quite clear that this is not a book on fly-tying techniques, but rather one on tying particular patterns and the techniques required to fish them. There are many excellent volumes available on basic fly-tying techniques and it was never my intention to add to the subject.

My primary goal was to provide for anglers who tie their own flies a manual which lists the pattern, identifies the insect being imitated, and describes the most effective method of fishing the imitation. (However, those anglers who do not tie their own flies can also benefit, as the fishing techniques described herein have broader applications: for example, the fishing techniques specified for the All-Rounder Damsel [pages 33–34] are precisely the same as those required for Hugh Huntley's Red-Eyed Damsel, which is available commercially.)

Although entitled *The South African Fly-Fishing Handbook*, the purpose of this book is to bring together in one volume not only a collection of indigenous patterns, but a variety of patterns, both local and foreign, suitable for South African streams and stillwaters, that I and other anglers have found effective over many years of fly-fishing. In deciding which patterns to include, I chose those which do not involve complicated tying procedures. I also included both aquatic and terrestrial insects, as well as several other food forms of importance to the diet of a trout, such as forage fish. Some of the patterns in this book have been in use for centuries, whereas others have only found their way into the fly-boxes of anglers in recent years. All, however, are tried and tested and I am confident that they will become widely accepted throughout the country.

I firmly believe that if a fly-tier works his way through this book, following closely the size and colour ranges specified, he will be able to go astream confident that most of the food types he finds can be imitated. Naturally, there will be days when the trout will outwit the angler, no matter how vast the selection of imitations involved, but it is this that lures anglers back to try again!

If anglers and fly-tiers derive as much pleasure from reading and using this book as I have had in researching and writing it, then I'm sure it will lead to fuller fly-boxes and greater success on the water. I believe that this volume may benefit all South African fly-fishers and I hope that it will stimulate local fly-tying.

DEAN RIPHAGEN
1998

Tools and Techniques

Tools

SELECTING THE CORRECT TOOLS for tying flies, and making sure that they are of good quality, is of paramount importance to your enjoyment and efficiency, and will save you endless hours of frustration each season.

After several years of fly-tying, I have found certain tools to be unnecessary (the most notable being the whip finish tool) and have dispensed with these because they merely clutter up the tying area and waste time. Below, however, is a list of tying tools that I consider indispensable.

Vice

A high-quality vice should, with the correct care, last a lifetime and will justify its extra expense. It should have the following features:

1. The vice should securely hold a range of the most commonly used hook sizes. The better vices on the market today hold a range of hooks from #2/0 to #28 which are more than adequate for fresh- and light saltwater use.

2. It should have a set of jaws that are strong and easily adjustable. Jaws that are brittle will chip – this is frustrating for the fly-tier. The Regal is difficult to beat for simplicity, durability and ease of use.

3. The vice should have a matt finish rather than a gloss one which may cause eye fatigue with prolonged use.

A useful but not essential additional feature is the ability to rotate the vice's jaws, allowing the fly-tier to view the fly through 360 degrees. For many years I used a Regal vice with fixed jaws but was given a Renzetti vice with a rotary jaw function and find this useful for viewing flies from all angles during certain stages of the tying procedure.

A vice on a pedestal base, while not as stable as a C-clamp vice, is useful for fly-tiers who spend time away from home or travel on extended fishing vacations, both in South Africa and abroad.

Bobbins

The durability of bobbins has been greatly improved in recent years. Just as graphite has replaced fibreglass in fly-rod construction, ceramic, with its superior durability, is replacing stainless steel and brass in the manufacture of bobbin shafts. Worn metal bobbin shafts cut tying silk, often at crucial stages, but this risk is greatly reduced in ceramic bobbins.

Griffin and other manufacturers make excellent ceramic bobbins which are well worth the small extra cost compared to the stainless steel variety. Standard-size bobbins, available in most shops in this country, are excellent for all fly-tying, regardless of the size of the fly being tied.

Hackle pliers

Several styles of hackle pliers are available and all have their merits; teardrop and English- or Danville-style hackle pliers are the two most commonly used.

English-style hackle pliers have an advantage over the teardrop pliers because their tension can be adjusted to suit the fly-tier, making for easier opening when grasping hackle. Teardrop hackle pliers, on the other hand, are almost impossible to adjust for tension but are lighter than the English-style pliers and are therefore better suited to winding hackle on small flies.

However, always try to wind hackle without hackle pliers if possible, as this allows you to skip the steps involved in picking up and replacing the pliers and thus reduces your tying time.

Scissors

Sharp scissors are an essential aid for the fly-tier and I carry several pairs for various applications. Many excellent makes are available and some of the better models, made specifically for fly-tying, have so-called 'ice-tempered' blades, making them durable and sharp. I have several pairs for general purpose work, a small, pointed pair for work on small flies, and a pair with curved blades for trimming hair bodies and for cutting in areas where space is restricted.

Griffin makes an excellent pair of all-purpose fly-tying scissors (available from most good fly-fishing specialist shops) and the famous knife manufacturer, Kershaw, has recently introduced an excellent design with serrated blades which are perfect for use as general fly-tying scissors.

Keep scissors sharp at all times, as there is nothing more frustrating than sitting down for a tying session only to discover they are blunt.

When weighting flies with lead wire, break the lead rather than cutting it with scissors. Fly-tying wire can be cut, but use the base of the blades rather than the points. (Readers will notice that in the photographic fly-tying sequences that follow the points of the scissors are used to cut wire, but this is merely for clarity.)

Hair stacker

For those fly-tiers who use hair, such as deer or elk hair, in many of their patterns, a hair stacker is an essential tool. Several models are available, with Renzetti making an excellent double-ended model that can be used to stack both small and large quantities of hair. The latest Renzetti models have rubber gaskets on the ends to dull the sound when the stacker is tapped on the tying surface – a feature which will also preserve the surface of your bench.

Dubbing teaser

Anglers know that a fly, particularly a nymph, that has taken a few fish seems to out-perform one that has not. It is

generally believed that this is because the teeth of the fish tease out the dubbing, giving the fly a 'buggier' appearance. The dubbing teaser is a useful tool as it enables the fly-tier to give the flies a 'buggy' appearance straight from the vice.

The dubbing teasers available in most shops are simple serrated pieces of wire, but are not particularly efficient. A small piece of coarse Velcro tape pasted onto the end of a tongue depressor or wooden ice cream stick is more effective and much cheaper.

Dubbing needle

The dubbing needle, with its many uses, is another essential tying tool. Use it to apply head cement to heads, tie half-hitch knots in thread, and to tease out dubbing on nymph bodies. Choose a needle with a base that has been squared off to prevent it from rolling off the tying surface.

Tying lamp

While nothing can replace good quality, natural light from behind your shoulder, a high intensity lamp with a concentrated beam will add greatly to your tying enjoyment and will substantially reduce eye fatigue, especially if you do your fly-tying at night.

Select a lamp with a pedestal base so that you can position it conveniently on the work bench and can transport it should you tie away from home.

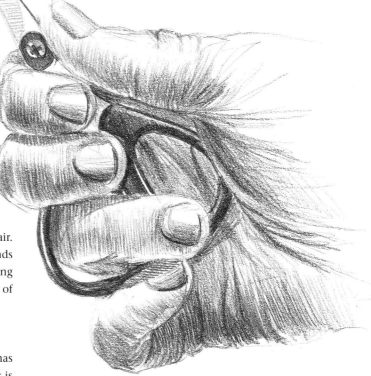

Speed-Tying Techniques

MOST FLY-TIERS I KNOW would prefer to spend their valuable free time fishing their flies rather than tying them. If a trick or method reduces tying time by even five minutes, I am sure that no fly-tier would pass up the opportunity to learn it. What at first may appear to be a trivial timesaver may ultimately save the fly-tier several precious hours each season.

The following is a list of short-cuts that I have learnt during my years at the vice, as well as several that I discovered by reading books and watching other experienced fly-tiers at work.

1. Always tie one specific pattern at a tying session, rather than several different ones. This allows you to maintain uniformity in terms of proportion, and prevents your tying surface from becoming cluttered with all the materials needed for many different patterns. (When tying a new pattern to stock my fly-boxes I generally try to tie fifteen flies of one pattern in a particular colour in a single session.)

2. Weight all hooks in advance.

3. If a certain pattern requires lengthy preparation, do this before you begin any tying session. (Examples include preparing burned monofilament eyes, lacquered wing-cases, and lacquered flight or body feathers for use as wings.)

4. Always select all the materials and the correct quantity of hooks required for a tying session before you start – and place them where they are readily accessible.

5. Tie with your scissors on the fourth or last finger of your tying hand as this eliminates the need to pick up and replace the scissors each time they are required. Initially this may feel uncomfortable, but you will soon adjust to it. (I consider this to be the greatest timesaver I have learnt during my years as a fly-tier.)

6. Use a half-hitch knot (a simple overhand knot) to complete the heads on your flies, instead of whip-finishing them. A head that is half-hitched and cemented is as durable as one that is whip-finished and cemented, and can be completed more rapidly. Furthermore, the use of the whip-finish tool merely involves picking up and replacing yet another unnecessary tool.

Above *A well-organised tying area will greatly enhance your tying enjoyment. This is a custom-built unit made especially for the author.*

MIKE SOMERVILLE

7. Try to tie patterns in stages, as this considerably reduces tying time. The Royal Wulff (see pages 114–116) is a good example: all the hair wings can be tied onto the hooks before starting the actual tying. Another good example is the Lake Dragon (see pages 24–27), where the underbodies can be built up before tying begins.

8. Clear your work area after a tying session, and always replace your tools.

9. Blend a large quantity of underbody dubbing (such as that used for the Kaufmann Lake Dragon), as this will save considerable time, and this versatile material has numerous applications, particularly for nymphs. Different colours of dubbing can be blended and kept in separate zip-lock bags for future use (this is particularly useful if you are travelling); one bag usually contains enough blended dubbing for several hundred nymphs.

Weighting Flies

CORRECT WEIGHTING OF TROUT FLIES is an important yet poorly understood aspect of fly-tying, and only with constant on-the-water experimentation will the fly-fisher discover the weighting combinations that best suit his fishing styles and techniques. The suggestions listed on the following pages should thus act as guidelines only and not as hard-and-fast rules.

Few anglers can agree on a universal weighting system for fly patterns and most have their own theories about when and whether to weight a fly, the amount of weight required and the placement of the weight on the hook. While anglers who buy mass-produced patterns are forced to make do with pre-determined weightings, those who tie their own flies can experiment with weight combinations to find those that best suit their specific needs. (This in itself is an excellent reason to tie your own flies.)

In order to cover comprehensively the problems of and solutions to weighting flies, the various pattern styles have been separated into two sections, namely stillwater patterns and stream and river patterns.

Weighting Stillwater Patterns

Over the years I have revised my weighting of stillwater flies and have slowly eliminated weight in almost all my still-water patterns; this has had a positive effect on my catch rate, as well as on the pleasure I derive from fishing these patterns. Observation of stillwater insects in their natural environment proved to me that my weighted imitations were not performing in the water anything like the live insect. Any angler who has taken the time to watch at close quarters the retrieve of a weighted fly will have noticed how rapidly it sinks during pauses in the retrieve. This is quite unlike the natural motion of an insect in the water: most aquatic insects do not sink, or else sink very slowly, when they stop swimming. Weighted imitations, however, sink unnaturally fast during pauses in the retrieve, and the heavier the fly the more pronounced is this deviation. (This is particularly true of the larger dragonfly nymph imitations which I used to weight with fifteen to twenty turns of lead wire, and which actually perform far better with no weight at all.)

In addition, weight should not be used to take an imitation into the feeding zone of the trout as the weighting makes them pass through this zone rather quickly. Instead, the fly-fisher should select from a vast assortment of fly-lines and braided leaders which are available in various densities and are designed to take the fly efficiently and effectively to a specific depth and to keep it at that depth for most of the

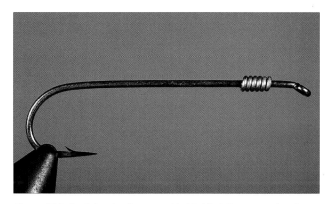

Above *This hook has lead wraps added behind the eye to give the fly a jigging, crippled or diving action.*

retrieve. It is thus far better to fish an unweighted or lightly weighted imitation together with a sinking or intermediate line designed to take the fly to the required depth than to use a weighted imitation, which will remain in the trout's feeding zone for a short time only, together with a floating line and rapid retrieve.

However, a small amount of lead can be used to impart action to the pattern. Three examples of the selective use of weight in stillwater patterns are the Woolly Bugger (pages 166–171) and leech patterns, and the attractor patterns which are tied to imitate baitfish. By adding a few lead wraps to the front third of the hook shank, a jigging action is achieved for the Woolly Bugger and leech patterns and a crippled effect for the baitfish imitation.

The advent of brass (and, more recently, tungsten) beads in the tying of trout flies has opened up a whole new dimension to the stillwater and stream angler, who can use beads instead of lead wraps or fly-lines. Presently, I use beads on my Woolly Bugger and leech patterns only, and then only to add flash and impart action to them, but this is a matter of personal preference and many anglers I know use beads in many of their stillwater patterns with great success.

Weighting Stream and River Patterns

It is along the streambed that the current moves most slowly and it is here that trout expend the least amount of energy to hold their position. As this is where for most of their lives the fish will be found in running water, it is therefore the level at which the angler should attempt to position the fly.

In running water specific situations may demand heavily weighted flies to take the imitations down to the feeding level of the fish. These flies should be used together with floating lines, which are easily mended to counteract the drag caused by water currents. (The intermediate and sinking lines recommended for stillwater fly-fishing are not effective in rivers and streams, as they are dragged by current

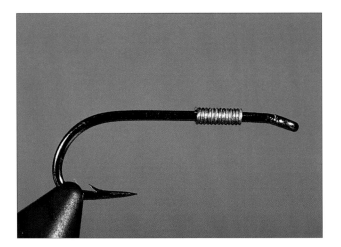

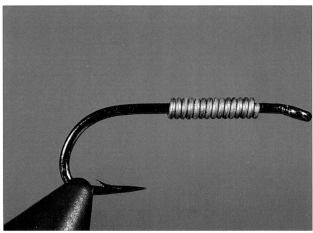

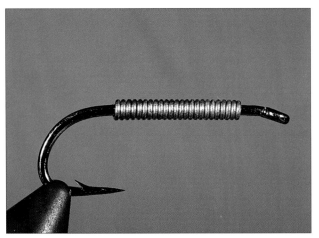

Various hook weightings to achieve different sink rates:
Top left *Light* **Above** *Medium* **Bottom left** *Heavy*

the materials used in the construction of the fly. Generally, the bulkier the fly, the more buoyant it will be and the more weight will be required to sink it.

Freshwater anglers who tie their own flies and who frequent a particular stretch of water will quickly master the weighting requirements of their flies for that stretch. Those who fish a variety of waters during a season, however, and who are unsure about the particular characteristics of each, should follow the general rule to underweight all their stream patterns. Nothing is more frustrating than fishing with flies that are too heavy for the conditions and that continually hang up on the stream bottom.

While your flies should not drag along the bottom they should occasionally touch it during the drift. If, because of insufficient weight on the hook shank, you do not occasionally feel the bottom during the drift of your fly you can add additional weight to the leader in the form of split-shot, Twistons or the like.

For those who do not believe in adding weight to their leaders, the most effective method of covering all water conditions is to keep each pattern in three or four weight combinations, ranging from unweighted through to heavily weighted. The angler can develop a marking system, using small dots of nail varnish in various colours on the underside of the pattern head or various thread colours for pattern heads, to distinguish between the differently weighted patterns. In this way most water depths can be catered for, and the angler merely has to select a suitably weighted pattern and to adjust his casting action for the heavier patterns by slowing down the casting stroke and opening up the loop. (When patterns are large and heavily weighted they often cannot be 'cast' in the conventional sense and must, instead, be 'lobbed'.)

flows and – because of their sinking properties – cannot be mended to counteract the effects of this drag. In addition, unweighted flies fished together with floating lines will seldom be effective in the boundary layer – that cushion of water directly above the river bottom where friction occurs between the water and the streambed; turbulent water currents will sweep the fly out of this zone and buoy it up towards the surface.)

The most common method of weighting flies for stream or river fishing is to wrap lead wire around the hook shank. Bead chain and lead barbell eyes (such as those used in many saltwater patterns) can also be used to simulate eyes on certain patterns and to take them down in deeper water. Brass, tungsten and similar beads have gained widespread acceptance in fly-tying in recent years and have proved themselves effective additions to many established fly patterns. As well as adding sparkle, they add valuable weight to those patterns which must quickly reach the streambed.

The amount of weight the fly-tier adds to the fly depends on several factors, the most important being water depth, current speed, water temperature (which affects trout mobility), fly size, leader and tippet diameter and the buoyancy of

Note: The only application for very heavily weighted patterns is in deep, powerful water or in fast pocket water where it is necessary to get the fly to the bottom quickly and to keep it there.

Additional Weighting Techniques

While most fly-fishers rely on lead wire on the hook shank or various densities of intermediate and sinking fly-lines to take their flies down to the trout, there are other methods which can be used to achieve similar results.

Probably the most common weighting technique for stream fishing is to add weight – usually in the form of split-shot, Twistons and Soft Lead – to the leader. I prefer to add extra weight a few inches from the fly, but have often caught trout with the weight tight up against the hook eye. Anglers who want to give their stillwater flies a jigging or crippled action should add the weight no more than two inches from the eye of the fly.

Anglers who enjoy fishing small, sub-surface patterns (#16 or smaller) in deep, fast water, can make use of a heavier dropper pattern on the leader to take their flies to the bottom. This is a popular technique in the western states of North America, where fish often key onto diminutive aquatic insects, such as midges, in fast water. A similar technique is used by New Zealand anglers who use a heavy bead head pattern on the dropper to take small nymph or pupa imitations down to fish feeding along the streambed in very fast, deep water. These smaller patterns are often tied directly to the bend of the bead head dropper fly with a foot-long length of tippet. (See also pages 59–61 and 88–91.)

Sink-tip lines are another addition to the fly-fisher's arsenal of techniques to get the fly into deeper water, but are, as Tom Sutcliffe calls them, '...the invention of the devil on our streams'. Although they do have a use on some of South Africa's larger rivers, such as the Kraai and Langkloof, they do not possess the advantages afforded by fishing a floating line coupled with a weighted fly, and are usually difficult to cast compared to full floating fly-lines.

Another technique is to use a small section of lead-core line, with loops added to both ends, to sink a fly to the required depth. One end of the lead-core is attached to the tapered end of the leader while the other end is attached to the tippet. A similar method is to use braided butt leaders that are designed to sink. Used together with a floating line they convert the system into a sinking-tip, which is not the most suitable technique where nymphs require to be fished with a natural, drag-free drift in rivers and streams and is not a system which I generally recommend.

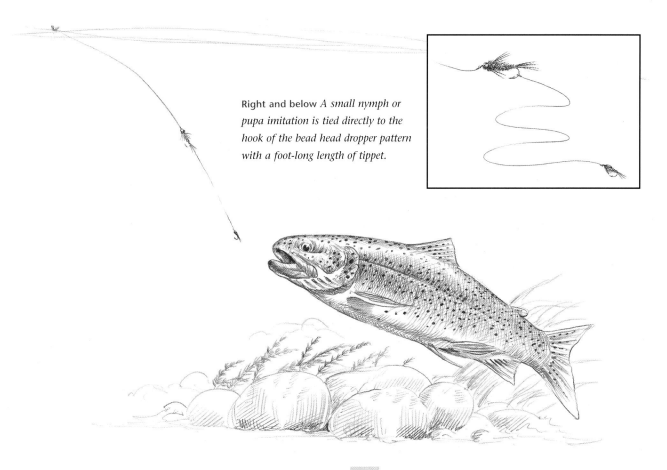

Right and below *A small nymph or pupa imitation is tied directly to the hook of the bead head dropper pattern with a foot-long length of tippet.*

Hook Comparison Chart

THERE ARE MORE HOOK MANUFACTURERS today than ever before, with an accompanying increase in hook styles designed specifically for fly-fishers. However, as in the past, manufacturers have done little to establish uniformity in hook specifications and styles. This has led to confusion amongst fly-tiers, particularly novices. Different makes of, for example, a #8 2X longshank hook will often vary not only in gape size, but also in shank length.

I believe that Tiemco currently have the widest range of fly-fishing hooks and their quality is superb. As a result, a Tiemco hook is specified for all patterns in this book. Tiemco are constantly expanding and updating their hook range, and also produce several barbless models for those who prefer them. The following hook comparison chart provides a means of selecting an alternative hook should the specified Tiemco one be unavailable.

HOOK COMPARISON CHART

* = Not an exact match, but still a reasonable substitute.

	DESCRIPTION OF HOOK	SPECIFIED HOOK Tiemco
1.	Dry fly, down eye, 1X fine, wide gape, forged, bronze.	100
2.	Dry fly, straight eye, 1X fine, wide gape, forged, bronze.	101
3.	Drys and wets, down eye, 1X heavy, wide gape, forged, bronze.	9300
4.	Dry fly, down eye, 1X fine, perfect bend, forged, bronze.	5210
5.	Dry fly, down eye, 3X fine, perfect bend, forged, bronze.	5230
6.	Hoppers and terrestrials, down eye, 2X long, 1X fine, perfect bend, forged, bronze.	5212
7.	Hoppers and terrestrials, straight eye, 2X long, 1X fine, slightly humped shank, forged, bronze.	2312
8.	Shrimps and caddis pupae, down eye, 2X wide, 2X short, fine wire, reversed, forged, bronze.	2487
9.	Shrimps and caddis pupae, down eye, 2X wide, 2X short, 2X heavy, bronze.	2457
10.	Wet fly and nymph, down eye, 2X heavy, sproat bend, bronze.	3769
11.	Wet fly and nymph, down eye, 1X long, 2X heavy, sproat bend, bronze.	3761
12.	Nymph and streamer, down eye, 2X long, 2X heavy, perfect bend, forged, bronze.	5262
13.	Nymph and streamer, down eye, 3X long, 2X heavy, perfect bend, forged, bronze.	5263
14.	Nymph and dry fly, semi-dropped point, forged, bronze.	200R
15.	Streamer, down eye, 6X long, heavy wire, forged, bronze.	300

NEIL HODGES

Above *A Western Cape rainbow just prior to netting.*

ALTERNATIVE HOOKS

Orvis	Kamasan	Daiichi (Senque)
extra-fine dry fly hook	B400/B401*	1100
straight-eye big-eye hook	B410*	–
–	B170*/B175*	–
extra-fine dry fly hook	B400/B401*	1100*
extra-fine dry fly hook*	B401*	1100*
2X dry fly hook	–	1710*
curved nymph hook*	B220	1270
shrimp/caddis nymph hook	B100	1130
heavy wire worm/caddis hook	B110	1130
heavy wet/nymph hook	B175	1530 (wet fly)
standard wet fly hook	B170	(wet fly)*
traditional nymph hook	B200	1710 (nymph)
muddler/stonefly hook	B800*	(nymph)*
curved nymph/bead head hook	B220	1270
streamer/4X streamer hook	B800*	2340 (streamer)*

21

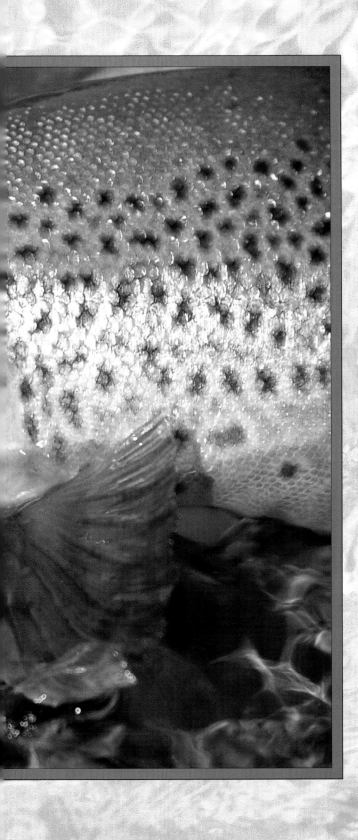

Tying
Instruction

NYMPHS

Lake Dragon

RANDALL KAUFMANN

THE LAKE DRAGON IMITATES the robust *Aeshnidae* dragonfly nymphs very well and it has become my standard dragonfly nymph imitation, particularly for deep fishing. I tie it unweighted, relying on intermediate or sinking lines of various densities to take the fly to the required depth. Through experience, I have found that unweighted patterns have the edge over weighted versions in stillwaters because of their more lifelike behaviour during the retrieve. Weighted patterns tend to sink too rapidly during pauses in the retrieve and are considerably more difficult to cast.

The Lake Dragon can be fished at various depths with floating, intermediate or sinking lines, but I use it to dredge the deeper bottom areas for the larger trout that seldom show in the shallower margins of a lake. However, due to low prey densities, low light intensity and lower oxygen levels, dragonfly nymphs are largely confined to water depths shallower than nine feet, so anglers should keep this in mind when fishing imitations of these insects.

The Lake Dragon is at its most effective when retrieved in short 'strips' of three to four inches, interspersed with pauses of a second or two to simulate the nymph's short rest periods while swimming. The dragonfly nymph is among our fastest aquatic insects, yet it is only capable of these short, propulsive bursts. It never ceases to amaze me, therefore, to see

Below *André Hamman took this six-pound rainbow hen from a lake near Underberg using a dragonfly nymph imitation.*

DRAGONFLY NYMPHS

*I*n South African stillwaters the dragonfly nymph is a readily available and important trout food, whereas the adult dragonfly is mostly taken opportunistically.

Dragonflies and their close relatives the damselflies constitute the order Odonata. The dragonflies are grouped under their own suborder Anisoptera, which is further divided into two super-families of interest to the South African fly-fisher, namely Aeshnoidea *and* Libelluloidea.

Dragonflies begin life as eggs which hatch into nymphs with voracious appetites. The life cycle of these nymphs ranges from several months to several years, depending on the species, environmental conditions, prey availability and other factors. They are among the largest aquatic insects the fly-fisher will come across, with some specimens attaining lengths of as much as three inches (these are probably Anax imperator *sp.*). They eat smaller aquatic insects – and fish in certain cases – by means of a highly developed, prehensile lower labium, which can be extended to grasp prey.

While dragonfly nymph species from the Libelluloidea *super-family are occasionally ingested by trout, it is species from the* Aeshnidae *family which are predominantly preyed upon by trout, perhaps because their larger size makes them more visible. In South Africa, it is thus the nymphs of this particular dragonfly family which are significant to the fly-fisher.*

These Aeshnidae *nymphs spend most of their lives clambering around weeds, using camouflage to conceal themselves from both prey and predator. The* Aeshnidae *nymph is stout and robust, with two large eyes situated at the front of the head. It has six spider-like legs, no tail, and an abdomen which is triangular in cross-section and which is markedly constricted as it approaches the head and thoracic region. These are some of the features fly-tiers should try to imitate in their flies.*

Nymphal coloration is highly variable, and is often related to the insect's species, the habitat in which it lives, its food, and its stage of development. Aeshnidae *nymphs are usually weed dwellers and may range in colour from olive to dark green, an attribute anglers can emulate by tying patterns in medium to dark olive. I use a medium olive pattern for most of my stillwater fishing from September through to April when there is abundant weed growth (the colour of which will be reflected by the colour of the nymphs) in most of the stillwaters around the country. However, when I have examined the stomach contents of trout caught during winter I have found that* Aeshnidae *nymphs eaten by the fish were very dark olive to blackish in colour, and so from May to August I rely on a dark olive pattern to deceive trout.*

Above Examples of *Aeshnidae* dragonfly nymphs, showing the distinctive bulbous eyes and elongated, cylindrical body.

A medium to dark brown pattern is also a useful addition to a dragonfly nymph imitation assortment, particularly for those anglers who concentrate their stillwater efforts on the waters of the Western Cape where weed growth is limited; in these waters nymphs have a distinct brownish hue because most of their lives are spent over weedless bottoms.

The dragonfly nymph has an anal area specially adapted for respiration by means of an internal rectal gill system. The nymph pumps water in and out of the rectal chamber; once it has removed the oxygen from the water it expels this water via the anal orifice. This expulsion of water is often used to great effect to propel the insect forward to attack prey as well as to avoid predation, and many stillwater anglers will have seen these large nymphs darting up to four inches in bursts. It is useful for the fly-fisher to imitate these short bursts of activity during the retrieve.

Local fly-fishing stores have, for many years, been preoccupied with supplying dragonfly nymph imitations with flattened bodies. I have never understood this, since most dragonfly nymphs eaten by trout are from the Aeshnidae *family, and have cylindrical rather than flattened abdomens.*

anglers retrieving their imitations in arm-length strips through the water; no aquatic insect is capable of movement this rapid, and such retrieves will only deter wary trout.

Due to the relatively fast retrieves required when fishing dragonfly nymph imitations, anglers should—be well prepared for savage takes. Match tippet size to the size of the fly being fished; as well as the size of the fish likely to be encountered. Since most of my dragonfly nymph imitations are tied on 6X longshank hooks, in the #2 to #8 hook range, I use 2X to 3X tippets. With the excellent new fly-lines manufactured by Airflo now on the market the use of appropriate tippet sizes has taken on increased significance, since their low- or non-stretch cores leave little margin for error when even moderate-sized trout hit an imitation at speed. Several years ago, while fishing a Lake Dragon along a drop-off at Mount Arthur using an Airflo sinking line with a non-stretch core, I was broken by a savage take, even though I was using 0X tippet material.

When exploring the depths with a fast-sinking line keep the leader and tippet short. A long leader used with a fast-sinking line will, to a large degree, defeat the purpose as it will buoy up the fly in the water: while the line may be fishing at the correct depth, an artificial on a long leader will invariably fish several feet above the line. Leaders need not exceed four to five feet when used with fast-sinking fly-lines.

LAKE DRAGON

HOOK: Tiemco 300, #2 – #10.

THREAD: 6/0 prewaxed, colour to match abdomen.

WINGCASE: Mottled light or white tip turkey feather lacquered with Dave's Flexament.

EYES: 100 lb burned monofilament.

TAIL: Marabou, or grizzly marabou, colour to match abdomen.

RIB: Copper wire.

UNDERBODY: Wool, colour to match abdomen.

ABDOMEN: Medium olive, dark olive or brown Hare-Tron dubbing, or similar, blended with the following colours of Angora goat dubbing for highlights: blue, purple, green, amber, olive, brown and rust.

LEGS: Pheasant rump or body feather to match the colour of the abdomen.

THORAX and HEAD: Same as abdomen.

1. Coat the turkey feather with Flexament and allow to dry completely. Once it has dried cut a thin sliver, approximately one-third of an inch wide, from the feather for the wingcase.

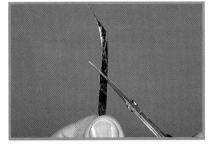

2. Fold this sliver in half lengthways and trim it at a 45-degree angle as shown.

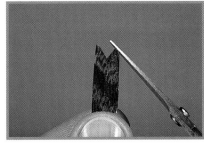

3. Open the feather up and trim the points of the wingcase.

4. Prepare the eyes by burning both ends of a one-inch strand of 100 lb monofilament.

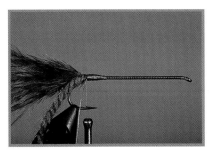

5. Take the thread to a position above the barb of the hook and tie in a thick bunch of marabou fibres, a length of copper wire and a single strand of wool.

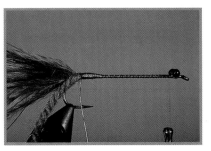

6. Tie in the eyes behind the hook eye using figure-of-eight wraps. Notice the spacing between the eyes and the hook eye.

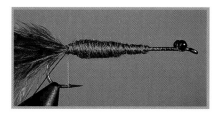

7. Form an underbody with the wool, tapering it as shown. Tie it off and return the thread to a position above the barb of the hook, taking several wraps of thread over the underbody.

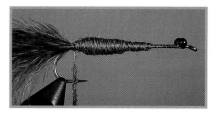

8. Spin a thin noodle of dubbing onto the thread. Do not apply too much dubbing to the thread as this will not allow for a neat, compact and well-tied fly.

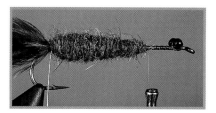

9. Form the abdomen, ensuring that it is reasonably sharply tapered towards the eye of the hook. The abdomen should cover approximately three-quarters of the hook shank.

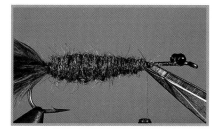

10. Wind the wire rib through the abdomen in seven to eight evenly spaced turns, secure with the thread and trim. This rib will provide segmentation and will strengthen the abdomen.

11. Select a body feather from a ringneck pheasant, strip off the webby flue at the base of the feather and stroke the fibres so that they stand out at right angles to the shaft of the feather.

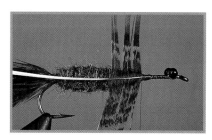

12. Tie in the feather by the tip in front of the abdomen, ensuring that the concave (dull) side of the feather faces the fly.

13. Take two turns of the feather in front of the abdomen and tie it off. Stroke the fibres down around the sides of the fly and secure them with a few wraps of thread.

14. Tie in the prepared wingcase in front of the abdomen, ensuring that it covers the legs on the side of the fly. The wingcase should extend over approximately one half of the abdomen.

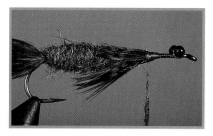

15. Spin a thin noodle of dubbing onto the thread for the head.

16. Form a sharply tapering head, ensuring that there is a prominent 'waist' between the head and abdomen. Half-hitch and trim the thread. Apply head cement to the thread wraps.

17. Break off the marabou so that a short tail is left. Do not cut the tail with scissors.

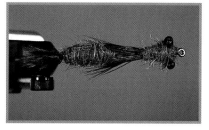

18. The completed Lake Dragon seen from above. Note the bulbous eyes and narrow 'waist'.

Floating Dragon

RANDALL KAUFMANN

MANY CONSIDER RANDALL KAUFMANN to be one of America's finest fly-tiers. He is the owner and operator of Kaufmann's Streamborn, a chain of mail-order and retail fly-fishing supply shops, and he has several innovative and effective patterns to his credit, including the Kaufmann Stone, the Stimulator and the Simulator.

The Floating Dragon is one of his more recent innovations, designed to be fished with a floating line over shallow, submerged weed, as well as in very shallow shoreline areas. Its application does not end there, however, and it has quickly gained a reputation as a pattern that will entice difficult, wary trout at all depths in a lake.

I have been using the Floating Dragon for six seasons now, and it has produced many respectable trout. It saved the day for Mark Yelland a few years ago by out-performing more conventional dragonfly nymphs being fished by two other very competent anglers at a private lake in the Kokstad area of East Griqualand. Probably the greatest advocate in this country of the pattern is Hugh Grieve, one of our finest leather craftsmen, who has recently had an extraordinary run of large trout, including a brown of over eight pounds from Kimber's 'Old Dam' in the Impendhle highlands.

While the Floating Dragon can be fished at all depths, I mainly use it over weedy lake margins and where weed reaches almost to the water's surface. Trout often cruise these areas in search of food, particularly in the early morning and late afternoon when the threat of predation is reduced. One of the features of the Floating Dragon is its 'neutral buoyancy' – once the pattern has been fished subsurface for a lengthy period and the deer hair has absorbed water, the fly, much like the natural, neither sinks to the lake bottom nor floats to the water's surface.

I prefer to use a floating or intermediate line when exploring shallower water with this fly, but it is also an extremely effective pattern when used with a fast-sinking line such as a Scientific Anglers Wet Cel Hi-D or Wet Cel Hi-Speed Hi-D.

Below *Tom Lewin, André Hamman and Mike Somerville pose with a large rainbow hen taken from a private lake in the Bushman's Nek area. The fish fell for a dragonfly nymph imitation fished deep.*

NEIL HODGES

Above *An example of a* Libellulidae *dragonfly nymph. The species pictured is* Orthetrum.

Right *Well-known fly shop owner Mark Yelland prepares to release a big rainbow taken from Kimber's 'Old Dam'.*

The Floating Dragon's greatest asset when fished with a sinking line is that once the deer hair body becomes water-logged, the fly has an almost neutral density and consequently behaves like the natural insect. When fished with a sinking line, the fly will ride above bottom weed and will not, like weighted flies, hang up.

With a floating line and long leader of up to fifteen feet, the fly can be cast out and allowed to float on the surface. I favour fishing the fly just sub-surface, using an intermediate line and a leader of up to twelve feet. The fly then fishes in the first few inches of water and takes can be seen as well as felt. I use the same retrieve for the Floating Dragon as I do for the Lake Dragon, giving the fly a few strips of up to three or four inches and then allowing it to settle in the water to simulate the resting insect. As with the Lake Dragon, anglers should gear tippet sizes to the size of the fly being fished and so 2X or 3X tippets should be used.

FLOATING DRAGON

HOOK: Tiemco 300, #2 – #10.

THREAD: 3/0 monocord, colour to match abdomen.

TAIL: Marabou, or grizzly marabou, dyed brown or olive.

ABDOMEN: Spun brown or olive deer hair.

EYES: 100 lb burned monofilament.

LEGS: Same as tail.

WINGCASE: Mottled light or white tip turkey feather, lacquered with Dave's Flexament (see page 26, steps 1 to 3 for preparation method).

THORAX and HEAD: Brown or dark olive Hare-Tron, or similar dubbing.

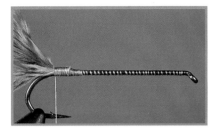

1. Tie in a thick bunch of marabou fibres on the top of the hook shank. Don't worry about the length of the fibres at this stage as the fibres will be broken off later in the tying procedure.

2. Place a section of deer hair with the diameter of a pencil on top of the hook shank and take two to three loose wraps of thread over the hair. Do not pull the thread tight at this stage.

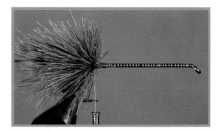

3. Slowly draw the thread wraps very tight, so that the hair flares and spins around the hook shank. Hold the hair back out of the way and take a few turns of thread directly in front of it.

4. Repeat steps 2 and 3 until three-quarters of the shank is covered in spun hair, ensuring at all times that the flared hair is compacted against the previous spinning.

5. Half-hitch and trim the thread. Remove the hook from the vice. Trim the deer hair on the upper and lower sides of the abdomen.

6. Cut the sides of the abdomen into a coffin shape as shown.

7. Once the sides have been trimmed, neaten off the edges of the abdomen with a pair of scissors.

8. Re-insert the hook into the vice and re-attach the tying thread at a point directly behind the hook eye. Using figure-of-eight wraps, tie in a pair of eyes directly behind the hook eye.

9. Tie in two thick clumps of marabou fibres on either side of the abdomen for the legs. Don't worry about the length of the fibres at this stage as they will be broken off later in the tying procedure.

10. Tie in the lacquered wingcase in front of the abdomen; it should cover three-quarters of the abdomen. Trim the butt of the wingcase.

11. Spin a thin noodle of dubbing onto the thread and form a neat, sharply tapering head. Half-hitch the thread and trim. Apply head cement to the thread wraps.

12. Break the marabou off to form the legs and tail. Do not cut the marabou with scissors. The photograph shows the Floating Dragon seen from above.

Filoplume Dragonfly

E.H. 'GENE' ARMSTRONG

THE FILOPLUME DRAGONFLY is an exceptional producer of trout and belongs in the fly-boxes of all stillwater anglers. The use of filoplume, those small, fragile, downy feathers occurring at the base of the main body feathers of game birds such as pheasant, grouse and partridge, has been one of the best-kept secrets in fly-tying. Filoplume feathers are usually found in a variety of dun colours and accept dye readily. Those of the cock ringneck pheasant are best for fly-tying. While some fly-tiers have used filoplume feathers with great success for many years, fly-tiers in general have only recently begun to appreciate their value in the construction of trout flies. It took two American anglers, Gene Armstrong and Jack Gartside, to bring them to the fore and to give them the publicity they rightfully deserve.

The Filoplume Dragonfly is one of many filoplume patterns devised by Gene Armstrong, and it is one of my favourite dragonfly nymph patterns for searching and probing a lake. I tie it unweighted for use in the top few feet of water, using a floating or intermediate line, or fish it with a sinking line to search a lake's deeper areas for bigger fish.

Imitations made with filoplume will consistently out-perform the flattened, commercially tied nymphs which are made with materials which provide them with little inherent movement. Filoplume feathers, on the other hand, are so mobile and soft that they have a tantalising action in the water which makes an otherwise lifeless pattern come alive, particularly when retrieved in a series of short, rapid strips interspersed with pauses. This causes the material to pulsate, enhancing the impression of life.

I tie this pattern in either olive or brown, and fish it in a similar fashion to the Lake Dragon – the olive version in weedy areas and the brown version over mud bottoms. Most takes on this fly have been hard – on several occasions the rod has almost been wrenched from my grasp. Many of the fish I have landed with this pattern have been hooked deep in the back of the throat, indicating that the fish has taken the imitation confidently. This has added to my own confidence in this wonderfully effective pattern.

FILOPLUME DRAGONFLY

HOOK: Tiemco 300, #2 – #10.

THREAD: 6/0 prewaxed, colour to match abdomen.

TAIL: A small wisp of ringneck pheasant rump marabou and six to eight wisps of mallard flank feather.

RIB: Fine copper wire.

ABDOMEN: Brown or olive filoplume feathers.

WINGCASE: Ringneck pheasant back feather in blue-green phase, or a sliver of white tip turkey feather.

THORAX: Angora goat dubbing, rabbit hair and Antron yarn, blended to obtain desired colour to match abdomen.

LEGS: Ringneck pheasant back feather.

Below *An example of a* Libellulidae *dragonfly nymph. The species pictured is* Trithemis.

NEIL HODGES

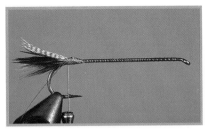

1. Tie in a short section of ringneck pheasant rump marabou, a few mallard flank fibres above the pheasant marabou and a length of fine copper wire.

2. Select a fluffy filoplume feather – the one on the left is a ringneck pheasant rump feather; on the right is its accompanying filoplume, or aftershaft, feather.

3. Tie in the filoplume feather above the hook barb by its tip. Once the feather has been tied in, take the thread to a position just in front of the feather.

4. Using hackle pliers, carefully wrap the filoplume feather forward towards the eye of the hook, tie the feather off with a few turns of thread and trim the excess.

5. Form the abdomen by repeating steps 3 and 4 until about two-thirds of the shank is covered with filoplume feathers, each time tying in the next feather straight in front of the previous one.

6. Wrap the copper wire through the abdomen, being careful not to trap the filoplume fibres with the rib. Tie off the rib and tie in a ringneck pheasant back feather for the wingcase by the tip.

7. Spin a thin noodle of dubbing onto the thread and form the thorax. Note the space left behind the hook eye where the hackle will be wound and a head formed.

8. Select another ringneck pheasant back feather for the legs and tie it in by the tip, ensuring that the concave side of the feather faces the hook shank.

9. Take two turns of the feather around the hook shank and secure the butt with a few turns of thread. Trim the excess.

10. Using your thumb and index finger, stroke the fibres so that they lie on the sides and bottom of the fly. Secure the fibres in this position with a few wraps of thread.

11. Pull the wingcase forward and tie it down with a few wraps of thread. Trim the butt of the feather as close as possible to the thread wraps to ensure a neat head.

12. Form a small, neat thread head, half-hitch and trim. Apply head cement to the thread wraps.

NEIL HODGES

All-Rounder Damsel

JOHN BARR

Above *An example of a damselfly nymph, showing the bulbous eyes and feathery tracheal gills at the rear of the slender abdomen.*

OCTOBER IS ONE OF THE PRIME stillwater fishing months in KwaZulu-Natal. It is also the month that the ubiquitous damselfly begins to make its presence felt in the stillwaters across the country.

It was a crisp October morning as Jimmy Baroutsos and I quietly eased our float tubes into the clear waters of Pappa's Lake, a Fly Fishers' Association water just outside the town of Mooi River. I made my way slowly across the lake towards the far bank where a dense mat of weed blanketed the water's surface. After a lengthy paddle, I found myself some twenty yards from the edge of the weed and, with a cool wind beginning to stir the water's surface, I anchored the tube.

There were no visible signs of fish and no indication of any insect activity. Although my rod was rigged with a floating line and long leader, I decided to prospect the deeper water using an intermediate line, short leader and an All-Rounder Damsel – this is my favourite damsel pattern for searching the water around weedbeds that are known to harbour these delicate yet ferocious insects.

I wet the fly with saliva to remove any air bubbles that would inhibit its sinking, and quartered the weedbed with a long cast. The fly broke cleanly through the surface and had hardly begun its descent when the line was suddenly wrenched taut and a silvery rainbow took to the air in a shower of spray. It was a powerful fish and used its strength to good effect, staying deep and transmitting its indignation by some violent head shaking. When I finally netted it, I was surprised that the scale registered only three pounds, for she had fought like a much larger fish. After a quick revival alongside the tube, I released her to drift off slowly.

We caught more than two dozen rainbows that day, the largest a fish of over five pounds which fell to the rod of my companion who, in the failing afternoon light, was also fishing an All-Rounder Damsel tight against a weedbed.

Takes occur at any time during the retrieve, often 'on-the-drop' when the fly is sinking just after entering the water, or during pauses in the retrieve.

Damselfly nymphs are fished most successfully with floating and intermediate lines. When fish are visibly feeding on nymphs near the surface I rely on a floating line and a long leader of about fifteen feet. Use the brightest floating fly-line available, as takes are sometimes quite subtle and may be signalled only by a slight movement of the tip of the fly-line. Usually, however, takes are very positive and trout will be well hooked when patterns are fished with a constant hand-twist retrieve.

The alternative is to use an intermediate fly-line with a leader of ten to twelve feet; this is the most effective technique for searching the water when fish are not actively feeding near the surface.

Takes vary from a subtle tightening of the line in the hand to a violent wrench. Generally, the power of a take is in direct proportion to the speed of the retrieve, which will usually make takes on damselfly nymphs quite – but not overly – solid. Takes can be so gentle that it appears as though the fly has fouled on a clump of weed.

I rely on 4X or 5X tippet diameters for most of my damselfly nymph fishing, occasionally stepping up to 3X when big fish, which must be kept away from weedbeds once hooked, are a possibility.

ALL-ROUNDER DAMSEL

HOOK: Tiemco 200R or 5263, #8 – #12.
THREAD: 6/0 prewaxed, olive.
TAIL: Olive marabou or olive grizzly marabou.
EYES: 35 lb burned monofilament.
RIB: Clear 4X monofilament.
BACK: Clear plastic strip, ⅛-inch wide, from a plastic bag.
ABDOMEN: Medium olive or olive brown dubbing.

LEGS: Olive grizzly hackle fibres, olive-dyed cock ringneck pheasant fibres or olive-dyed mallard flank fibres.
THORAX: Same as abdomen.

1. Tie in a bunch of marabou above the barb of the hook for the tail, and take the thread to a position behind the hook eye.

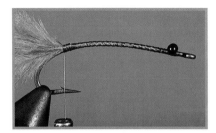

2. With figure-of-eight wraps, tie in a pair of eyes directly behind the eye of the hook. Return the thread to a position above the barb of the hook.

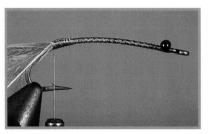

3. Tie in a length of clear monofilament for the rib and the clear plastic strip for the back above the hook barb.

4. Spin a thin noodle of dubbing onto the thread and form a thin, tapering abdomen, covering approximately three-quarters of the hook shank.

5. Tie in approximately five hackle or ringneck pheasant fibres on either side of the abdomen, keeping them fairly short, for the legs. Spin a thin noodle of dubbing for the thorax onto the thread.

6. Form the thorax with the dubbing, ensuring that it is slightly thicker than the abdomen.

7. Pull the strip of clear plastic tightly over the top of the abdomen and thorax, tie the strip off in front of the thorax, and trim the excess.

8. Wind the monofilament rib tightly over the abdomen and thorax in six to nine evenly spaced turns. Tie the rib off. Do not trap the legs when wrapping the rib through the abdomen and thorax.

9. Form a neat thread head, half-hitch and trim the thread. Apply head cement to the thread wraps. Break off the marabou to form a short tail.

Filoplume Damsel

E.H. 'GENE' ARMSTRONG

SEVERAL YEARS AGO I spent a memorable spring day with Terry Andrews fishing Mt. Arthur, a fabulous, high-altitude lake in East Griqualand. A blizzard-like hatch of tiny *Tricorythidae* mayflies was in full flurry on our arrival, and fish were bulging and porpoising all over the shallows of the lake, apparently taking the small emerging nymphs as they made their way to the water's surface to hatch.

We launched our float tubes off the wall and made our way to the shallows as fast as our fins would get us there, high with the anticipation of the action that was to follow.

Right *Mike Somerville with a fat rainbow hen taken during autumn from a private lake in KwaZulu-Natal.*

DAMSELFLY NYMPHS

*L*ike dragonflies, damselflies are part of the order Odonata but occupy their own suborder, Zygoptera. They are among the most abundant of all the aquatic insects found in South African still-waters, and are also present in slow-moving rivers and streams, making them significant to all trout fishermen, particularly those who enjoy fishing during the hotter months of the year.

Mating takes place and eggs are laid during the hot months from summer through to mid-autumn. The egg hatches into a nymph which, like the dragonfly, has a prehensile lower labium which can be extended to capture prey. The damselfly is a relatively slow-moving insect and captures its prey by stalking slowly through the weed. In this sheltered environment the damselfly is an elusive target for a trout on the lookout for a meal, but they become easily available in open water during their migrations from one area of a lake to another, as well as during hatching periods, when the nymphs migrate en masse towards the shore in search of a perch on which to complete the metamorph-osis from nymph to adult. They are, however, most abundant in and around weedbeds, and anglers should concentrate their efforts in these areas. Damselfly activity reaches its peak from November to January and it is during these months that the heaviest bags of the season – certainly in terms of the number of fish caught – can be taken if damselfly patterns are used.

Damselfly nymphs usually range from one-half to an inch in length and are slender, delicate insects with abdomens that end in two or three tails. These tails are, in fact, caudal lamellae (gills),

used to extract oxygen from the water. The nymph swims with a side-to-side wiggle greatly aided by the gills at the end of the abdomen. It has two large eyes on the sides of the head, as well as three pairs of spidery legs which are tucked away while swimming. Nymphs vary greatly in colour and match the colour of their surroundings. The most prevalent colours are shades of olive or tan, but for the greater part of the season it is best to use a medium to bright olive pattern.

The nymph swims up to ten inches before resting. This swimming motion is best imitated by an erratic hand-twist retrieve, interspersed with pauses of up to five seconds.

When conditions are favourable, trout will move to the surface and feed avidly on damselfly nymphs migrating to the shore. While these nymphs usually stay close to the protection of weedbeds, trout will cruise inches above the weed picking off the nymphs as they leave the weed to begin their migration. In these situations, trout will betray their presence in several ways, sometimes by a mere dimpling or slight upwelling of the water, but more often by powerful sub-surface surges that push bow waves ahead of their heads. These surface disturbances during the warmer periods of the day are often a sign that trout are intercepting shore-bound damselfly nymphs.

Although damselflies usually hatch during the morning, I have often found them hatching after midday on hot, bright days and, consequently, anglers taking a break from the midday heat may miss some of the finest action a stillwater can provide.

Above *The stomach contents of a trout taken from a lake in East Griqualand during summer show signs of opportunistic feeding – small mayflies, a* Platana *frog, and dragonflies – and selective feeding on damselfly nymphs, which numbered in their hundreds.*

But though we fished all the appropriate patterns to imitate the diminutive mayflies, we failed to hook any fish. Looking for an answer, I stared into the water and saw, in addition to the multitude of tiny *Tricorythidae* mayfly nymphs, several bright olive damselfly nymphs, wriggling quickly over the weed. When I took a closer look at the rises I saw they weren't the subtle, slow, porpoising rises normally associated with trout feeding on emerging *Tricorythidae* nymphs: they were powerful, surging boils that anglers often associate with trout feeding on damselfly nymphs.

Removing the Trico nymph imitation, I replaced it with a Filoplume Damsel and selected my first victim, a large rainbow feeding tight to the bank along a line of reeds. This fish was feeding hard near the surface, turning left and right and pushing small bow waves as it chased the wriggling damselfly nymphs making their way to the shore. The fish moved in a succession of rises but, just as I was preparing to cast, it

disappeared. Several others were feeding at the surface, but the fish I had targeted was worth waiting for so, rather than chase these, I cast blindly into the area where I suspected the trout to be feeding, and allowed the pattern to settle.

The fly had hardly landed when the line was wrenched taut and a powerful fish ripped coils of line from the line tray as it headed for the sanctuary of deeper water. The fish, a rainbow cock of five-and-a-quarter pounds, was one of eighteen I hooked that day, a day which ranks amongst my most memorable stillwater fishing. All fish, bar one, fell for what is in my opinion one of the finest producers of stillwater trout in South Africa during the warmer months, the Filoplume Damsel.

The Filoplume Damsel is one of several patterns devised by Gene Armstrong to incorporate filoplume or aftershaft feathers, and it fills the gap in my fly-box for a fly that fishes close to the water's surface. Its materials allow it to sink extremely slowly, making it my favourite pattern when fishing above weed which reaches almost to the water's surface.

The Filoplume Damsel's greatest asset is the palmered thorax hackle, which allows it to be fished inches above weed without fouling in it. It should be tied unweighted and fished over and around the weed, using a hand-twist retrieve interspersed with several pauses to simulate the frequent rests taken by a damselfly nymph swimming to shore.

When fishing this pattern over weed which is only a few feet below the surface, I use a high-visibility floating line and long leader of twelve to fifteen feet, depending on the conditions. Clear, flat water will mean the trout will be very aware of careless casts and anglers should be careful not to line fish feeding actively near the surface and should cast ahead of them by an appropriate distance. Takes are normally positive, and since the fly is usually fished only inches below the surface, they are frequently visible as well, resulting in some of the most exciting action of the year.

FILOPLUME DAMSEL

HOOK: Tiemco 200R, 2312 or 5263, #8 – #10.

THREAD: 6/0 prewaxed, olive.

TAIL: Medium to light olive marabou.

RIB: Silver wire.

ABDOMEN: Medium to light olive marabou.

LEGS: Silver or golden badger saddle hackle.

THORAX: Filoplume feather, colour to match abdomen.

HEAD: Peacock herl.

1. Tie in a thin clump of marabou along the entire length of the hook shank – this ensures a tapered abdomen in subsequent steps. Break off the marabou to form a short tail.

2. Tie in a length of wire for the rib and four or five marabou fibres by their tips for the abdomen. Take the thread to a point approximately one-third of the shank length from the eye of the hook.

3. Twist the marabou fibres into a rope, wind the rope forward so as to cover two-thirds of the hook shank, tie off and trim the excess.

4. Select a saddle hackle for the legs with fibres which are one-and-a-half to twice the width of the hook gape. Tie it in at the base so that its concave side faces outwards.

5. Select a fluffy filoplume feather for the thorax and tie it in over the hackle by the tip.

6. Wind the filoplume feather forward towards the eye in close turns and tie it off, leaving enough room for a peacock herl and thread head.

7. Wind the hackle forward through the filoplume feather toward the eye in three evenly spaced turns and tie the feather off.

8. Tie in four or five peacock herls directly in front of the filoplume feather and saddle hackle and take the thread to a point directly behind the hook eye.

9. Twist the herls into a rope and form a head with them. Wrap the rib through the abdomen, thorax and head, and tie it off. Form a thread head, half-hitch and trim. Apply head cement to the thread wraps.

Wiggle Damsel

FRED ARBONA JR.

WHILE DAMSELFLIES account for some of the most frenzied feeding activity in our lakes, they also cause some of the most frustrating fishing of the season, particularly for those anglers who lack the correct patterns to imitate these abundant aquatic insects. Although I prefer more suggestive patterns for most of my angling, a selective rainbow several seasons ago convinced me that an angler armed with a wide variety of patterns – ranging from exact to suggestive flies – stands a better chance of success than one with only a small selection.

An angling companion and I had spent a productive morning on one of KwaZulu-Natal's high altitude lakes and had found a nondescript damselfly nymph imitation to be particularly effective on the rainbows we could see cruising along a thick weedbed, thirty yards off the bank.

As the weather warmed towards midday and the damselfly activity began to increase, our catch rate started to drop off and we realised that the imitation, which until then had proved so successful, was no longer catching any fish.

I waded back to the shore for a softdrink and watched as my partner pitched the small nymph out to the fringe of the weedbed. One fish in particular continued to show regularly along the weed in a series of rhythmical rises, and on several occasions I had the pleasure of watching this fish follow the imitation towards the shore only to refuse it at the last moment. It would then continue to slowly patrol the perimeter of the weedbed.

I could find nothing wrong with my companion's presentation or his method of retrieve, so I thought perhaps the fault lay in the fly and waded back to discuss the matter with him. A glance into the margins of the lake showed extensive damselfly nymph activity and it was obvious that there were so many naturals to choose from that a more specific imitation was necessary to deceive the fish.

I removed a box containing damselfly nymphs from my vest and offered my companion what I consider to be the ace up my sleeve during heavy damselfly activity – a Wiggle Damsel.

After tying on the fly, we waited for the fish to show itself again. Like clockwork the trout appeared along the weed, and my partner's first presentation landed several feet ahead of it. The fish was aware immediately of the disturbance in the water, finned nonchalantly over to the imitation and took it.

After a brief struggle, the rainbow was netted. The hook had lodged deep in the throat – a sure sign that the pattern had been taken as confidently as a natural insect would have been.

I believe that Fred Arbona Jr., best known for his excellent book *Mayflies, the Angler and the Trout*, made his greatest contribution in terms of pattern development with his series of Wiggle Nymphs which were designed to imitate the motion of *Ephemerella* and *Baetis* mayfly nymphs. Arbona was not satisfied with the motion of the two-part Wiggle Nymph joined by piano wire created by Doug Swisher and Carl Richards, two famous American angler/entomologists, and so designed an imitation that would improve on theirs.

Below *The Wiggle Damsel seen from above. The clear plastic scoop or lip in front of the hook eye ensures that the pattern 'swims' through the water with a lifelike wiggling motion.*

Below *The author took this healthy Mt. Arthur rainbow on an Arbona Wiggle Damsel fished just under the surface during a heavy hatch of damselfly nymphs.*

Above *Mike Somerville watches as a powerful Waterford rainbow runs backing off the reel.*

He was convinced that trout based their decision to take a nymph – either natural or artificial – on the nymph's motion, particularly in tranquil waters where trout follow a nymph for a distance before accepting or rejecting it.

Arbona overcame the problems associated with the Swisher/Richards Wiggle Nymph by extending the body and tying in a tiny plastic scoop or lip, cut from hard, clear plastic, just above the hook eye, which resulted in an extremely lifelike, side-to-side wiggling motion. He found that under demanding conditions his patterns consistently outperformed traditional ones.

The original Arbona Wiggle Damsel called for an abdomen and thorax of olive ostrich herl, but I have modified the pattern somewhat, using a dubbed abdomen and thorax. In addition, I have also added burned monofilament eyes, which I feel greatly enhance its appearance. Although this pattern appears to be difficult to tie, it is in fact relatively easy to master, if time consuming. The fly has great visual appeal and obvious fishing potential.

The Wiggle Damsel should be fished in the same manner as other damselfly nymphs. A steady hand-twist retrieve will cause the pattern to move through the water in a side-to-side motion quite similar to that of the natural damselfly nymph. In addition, the scoop forces the angler to slow down the retrieve to a speed more in line with that of the natural insect. (Most fly-fishers retrieve their imitations far too rapidly, which will cause the Wiggle Damsel to spin in the water and twist the tippet.)

WIGGLE DAMSEL

HOOK: Tiemco 3769, 3761 or 5262, #10 – #14.

THREAD: 6/0 prewaxed, olive.

SCOOP: Clear, rigid plastic.

EYES: 35 lb burned monofilament.

TAILS: Olive hackle tips.

ABDOMEN: Medium to light olive dubbing.

THORAX: Medium to light olive dubbing, slightly thicker than abdomen.

WINGCASE: Hen or cock pheasant central tail.

LEGS (OPTIONAL): Olive-dyed partridge hackle.

1. Cut a plastic scoop into the spade-like shape shown here. The top part of the scoop is ± 3 mm wide, the tail-end ± 1 mm wide, and the length ± 4 mm.

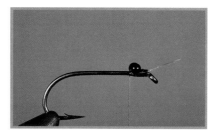

2. Tie in the end of the scoop behind the hook eye with the top extending forward. Leaving space for a head behind the hook eye, tie in the monofilament eyes.

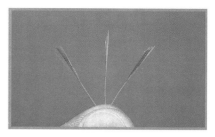

3. Strip the fibres from three hackles, leaving behind only the tips. The tail-ends plus stripped hackle stems should be about twice the length of the shank.

4. Tie in the stripped hackle stems above the barb, ensuring that the stripped portion equals the shank-length. Spin a thin noodle of dubbing onto the thread.

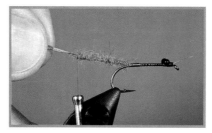

5. Grasp the hackle tips with your left hand and, using your right hand, wind the noodle of dubbing around the stripped stems until you reach the tails.

6. Continue wrapping the stripped stems with dubbing until a thin, tapered, extended abdomen is formed.

7. Spin a noodle of dubbing onto the thread and form the remainder of the abdomen, covering half the hook shank with dubbing.

8 Tie in the wingcase directly in front of the abdomen and spin a noodle of dubbing onto the thread.

9. Form the thorax, taking figure-of-eight wraps between the eyes. The thorax should be slightly thicker than the abdomen.

10. Pull the wingcase over the top of the thorax, tie off and trim the excess.

11. Form a small thread head, taking a few wraps of thread under the scoop to ensure it stands at a 45-degree angle to the shank. Half-hitch and trim the thread. Apply head cement to the thread wraps.

12. Pick out the dubbing in the thorax area to represent legs.

Gold Ribbed Hare's Ear Nymph (American)

ANON

THE GOLD RIBBED HARE'S EAR NYMPH, or Hare's Ear as it is commonly called, is a pattern that deserves a place in every angler's fly-box because it is simple to tie, requires no exotic tying materials and, most important, it is one of the most effective nymph patterns.

The Hare's Ear Nymph is a classic impressionistic nymph, imitating no aquatic insect in particular but several in general. I use it as a general mayfly nymph imitation because its overall brownish-grey colour matches many of the *Baetidae* mayfly nymphs found in South African lakes and streams. The Hare's Ear can be tied in various sizes and colours to represent many other food forms. In a mustard colour, for example, it mimics the yellow stoneflies found in some of our headwater streams. It is an extremely versatile pattern and I fish it in all waters.

A recent development that has further enhanced the appeal of this pattern is the slight changes introduced by Randall Kaufmann, which include the addition of a peacock sword wingcase and copper-wire rib. This variation appeals to me so much that I find myself using it more than the original pattern and, tied in a variety of colours, it imitates several species of nymphs. This Kaufmann Hare's Ear Nymph, tied in different sizes and colours, imitates most of

Top *This beautiful rainbow, caught by Fred Steynberg from the Bell River above Rhodes, was taken on a small nymph fished deep alongside an undercut bank.*

Above *Terry Andrews, a proponent of the Gold Ribbed Hare's Ear Nymph, releases a tagged rainbow in a KwaZulu-Natal lake.*

Above *Terry Andrews removes the stomach contents of a trout with a stomach pump to ascertain what food-forms the captured trout was feeding on. This is a relatively harmless method of removing stomach contents and means that the angler does not have to kill the fish he captures to inspect the aquatic and terrestrial foods they have eaten.*

the mayfly nymphs an angler can expect to encounter in a season. For the fly-fisher who wishes to reduce his pattern selection, this is a very good fly to start with.

When fishing rivers and streams I always fish the Hare's Ear Nymph on a floating line with a leader of up to twelve feet, and a strike indicator. A strike indicator is essential when nymphing our fast freestone streams, as they relay takes that would otherwise go unnoticed by the angler. For many years I used indicators made from a wide variety of materials, including cork and foam. While they did a serviceable job they were not the answer, and it was during a trip to New Zealand that a guide introduced me to yarn indicators. These yarn indicators are all the nymphing angler will ever need. The yarn used for steelhead patterns, called Glo-Bug Yarn, makes excellent indicator material, is available in a wide variety of colours and is inexpensive. I soak the yarn in a liquid floatant for a few hours, after which it is virtually unsinkable, even with the heaviest of nymphs suspended below it. I attach the indicator to the leader or tippet with a simple slip knot, which means the indicator can be removed when I wish to fish dry flies or streamers. The distance the indicator is placed from the fly and the size required to drift nymphs through rough water without the yarn sinking are things that one can determine only

through on-stream experience. The nymph should be cast upstream, or across and upstream, and allowed to drift naturally downstream, thereby imitating a helpless nymph that is being swept along by the current.

In stillwaters, I fish the Hare's Ear on a long leader of up to fifteen feet. It is a fine prospecting nymph as well as one that can be cast to visible fish feeding near the surface. I do not weight my Hare's Ear Nymphs for stillwater use, relying on the natural absorbency of the fur to sink the pattern. When fishing them on a floating line I use a slow hand-twist retrieve and, as a result, takes can be extremely subtle. Anglers should consequently choose the highest floating and most visible fly-line for this particular style of fishing.

One of my favourite methods when fishing small mayfly nymph imitations on a floating line in stillwaters is to wade carefully along the shoreline, searching the water ahead of me. Most anglers neglect the productive shoreline area, thinking instead that the further they cast, the more chance they have of taking fish. However, trout are particularly fond of the shallow margins of lakes with their abundant food, and by wading parallel to the bank and systematically fanning casts ahead of a predetermined wading route, the angler will hook a surprising number of trout in this often ignored shallow water.

GOLD RIBBED HARE'S EAR NYMPH

HOOK: Tiemco 200R, 5262 or 5263, #8 – #18.

THREAD: 8/0 prewaxed, brown.

TAIL: Hare's ear fur.

RIB: Flat gold tinsel.

ABDOMEN: Blended hare's ear fur.

WINGCASE: White tip turkey tail segment.

THORAX: Same as abdomen.

Variation: KAUFMANN HARE'S EAR NYMPH (right)

HOOK: Tiemco 200R, 5262 or 5263, #8 – #18.

THREAD: 8/0 prewaxed, colour to match abdomen.

TAIL: Hare's ear fur, colour to match abdomen.

RIB: Copper wire.

ABDOMEN: Blended hare's ear fur. The most widely used colours are natural, black, rust, mustard and various shades of olive and brown.

WINGCASE: Peacock sword.

THORAX: Blended hare's ear fur, colour to match abdomen.

1. Tie in a thick tail, which should be one-third to one-half the length of the hook shank, above the barb of the hook.

2. Tie in the rib and spin a thin noodle of dubbing onto the thread for the abdomen.

3. Form a neat, tapering abdomen over two-thirds of the hook shank. Wind the rib through the abdomen in four or five evenly spaced turns, tie it off and trim the excess.

4. Tie in a wingcase directly in front of the abdomen. Spin a thin noodle of dubbing onto the thread for the thorax.

5. Form the thorax, ensuring that it is slightly thicker than the abdomen. Note the space left behind the eye of the hook for a small head.

6. Pull the wingcase over the top of the thorax, tie off and trim excess. Form a small thread head, half-hitch and trim. Apply head cement. Pick out the thorax with a dubbing needle to simulate legs.

Pheasant Tail Nymph

FRANK SAWYER

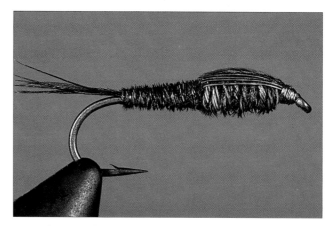

Above *Sawyer's Pheasant Tail Nymph.*

THE PHEASANT TAIL NYMPH was one of the first nymphs that I taught myself to tie and is still one of my firm favourites. The original Pheasant Tail Nymph was designed in the 1950s by Frank Sawyer to imitate the abundant *Baetis* mayflies that he encountered, and is simplicity itself to tie, as the only components are cock ringneck pheasant tail fibres and copper wire.

Sawyer used copper wire as the tying thread to reduce tying time and to produce a slender, weighted nymph which would quickly penetrate the water's surface and sink rapidly. Almost all of Sawyer's patterns reflect this streamlined approach to design. Although his Pheasant Tail Nymph is his best-known and most popular pattern, he was responsible for several other important patterns, such as the Grey Goose Nymph and Killer Bug which, over the years, have fallen into relative obscurity.

Sawyer, a professional river keeper, gained a reputation as one of England's finest nymph fishermen and spent many years fishing the famous River Avon, a chalkstream that flows through Hampshire in southern England. While perhaps not as well known as other Hampshire chalkstreams, such as the Test and Itchen, the Avon provides excellent hatches equal to those of its better-known counterparts. Sawyer's thoughts and experiences are well chronicled and his books make interesting reading, particularly *Nymphs and the Trout* and *Keeper of the Stream*.

Below *Terry Andrews nymphing the crystal-clear waters of the Sterkspruit River in the Rhodes/Barkly East area during autumn.*

Above *Well-known Natal angler Terry Andrews nymphing a beautiful section of the Sterkspruit River in the Rhodes/Barkly East area.*

The original Pheasant Tail Nymph spawned a host of variations; one of the most popular contemporary versions is Al Troth's, which has a peacock herl thorax. Although I carry both the Sawyer and Troth versions, I find that I use the latter more frequently as I consider it more versatile because of its buggier appearance and the added appeal of the iridescent peacock herl in the thorax. These attributes make it suitable both for fishing to visible fish or as a prospecting pattern. I use the Sawyer Pheasant Tail Nymph solely for fishing to visible trout.

The Pheasant Tail Nymph is used worldwide to imitate the nymphs of the ubiquitous *Baetidae* mayfly family, as well as a host of other small brown mayfly nymphs. These mayflies emerge by swimming to the water's surface where the dun breaks free of the nymphal exoskeleton. When trout are deep a weighted Pheasant Tail Nymph is ideal, as it sinks quickly to the feeding level of the trout. Once it has reached this level, a response from the fish can be 'induced' by raising the tip of the rod, causing the nymph pattern to rise towards the surface. On rivers and streams, this is usually done as the imitation approaches the trout after it has been dead-drifted with the current for several yards. A similar approach can be applied to trout that are feeding fairly deep in stillwaters: the nymph pattern is pitched out in front of the cruising trout and allowed to sink to the bottom. As the trout approaches the imitation, the rod is lifted to simulate the rising motion of the natural in the water. This particular style of fishing is best practised from the bank, where the angler is able to use the advantage of height to spot the fish. Float tubes and similar low-floating craft do not always afford this advantage, in which case a strike indicator is a useful aid in stillwaters.

Fishing small nymphs to visible stillwater trout, using light tippets, offers some of the most demanding fishing available, but the rewards can be great and there are few

PHEASANT TAIL NYMPH (SAWYER)
HOOK: Tiemco 5262 or 5263, #10 – #18.
THREAD: Copper wire.
TAIL: Cock ringneck pheasant tail fibres.
ABDOMEN: Same as tail.
WINGCASE: Same as tail.
THORAX: Cock ringneck pheasant tail fibres and
   copper wire, twisted together.

PHEASANT TAIL NYMPH (TROTH)
HOOK: Tiemco 5262 or 5263, #10 – #18.
THREAD: 8/0 prewaxed, brown.
TAIL: Cock ringneck pheasant tail fibres.
RIB: Copper wire.
ABDOMEN: Same as tail.
WINGCASE: Same as tail.
THORAX: Peacock herl.
LEGS:·Same as tail.

experiences that equal that of seeing a large trout rushing over to take a small nymph rising through the water. This 'induced-take' technique was popularised by Oliver Kite through his book *Nymph Fishing in Practice*. It is an extremely effective method if you can see the trout in rivers or predict their feeding paths in lakes.

Note: Ed Herbst often includes one or two strands of marabou with the pheasant tail fibres used in the abdomen. He clips the marabou top and bottom, leaving the tufts projecting from the sides of the fly only, thereby simulating the fluttering gills of the mayfly nymph. (These gills are most prominent on nymphs living in slow-flowing or still water.)

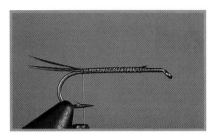

1. Tie in a few pheasant tail fibres above the barb of the hook to form the tails. The tails should be one-third to one-half the length of the hook shank.

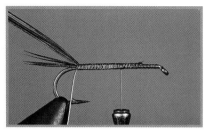

2. At the same point, tie in a fine copper wire rib and three to four pheasant tail fibres by their tips for the abdomen. Take the thread to a point approximately one-third of the hook shank from the eye.

3. Twist together the pheasant tail fibres to form a rope and wind the rope forward in close turns to form the abdomen, which should cover approximately two-thirds of the hook shank. Tie off and trim the excess.

4. Wind the rib forward through the abdomen, tie it off and trim the excess. This will add segmentation and strength to the abdomen.

5. Tie in the wingcase and, for the thorax, approximately five peacock herls by the tips directly in front of the abdomen. Take the thread to behind the eye.

6. Twist the peacock herls into a rope and wind it forward towards the eye to form the thorax. Tie it off and trim the excess.

7. Pull the wingcase forward over the top of the thorax, tie it off and trim the excess. Note that enough space has been left behind the hook eye for legs to be tied in and a small head to be formed.

8. Select approximately ten pheasant tail fibres and tie them in in front of the thorax, with the tips facing back towards the tail. The tips should be one-third the length of the hook shank.

9. Divide the pheasant tail fibres and pull them down on either side of the thorax to form the legs. Trim the excess, form a small, neat head, half-hitch and trim the thread. Apply head cement to the thread wraps.

Brown Nymph

ROBIN FICK

WHEN I FIRST FISHED the streams of the Western Cape several years ago I relied almost exclusively on nymphs to deceive the majority of my fish. Dry flies were extremely effective, but the largest fish generally fell for deeply sunken nymphs. For most of my nymph fishing I used the Brown Nymph as a deep, searching pattern, and it proved to be an impressive producer of trout.

This pattern was designed by Robin Fick, one of South Africa's most talented and innovative fly-fishers and someone who, on stillwaters, had few equals. (The last I heard of Robin was that he had given up trout fishing in favour of saltwater fly-fishing. This has lost an innovative fly-tier and -designer to the freshwater angling fraternity.) Born and educated in Cape Town, Robin has fished widely throughout the country and his knowledge of trout fishing, and its allied subjects, is vast. Robin's patterns are simple, easy to tie and appear to have been through the teeth of a trout rather than to have come from the jaws of a vice!

The Brown Nymph was designed to imitate the many small brownish mayfly nymphs – particularly the clinger nymphs – found in our rivers and streams. Most of these nymphs are of the family *Heptageniidae*; in South Africa these nymphs are most commonly found in the faster stretches of freestone streams. The nymphs have adapted to life in fast, turbulent waters by developing a flat body. It never ceases to amaze me how adept they are at clinging onto river-bed rocks and stones, even in the fastest currents. Nevertheless, some lose their grip and, before they are able to regain their hold on another obstruction, they are swept downstream at the mercy of the current. They still have an amazing ability to

Above *Terry Andrews nymphing the fast waters of a stream in the north-eastern Cape while Elwin Love and Mosey look on.*

make instinctively for the bottom, and thus an imitation that enters the water and immediately sinks towards the bottom will effectively duplicate this downward swimming motion.

Despite what has been written in other countries about the importance of caddisflies in the trout's diet, it is mayfly nymphs that have consistently turned up in the stomach analyses I have done on trout taken from South African rivers and streams, albeit – in many cases – in limited numbers. Caddisflies and other aquatic insects, on the other hand, have appeared in only limited numbers, and in many cases were completely absent. Research by Bob Crass

on the stomach contents of trout supports my observations regarding mayflies – although he found 5 407 different food forms in the stomach contents of 235 KwaZulu-Natal trout, 75 percent of the stomach contents was made up of mayfly nymphs. Hence the need for having a serviceable mayfly nymph imitation in your fly-box.

Above and left *These different species of mayfly nymphs show how their appearance differs in different waters. The species above has evolved a flattened body to accommodate life in fast water, while the nymph on the left has enlarged gills for life in slower currents.*
Below *Maclear angler Elwin Love nymphing the Sterkspruit River in the Rhodes/Barkly East area.*

I fish the Brown Nymph on a twelve to fifteen foot leader, depending on current velocity and stream depth. Soft, thin tippet materials will enable the nymph pattern to react more naturally to minor currents in the main flow, and will allow the nymph to rise and fall naturally as it drifts along. A strike indicator is extremely important when fishing nymphs in fast water. It facilitates strike detection and allows the angler to control the depth at which the nymph drifts in the water. For our fast freestone streams I like to fish bright orange indicators as they are easy to follow.

BROWN NYMPH

HOOK: Tiemco 5262, 5263 or 200R, #12 – #16.

THREAD: 8/0 prewaxed, brown.

TAIL: Cock ringneck pheasant tail fibres.

RIB: Copper wire.

ABDOMEN: Medium to dark brown dubbing.

WINGCASE: Cock ringneck pheasant tail fibres or white tip turkey tail segment.

THORAX: Same as abdomen.

LEGS: Brown hen or brown partridge hackle.

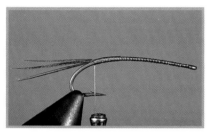

1. Tie in three to four pheasant fibres above the barb of the hook for the tail. The tail should be one-half to a full hook shank in length.

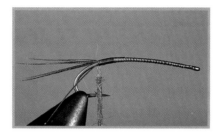

2. Tie in the rib and spin a thin noodle of dubbing onto the thread for the abdomen.

3. Form a thin, neatly tapering abdomen, covering two-thirds of the hook shank.

4. Wind the wire rib over the abdomen in six to eight tight turns, tie it off and trim the excess. This will provide the abdomen with segmentation.

5. Tie in a wingcase directly in front of the abdomen and spin a thin noodle of dubbing onto the thread for the thorax.

6. Form the thorax, ensuring that it is slightly thicker than the abdomen. Note the space left behind the eye for the head and to wind a hackle for the legs.

7. Select a partridge hackle and tie it in by its tip with the concave side facing the fly.

8. Take two turns of hackle around the shank, tie off and trim. The fibres should not extend beyond the point of the hook. If any fibres are above the hook, stroke into place and tie down.

9. Pull the wingcase over the top of the thorax, tie it off and trim the excess. Form a small, neat thread head, half-hitch and trim the thread. Apply head cement to the thread wraps.

Zak Nymph

TOM SUTCLIFFE

Above *A Zak Nymph tied by Tom Sutcliffe.*

TO MY KNOWLEDGE, THE ZAK NYMPH – or simply Zak, as it is best known – was until recently unheard of by most fly-fishers. I do, however, recall Tom Sutcliffe speaking of a similar nymph pattern many years ago when I fished Mick Kimber's 'Old Dam' with him and Hugh Huntley, and the Zak Nymph that most anglers use today is probably an evolution of the fly he spoke of. According to Tom, the pattern was developed in the late 1980s as an all-purpose nymph and, rather than being a new pattern, was intended to be a method of tying a more buggy-looking nymph. The pattern was named for the Zulu gentleman who took care of the cottage at the Kimber's syndicate.

Tom was looking for a fly with strong contrast, plenty of movement and as much naturalness as he could incorporate into a pattern. He was also looking for an imitation that he could tie quickly, without much fuss and which required no exotic materials.

The peacock herl he settled on is a wonderful material with which to tie flies, but used on its own as a body material it lacks clear segmentation. However, as the

segmentation on an insect's abdomen is fairly subtle, a quality Tom was trying to replicate with his artificial, peacock herl is quite suitable. It is not a bad idea, though, to tie in a fine wire rib with this pattern to add durability.

In the short time that the Zak Nymph has taken to rise from relative obscurity to popularity with a broad spectrum of South African fly-fishers, many changes have been made to it, the most interesting of which are the changes to the tying procedure. In the first Zak Nymphs the materials were tied in behind the hook eye and the thread was taken to a point above the hook barb. The materials were then wrapped towards the thread and tied off. The thread was then used as a rib as it was wrapped back towards the hook eye. Tom now uses the more conventional method of tying the materials in above the hook barb and wrapping them towards the eye. Also, the fibres from the one side of the hackle are now stripped so that the palmered hackle appears less dense. As a result of this rather unorthodox tying

Above *Well-known Rhodes angler Fred Steynberg poses with a fine rainbow taken from the Bell River just above Rhodes.*
Left *Fred Steynberg nymphing the sparkling waters of the Bell River.*

method, the fly has little aesthetic appeal. It is an untidy pattern lacking any semblance of symmetry – which is precisely what Tom had in mind when developing it.

Tom also had a rather unusual method of forming the body: he plaited the peacock herls, stripped peacock herls and hackle which made up the body. These days, however, Tom seems simply to twist the materials together, probably to reduce his tying time, but the plaiting appeals to me and is the method demonstrated here.

The materials used have also changed a fair deal since I first read about this pattern in *Flyfishing* magazine several years ago. The tailing fibres originally used to tie the fly were from a water mongoose, but these fibres were found to be too hard and have been replaced by a few wisps of softer hackle fibres which react better to water currents and give the fly better movement during its drift.

When Tom first wrote of this pattern in *Flyfishing* magazine, he did not encourage the addition of a bead in the pattern as he believed it merely added angler appeal. Nowadays he ties his patterns both with and without a metal bead at the head – testimony to the effectiveness of beads in fly patterns.

Tom likes to cast the fly upstream on our freestone streams, fishing it on a dead drift, or retrieving it only after it has drifted well down from his position, and then giving it a twitch or two. He likes to fish the fly using a small strike indicator to relay the subtlest of takes.

On stillwaters, Tom likes to add only a small amount of weight to the fly and to fish it slowly around weedbeds using a floating line, long leader and strike indicator. When fished like this the fly will often be taken 'on-the-drop', so the end of the leader must be watched at all times.

While the Zak Nymph has outperformed certain patterns and failed against others, it has worked consistently well for Tom, who believes it to be the most successful nymph he has ever used. It is a quick and easy pattern to tie and, like his DDD (pages 149–151), belongs in every South African fly-fisher's box.

ZAK NYMPH

HOOK: Tiemco 5262 or 5263, #8 – #16.

THREAD: 6/0 prewaxed, black.

HEAD (OPTIONAL): Metal bead.

TAIL: Black or dun cock hackle fibres.

BODY: Three stripped peacock herls, two peacock herls, single strand of Krystal Flash, and black or dun cock hackle with the fibres stripped from one side.

Above *Tom Sutcliffe poses with a rainbow taken from the Willow Stream in the Barkly East area.*

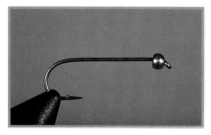

1. Slip a small bead onto the hook and fit it snugly against the eye.

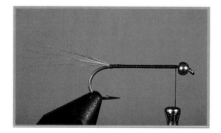

2. Above the barb, tie in 10 to 12 hackle fibres for the tail; the tail should be the same length as the hook shank but the fibres should not all be of uniform length. Return the thread to a position behind the bead.

3. Tie in the three stripped peacock herls together with the two peacock herls, a strand of Krystal Flash and the prepared hackle.

4. Return the thread to the tail tie-in position. Plait or wind the body material into a rope and form a neatly tapered body as shown.

5. Trap the body materials above the barb with the thread, and continue winding the thread forward through the body materials towards the bead. Note the length of the hackle fibres.

6. Trim the excess hackle tip. Half-hitch and trim the thread. Apply head cement to the thread wraps.

Flashback Nymph

ANON

THE CONCEPT OF USING BRIGHT MATERIAL in the wingcase of a nymph has been around for many years – I have been tying and fishing these Flashback Nymphs, as they are known, for over a decade – but only in recent years have they gained well-deserved popularity.

My research indicates that British anglers have, for many years, experimented with tinsel wingcases in nymph patterns, but it was only when I visited New Zealand in 1994 that I realised how popular these patterns had become (due to the efforts of local guide Frank Schlosser) and how effective they are at deceiving trout. Across the Pacific another angler, Tim Tollett, has done much for the fly's popularity in the western United States, particularly in his home state of Montana, where it is used either as a search-and-probe pattern or to cast to shy, selective trout feeding visibly in the current. Tim owns and operates Frontier Anglers, a full-service fly shop located in Dillon near the famous Beaverhead River where the pattern has proved successful. His store stocks Flashback Nymphs in a wide variety of colours and sizes, imitating most of the mayfly nymphs found in North American streams.

The 'flashback' principle uses flat tinsel materials – popular for decades – to enhance patterns. The Flashback Nymph is based on the premise that the highly visible tinsel wingcase acts as a trigger mechanism, causing trout to strike. The tinsel wingcase reflects light penetrating the water, making it highly visible, particularly under bright, sunny conditions. Whatever the reason, it is an exceptional producer of trout, particularly in deep, fast rivers and streams where trout have scant time to inspect food drifting by.

Top right *A Flashback Nymph seen from above. The tinsel reflects light and thereby acts as a trigger mechanism to trout.*
Right *Flashback Nymphs tied by professional New Zealand guide Frank Schlosser.*

In larger sizes, the Flashback Nymphs are amongst my favourite patterns for searching deep, fast stretches of our rivers and streams. They have produced excellent results for me on streams such as the Jan du Toit's in the Western Cape and various sections of the Umzimkulu River near Underberg. On a recent trip to the Rhodes area in the north-eastern Cape, Terry Andrews and I fished these patterns with great effect on streams like the Bell, Kloppershoekspruit and Sterkspruit.

I began fishing Flashback Nymphs on stillwaters several years ago after sitting out a blizzard-like hatch of tiny hyaline-winged mayflies *(Tricorythidae* family) at Mt. Arthur in East Griqualand. Fish were feeding all over the lake but I could not connect with them. The fish were bulging softly to take the emerging nymphs in the surface film but were not taking the adults off the top. I went through the ritual of trying the flies that usually work during emergences of these tiny mayflies but failed to interest any of the fish, which continued to feed in slow, languid rises. When I

MAYFLIES

Mayflies do not go through a pupal stage but hatch directly from the water-dwelling nymph into the adult, which emerges from the water to a life in the air. The adult, however, has two stages. In its sexually immature stage it is called a dun (subimago). This dun (subimago) moults into a sexually mature adult called the spinner (imago). The adults mate in the air, and the females then lay their eggs in a number of ways, two of which are of interest to the fly-fisher: the females may touch the surface of the water with the tips of their abdomens or they may swim or crawl down aquatic vegetation to lay their eggs before dying. The term 'spinner' is derived from the apparent spinning action of these mature females as they fall to the water to lay their eggs.

Above *Mike Somerville battles a Mt. Arthur rainbow which fell for a small Flashback Nymph during spring.*

finally settled on a #16 *Callibaetis* Flashback Nymph, I started hooking a fish on almost every cast, so effective was the fly.

When we fish Mt. Arthur now all my fishing companions have their fly-boxes crammed with these small imitations. Mike Somerville and I took over seventy rainbows, most in the three-pound range, during a weekend at Mt. Arthur using only small *Callibaetis* Flashback Nymphs. During another memorable day at Mt. Arthur, I caught twenty-five rainbows during a day's fishing, all but one taken on a small Flashback Nymph.

When using these patterns on stillwaters, I fish them with a floating line, long leaders of between twelve and fifteen feet, and light tippets of up to 5X. I usually fish the unweighted imitation with a slow hand-twist retrieve, or merely retrieve the slack that forms in the line when imitations are fished static with a floating line. Takes are almost always positive, resulting in solid hook-ups.

Another favourite stillwater application for the Flashback Nymph is during the emergence of a South African stillwater mayfly which closely resembles the North American *Callibaetis* mayfly (an abundant slow-water mayfly commonly found in stillwaters in the western United States, where trout feed frantically on the emerging nymphs). In our stillwaters, particularly those in KwaZulu-Natal and the Kokstad area of East Griqualand, we have a similar mayfly which can also stimulate heavy surface feeding, often leaving anglers frustrated and fishless. These nymphs may be mistaken for juvenile damselfly nymphs because they swim in a similar manner and have the same colours, ranging from a medium greyish-brown to tan. While the duns of this mayfly are of little value to the fly-fisher because they are able to escape easily once they have emerged, the nymphs and emerging duns, on the other hand, form an abundant food source as they struggle in the surface film for several minutes to free themselves from the nymphal shuck.

Trout feed right up in the film under these circumstances and show themselves with strong sub-surface swirls, leaving no bubbles on the surface. This is the cue to tie on an unweighted Flashback Nymph and work the pattern slowly at the surface using a slow, hand-twist retrieve.

As a deep, probing nymph in fast rivers and streams, I fish Flashback Nymphs on a leader of between ten and twelve feet together with a strike indicator. Currents at the streambed are slower than those at the surface and it is here that trout hold, and where nymphal imitations should be fished.

Split-shot will take a nymph into this layer and should be crimped on two to three inches above the pattern for maximum effect. A downstream, drag-free drift, preceded by a 'tuck' cast – a cast where the leader and fly 'tuck' under the fly-line before the line lands on the water, thereby enabling the fly to reach the streambed quickly – will enable the pattern to get quickly to the bottom and once there to drift without drag.

I have not given a specific dressing for a Flashback Nymph in the tying procedure, since almost any nymph can be converted to the Flashback Nymph's style (a good example is the Hare's Ear Nymph). However, the list of dressings on this page (see right) and overleaf are those stocked by Tim Tollett in his shop in Montana and will provide the fly-fisher with a wide variety of Flashback Nymphs.

Top *A beautifully coloured Mt. Arthur rainbow which was deceived using a small Flashback Nymph in spring.*

Above *The author watches as a three-and-three-quarter-pound rainbow swims off, having fallen for a small Flashback Nymph fished just below the surface.*

HARE'S EAR FLASHBACK

HOOK: Tiemco 3769, #10 – #16.

THREAD: 8/0 prewaxed, brown.

TAIL: Hare's ear guard hairs.

RIB: Gold or copper wire.

ABDOMEN: Hare's ear fur or hare's ear sparkle blend dubbing.

WINGCASE: #10 flat silver mylar tinsel.

THORAX: Same as abdomen.

DARK OLIVE-BROWN FLASHBACK

HOOK: Tiemco 3769, #10 – #16.

THREAD: 8/0 prewaxed, dark olive.

TAIL: Brown partridge or cock ringneck pheasant tail.

RIB: Copper wire.

ABDOMEN: Dark olive-brown sparkle blend dubbing.

WINGCASE: #10 flat silver mylar tinsel.

THORAX: Same as abdomen.

57

PHEASANT TAIL FLASHBACK

HOOK: Tiemco 3769, #10 – #16.

THREAD: 8/0 prewaxed, brown.

TAIL: Cock ringneck pheasant tail.

RIB: Copper wire.

ABDOMEN: Same as tail.

WINGCASE: #10 flat silver mylar tinsel.

THORAX: Same as tail.

BLACK FLASHBACK

HOOK: Tiemco 3769, #10 – #16.

THREAD: 8/0 prewaxed, black.

TAIL: Black ringneck pheasant tail, or similar.

RIB: Copper wire.

ABDOMEN: Black sparkle blend dubbing, or similar.

WINGCASE: #10 flat silver mylar tinsel.

THORAX: Same as abdomen.

PEACOCK FLASHBACK

HOOK: Tiemco 3769, #10 – #16.

THREAD: 8/0 prewaxed, black.

TAIL: Cock ringneck pheasant tail.

RIB: Copper wire.

ABDOMEN: Peacock herl.

WINGCASE: #10 flat silver mylar tinsel.

THORAX: Peacock herl.

CALLIBAETIS FLASHBACK

HOOK: Tiemco 5262, #14 – #16.

THREAD: 8/0 prewaxed, brown.

TAIL: Brown partridge.

RIB: Copper wire.

ABDOMEN: Greyish-brown dubbing blend.

WINGCASE: #10 flat silver mylar tinsel.

THORAX: Same as abdomen.

1. Take the thread to a position above the hook barb and tie in the tail, which should be about half the length of the hook shank.

2. Tie in a wire rib and spin a thin noodle of dubbing onto the thread.

3. Form a thin, neatly tapering abdomen over two-thirds of the hook shank. Wind the rib over the abdomen in five to seven evenly spaced turns, tie off and trim the excess.

4. Tie in a length of flat tinsel and spin a thin noodle of dubbing onto the thread.

5. Form the thorax, ensuring that it is slightly thicker than the abdomen.

6. Pull the tinsel over the top of the thorax, tie off and trim excess. Form a small, neat thread head, half-hitch and apply head cement. Pick out the thorax with a dubbing needle to simulate legs.

Hare and Copper

ANON

NEW ZEALAND IS A COUNTRY renowned for its superb fly-fishing, and for the angler looking for the opportunity of going one-on-one with large trout, there are few countries to equal it. Essentially, most of the fishing is a hunting style of angling where the trout must first be located before they can be cast to. The trout are large – larger than anything the South African fly-fisher will ever see in local waters – but the lessons learned there are as valid in South Africa as they are in New Zealand. Though I have visited New Zealand on several occasions now, it was during my first trip to the South Island that I was taught how small, simple patterns can deceive large trout.

We spent a week in Omarama, a small town in the central region of the South Island, fishing some of the fantastic rivers and streams in the area. On our arrival in the town we hired one of New Zealand's most respected fishing guides, Frank Schlosser. During our first morning with him I managed to land a twenty-seven-and-a-half-inch brown cockfish which had been holding in the centre of a long, shallow run. We spent the rest of the week exploring the surrounding waters on our own and concentrated our efforts mainly on one stream: a small, thin piece of water flowing between high sand bluffs. One day in particular stands out clearly, because it proved the ability of small flies to take big trout.

Tom Lewin and I had begun our day's fishing in the late morning, working our way slowly upstream looking for fish in all the likely lies. We had been walking and looking for trout along the centre of the same run where earlier in the week I had taken the big cockfish, when we froze in our tracks. Lying directly ahead of us, tight to the bank and completely out of the main current flow, was a large brown, his huge spots clearly visible in the clear currents. The fish did not appear to be feeding and was lying almost motionless, the only sign of life the slow movement of its gill covers and tail.

We backed away quietly and decided that Tom would try for the fish. It was not an easy proposition: the fish was a very difficult prospect in the lie it was holding in, with almost no current to deliver the fly to the trout. While I kept an eye on the fish, Tom walked well downstream and then retraced his steps carefully, working himself into a casting position behind the fish.

His first few casts were accurate and delicate, but the trout moved off slowly into the current, obviously unhappy with the proceedings, though none of the casts had lined his position and Tom was casting from well behind the fish.

Above *Tom Lewin and Terry Andrews prospecting the Witte River in Bain's Kloof Pass. The Witte River offers anglers a unique opportunity to sight-fish to trout using dry flies and small nymphs like the Hare and Copper.*

Moving up, Tom put a few more drifts through the brown's new lie, but again the fish moved off, this time upstream into slightly deeper, faster water.

Moving up again, Tom cast the small nymph upstream of the trout's lie. By this stage we were both convinced that the trout was spooked and the chances of hooking it seemed slim. The indicator continued to drift unhindered downstream past the brown's lie, when suddenly the fish moved to the side and the tiny wool indicator dipped beneath the water's surface.

The brown put up a fantastic battle on the 5X tippet material, racing all over the shallow run in an attempt to rid itself of the stinging fly in its jaw. When Tom finally slipped the net under the hook-jawed fish I don't know who was more relieved, he or I. The tiny fly was lodged firmly in the tip of the trout's upper jaw. After a brief photographic session, we released it and it swam away wiser, I hope, for the experience.

Above *This bright Bell River rainbow took a Hare and Copper fished deep through a fast run with a Bead Head Nymph to take it down.*
Left *The author took this twenty-four-inch, seven-and-a-quarter-pound brown on a #16 Hare and Copper from the headwaters of a South Island stream in New Zealand.*
Below left *A tiny Hare and Copper deceived this twenty-seven-and-a-half-inch New Zealand brown. Note the fly lodged in the tip of the trout's upper jaw.*

The fish was a replica of the brown I had taken earlier in the week, a magnificent cockfish of twenty-seven-and-a-half inches; however it was not the size of the fish that impressed me but rather the fly that had fooled it – the Hare and Copper, a simple impressionistic nymph that I now use with supreme confidence on rivers and streams throughout South Africa.

Since my first trip to New Zealand, I have caught many larger fish in New Zealand using this pattern. However, it was those first few experiences with it that made a lasting impression and whenever I have the opportunity to sight-fish for trout, I reach for this simple yet highly effective pattern. I think the confidence with which I fish this pattern has much to do with its effectiveness.

It is not in any way a revolutionary pattern that has turned the fly-fishing world on its head; rather, it is a general impressionistic nymph that, tied in a variety of sizes and colours, will imitate many insects the angler will find during the season, particularly mayfly nymphs. The fact

Right *The author, Elwin Love and Mosey pose with a Kloppershoekspruit rainbow taken on a Hare and Copper fished together with a Bead Head Nymph.*

that The Fly Shop, the well-known store in Redding, California, now advertises this pattern in its catalogue is testimony to the fly's worldwide status as a proven pattern.

The Hare and Copper is as effective on rivers and streams as it is on stillwaters. Whenever sight-fishing situations prevail, as they often do on many rivers and streams in the Western and north-eastern Cape, this pattern, in smaller sizes, is the first I reach for. It is also most effective when fished as a searching pattern on its own, or when fished on the point together with a bead head pattern (see page 88).

When fishing this fly together with a bead head pattern, I like to use them unweighted, allowing the bead head fly to take the Hare and Copper to the bottom. Unweighted, it reacts more easily to subtle currents than if it were heavily weighted, and has proved an excellent taker of trout when fished as an emerger at the surface in both lakes and streams. I like to fish it during hatches of the tiny *Tricorythidae* mayflies using a floating line, long leader and fine 5X tippet.

HARE AND COPPER

HOOK: Tiemco 3761, 3769 or 5262, #10 – #16.

THREAD: 8/0 prewaxed, brown.

TAIL: Hare's ear guard hairs or brown hackle fibres.

RIB: Copper wire.

ABDOMEN: Hare's ear fur, Australian opossum, or similar fur.

THORAX: Same as abdomen.

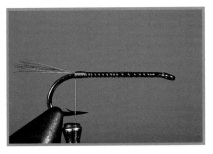

1. Take the thread to a position above the barb of the hook and tie in 10 to 15 hackle fibres, which should be approximately half the length of the hook shank.

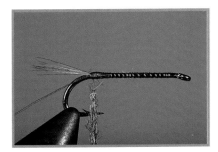

2. Tie in a wire rib and spin a thin noodle of dubbing onto the thread for the abdomen.

3. Form a tapered abdomen over approximately two-thirds of the hook shank.

4. Wind the rib through the abdomen in four or five evenly spaced turns, tie off and trim the excess.

5. Spin a thin noodle of dubbing onto the thread and form the thorax, which should be slightly thicker than the abdomen.

6. Form a small, neat thread head, half-hitch, and trim the thread. Apply head cement to the thread wraps. Pick out the dubbing in the thorax area.

TERRY ANDREWS

Floating Nymph

DOUG SWISHER/CARL RICHARDS

Above *The author and Tom Lewin sight-fishing on the Witte River in Bain's Kloof Pass.*

IT WAS A PERFECT SPRING DAY with clouds drifting slowly across a bright blue sky as Tom Lewin and I eased into the crystal-clear currents of the Witte River near the old hotel site at the top of Bain's Kloof Pass. Taking turns with a single rod allowed the person not fishing to act as observer and increase the odds of us spotting a trout feeding or holding in the current. We carefully fished upstream, searching all the likely holding water with a small dry fly. By midday, however, we had released only two trout and decided to take a break just below the forestry hut. We ate lunch atop a large flat rock in midstream and discussed our lean pickings, despite the perfect weather and water conditions. At dusk, when we reached the last long pool before the lower weir, we had taken only half-a-dozen browns, but it was the capture, in difficult stream conditions, of one of these fish that is noteworthy.

After lunch we had continued up the valley beyond the hut. After several disappointing hours astream, we finally reached the site of the old monument (dedicated to several people who drowned during a severe winter flood) situated on a hill overlooking the stream. Directly below the monument we found a long, slow, flat pool that gradually sped up before it tailed out into a riffle.

Approaching the pool we scanned the water and saw a fish rise in mid-stream. We immediately froze, backed off behind a clump of bankside vegetation and watched, captivated, as a large brown cockfish held station in water not more than two feet deep. It swept from side-to-side in the current, capturing minute insects as they drifted by, and every now and then it would tip up and intercept some morsel drifting in the surface film.

'Nice fish,' whispered Tom as he handed me the rod, giving me the opportunity of going one-on-one with the brown. I opened a box of dry flies and selected a #16 brown Floating Nymph with a medium dun polypropylene dubbing ball. After rubbing some silicone paste into the poly ball, I lengthened the tippet, adding a fifty-inch section of 6X material. It was a pattern I had come to rely on in demanding situations where the instincts of wary trout have been honed by years of angling pressure.

Rather than casting the nymph immediately, we waited and watched as the trout continued to feed. It would tip up intermittently to capture some insect which we could not see, and although we were unable to establish whether the surface food was of a terrestrial or aquatic nature, I was nevertheless confident that if any pattern would dupe the fish under the conditions, it would be the Floating Nymph.

There was only a hint of an upstream breeze, and because the trout had chosen a feeding lie rather than a protective, holding position towards the tail of the shallow pool, it made for one of the most demanding situations I had faced on the Witte. I knew the trout would allow me only one chance, with no margin for error, and so I waited for it to move to the surface again. By rising to the surface the trout's window of vision would be reduced, thereby diminishing the chances of it being spooked by casting, or by the line or leader landing on the water. Once it had just begun its descent to its station I pitched out the tiny imitation.

The line turned over slowly in the air, unfurling the leader and tippet so that it landed gossamer-like on the water's surface in lazy, serpentine curves. The nymph landed approximately two feet to the left of the fish, in a position almost level with its head. It was immediately obvious that the disturbance had been noticed by the fish. Its fin movements quickened, and we watched as the trout eased slowly across the current, inspected the imitation briefly as it drifted downstream, and then sucked it in with a clearly audible gulp.

'He's taken it,' said Tom as I tightened up, mindful of the frail tippet. The fish shot upstream, taking twenty yards of line in its first frantic bid for freedom. His attempt, however, was in vain and soon Tom slipped the net beneath a butter-yellow brown cockfish, which, at sixteen and a half inches, was a fine example of this river's hardy inhabitants.

Ted Rogowski was probably the first fly-tier to popularise Floating Nymphs, his patterns featuring stocking mesh material tied on the upper side of the fly in the thorax area. American angler and author Charles Brooks took Rogowski's pattern a step further with his Natant Nylon Nymph, which featured either two tiny hollow quill tips tied upright or a small ball of polypropylene enclosed in a nylon-stocking-mesh pouch. It was, however, the two well-known American

DEAN RIPHAGEN/MIKE SOMERVILLE

Above *The stomach contents of a small rainbow taken from the Bell River in autumn. Apart from eating two dance flies (*Empididae *family), an adult caddisfly and a caddis larva, this trout had been feeding highly selectively on dark mayfly emergers in the surface.*

angler/entomologists, Carl Richards and Doug Swisher, who brought these effective patterns to the attention of a much wider audience through their book *Selective Trout*. Their Floating Nymph was designed for use on smooth, clear, fertile waters such as the Paradise Valley spring creeks that flow through the Armstrong (O'Hair), Nelson and De Puy ranches in Montana, as well as Silver Creek and the Railroad Ranch (Harriman State Park) water on the famous Henry's Fork in south-eastern Idaho. These waters have vast, diversified insect hatches. Under these near-Utopian conditions trout become extremely selective and wary in respect of insect type, size and colour, and it is here that the Floating Nymph and similar emerger patterns have few equals. Swisher and Richards initially used a ball of polypropylene dubbing above the thorax to simulate the unfurling wings of the emerging mayfly – a concept which was developed further by Idaho angler and fly-tier, René Harrop.

The Floating Nymph was tied specifically to imitate mayflies of the *Baetidae* and *Ephemerellidae* families that rise to the surface to emerge. Duns may take several minutes to extricate themselves from the nymphal skin and often float great distances before their wings dry and they can fly off. When their wings break free from the nymphal skin they are initially crumpled and deformed. These incipient wings are nicely imitated by the dubbed ball of polypropylene.

I tie my Floating Nymphs in a range of body colours to imitate a variety of naturals. A dubbed ball in colours ranging from a medium to dark dun will suffice for most situations. It can also be tied with a white polypropylene ball to make it more easily visible, particularly in faster currents. The pattern is best fished on an upstream cast followed by a downstream dead-drift. Generally speaking, this is not a searching pattern and I reserve it for clear, flat water where the conditions are particularly testing.

It is surprising how well the pattern floats and how easy it is to follow, even though the imitation itself rides in the meniscus (the top layer of water created by surface tension). Only the dubbing ball should be greased with floatant – not

Below This magnificently marked sixteen-and-a-half-inch brown cock was caught by the author from the Witte River in Bain's Kloof Pass, and took a Floating Nymph on its first drift. The imitation can be seen lodged firmly in its upper jaw.

the thorax or the abdomen of the nymph. In this way, a realistic, low-floating profile, essential to the effectiveness of the fly, is achieved.

It is important to use soft, supple tippet materials when presenting the fly, and anglers should, at all times, try to use the lightest tippets for the prevailing conditions. All techniques available to the angler should be used to avoid drag, which would immediately arouse the suspicion of a wary trout whose survival depends on its ability to distinguish a fraud from the natural. Drag-free drifts and delicate presentations are always important, but never more so than when trout are feeding at the surface in flat, shallow water.

FLOATING NYMPH

HOOK: Tiemco 100, 5210, 5230, 5212 or 2312, #12 – #18.
THREAD: 8/0 prewaxed, colour to match abdomen.
TAIL: Hackle fibres, colour to match abdomen.
ABDOMEN: Natural fur dubbing (my favourite colours are brown, tan and olive).
LEGS: Hackle fibres, colour to match abdomen.
WING: Polypropylene dubbing in medium to dark dun colours, or white for better visibility.
THORAX: Same as abdomen.

TOM LEWIN

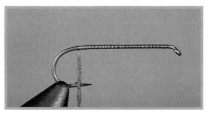

1. Take the thread to a position above the barb of the hook and spin a short, thin noodle of dubbing onto the thread.

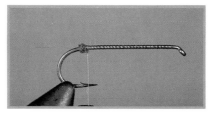

2. Wrap the dubbing to form a small ball above the hook barb. (This ball will serve to divide the tails of the pattern.)

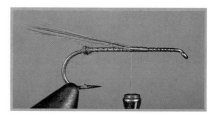

3. Take the thread to a position halfway along the shank. Strip 10 to 12 fibres from a hackle and tie them in at this halfway point. The part of the tail that extends beyond the hook shank should be half the length of the shank.

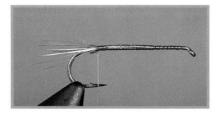

4. Wind the thread over the stripped hackle fibres back towards the dubbing ball. As you approach the ball, divide the tail fibres in half on each side of the ball and wrap the thread to secure them.

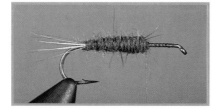

5. Spin a thin noodle of dubbing onto the thread and form a thin, neatly tapering abdomen over approximately two-thirds of the hook shank.

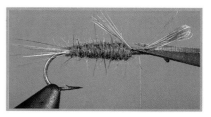

6. Strip 10 to 12 fibres from a hackle. Tie them in on top of the shank directly in front of the abdomen, with the fibre tips facing the bend. Trim the excess. These hackle fibres will form the legs.

7. Divide the fibres in half on each side of the abdomen and wrap the thread to secure them. The legs should be half the shank length; trim any excess.

8. Spin a loose noodle of polypropylene dubbing onto the thread for the wing.

9. Lift the dubbing noodle above the shank. With your left hand, push the dubbing down on the thread to form the wing. Secure in place with thread wraps.

10. Spin a thin noodle of dubbing onto the thread for the thorax.

11. Wrap the dubbing to form the thorax, which should have the same diameter as the abdomen. Form a small thread head, then half-hitch and trim. Apply head cement to the thread wraps.

12. A simple emerger pattern showing the use of CDC feathers to represent the unfurling wings of the emerging mayfly.

Golden Stonefly Nymph

DEAN RIPHAGEN

MOST ANGLERS IN THIS COUNTRY are under the impression that stoneflies (*Plectopera*) are absent or scarce in our streams and are, consequently, of little importance to trout or the fly-fisher. However, I have found good populations of stoneflies in many freestone streams across the country. Tom Sutcliffe has found populations of stoneflies in the Bushmans River where it flows through the KwaZulu-Natal Nature Conservation Service camp, the upper Yarrow, the upper Sterkspruit (Drakensberg) and in several other streams. He found the most abundant populations to be in the upper Bokspruit in the Barkly East district.

Unlike other countries that experience prolific stonefly hatches (such as the giant *Pteronarcys californica* stonefly hatch found in many rivers in the western United States), South Africa is not blessed with significant stonefly hatches. Hatches that do occur happen in some of our faster flowing rivers or in the faster sections of generally slower flowing waters. A sampling of the SAFFA waters on the Lunsklip River in Mpumalanga a few seasons ago revealed a surprising number of dirty-yellow stoneflies in a shallow riffle at the tailout of a deep, sluggish pool.

Stoneflies generally require unpolluted, well-oxygenated fast water to survive, and are usually good indicators of the state of a river. Certain species in KwaZulu-Natal, however, are found in warm, turbid, sluggish waters. The one area in which I have not found these aquatic insects is the Western Cape. This has always puzzled me as the fresh, tumbling mountain streams – such as the Jan du Toit's, and the Witels in Michell's Pass near Ceres – would seem to be ideal stonefly habitats.

Most stoneflies have a nymphal life cycle of three years and, as a result, the nymphs within any given river vary greatly in size. The largest specimens I have collected locally – which were dark brown – came from the Umzimkulu River below Underberg and measured almost an inch. Most frequently, however, I have come across a dirty-yellow specimen (possibly *Perlidae*); these are reasonably large insects and trout can therefore readily detect them in the drift along the streambed. I have fished an imitation of these robust aquatic insects for several seasons now with good results. A small black stonefly is also quite common in many of South Africa's freestone streams.

Stoneflies are usually to be found on the underside of rocks and stones on the streambed. In this habitat they are inaccessible to trout as food. However, trout can feed on them when they migrate along the streambed, during

Below *A golden stonefly nymph, showing the long antennae and tails, distinctive banded abdomen and the pronounced wingcases.*

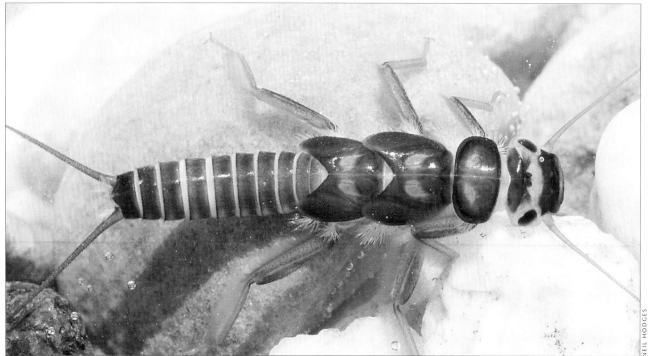

Above and right *Tom Lewin nymphing Gerhard du Toit's section of the Spekboom River in Mpumalanga. This particular river holds surprising numbers of small stonefly nymphs.*

hatching periods when they move to the shore or when these poor swimmers lose their grip on the rocks and stones they usually cling to and are swept helplessly downstream.

Imitations are best fished close to the bottom on an upstream cast with a floating line and a strike indicator, so that the nymph drifts downstream without drag. I weight my stonefly nymph patterns heavily, so they sink quickly to the bottom and remain there for most of their drift. It is essential that the fly reaches the bottom and remains there during its downstream drift, since an imitation that does not occasionally touch the bottom is missing this 'strike zone' and is likely to be disregarded by the trout.

Because the nymph pattern is usually fished in fast, broken water, a fairly large indicator is required to float the pattern without being dragged under. Glo-Bug Yarn is my indicator material of choice when drifting these heavy nymphs through fast currents. I usually select an approximately half-inch section of flame-orange or chartreuse yarn, which I soak in floatant for a few hours before use; thereafter it is seldom dragged under, even in rough water.

Below *Small Brown Stonefly Nymph*

GOLDEN STONEFLY NYMPH

HOOK: Tiemco 200R, 5262 or 5263, #10 – #14.

THREAD: 6/0 prewaxed, yellow or mustard.

ANTENNAE: Yellow or mustard goose biots.

TAIL: Same as antennae.

RIB: Medium transparent amber Swannundaze or copper wire.

ABDOMEN: Mustard fur dubbing.

WINGCASE: White tip turkey tail segment.

THORAX: Same as abdomen.

HEAD: Same as abdomen.

Variation: SMALL BROWN STONEFLY NYMPH

HOOK: Tiemco 200R, 5262 or 5263, #12 – #14.

THREAD: 6/0 prewaxed, brown.

ANTENNAE: Black goose biots.

TAIL: Same as antennae.

RIB: Dark transparent brown Swannundaze or copper wire.

ABDOMEN: Chocolate brown fur dubbing.

WINGCASE: White tip turkey tail segment, or similar.

THORAX: Same as abdomen.

HEAD: Same as abdomen.

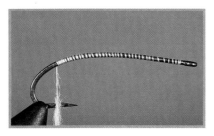

1. Take the thread to a position above the barb of the hook and spin a short, thin noodle of dubbing onto the thread

2. Wrap the dubbing to form a small ball above the barb of the hook. Take the thread to a point directly behind the eye of the hook.

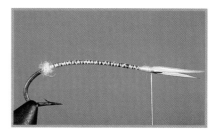

3. Select two goose biots half the length of the shank for antennae. Tie them in on either side of the eye, with concave sides facing outward and tips forward.

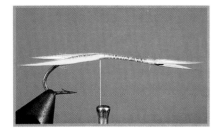

4. Take the thread to halfway along the shank. Tie in two biots for the tails, one on each side of the shank, with concave sides facing out and tips backward. The tails should extend past the hook bend for one-quarter the length of the shank.

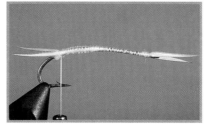

5. Wrap the thread over the tail biots along the hook shank towards the dubbing ball. This will cause the biots to flare apart at the dubbing ball.

6. Tie in a rib and spin a thin noodle of dubbing onto the thread.

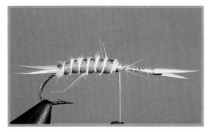

7. Form a robust dubbed abdomen over approximately two-thirds of the hook shank. Wind the rib through the abdomen in five to six evenly spaced turns, tie off and trim the excess.

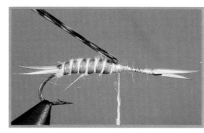

8. Tie in the wingcase directly in front of the abdomen and spin a thin noodle of dubbing onto the thread for the thorax.

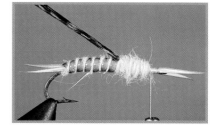

9. Form a robust thorax over about one-quarter of the hook shank. The thorax should be slightly thicker than the abdomen. (Note the space left for a dubbed head.)

10. Pull the wingcase over the top of the thorax, tie off and trim the excess. Spin a thin noodle of dubbing onto the thread.

11. Form a small dubbed head in front of the thorax.

12. Half-hitch the thread and trim. Apply head cement to the thread wraps. With a dubbing needle/teaser, pick out the thorax to represent legs.

Red Butt Woolly Worm

JOHN BEAMS

THE WOOLLY WORM is one of the most versatile patterns available today, effective in both stillwaters and streams. I originally came across this particular pattern while browsing through one of Gavin Grapes' fly-boxes several seasons ago, and have used it to great effect in streams and stillwaters. Although not a specific imitation of any particular insect, the enticing movement in water of its palmered body hackle gives the impression of life. By varying the body colours between black, brown and olive, or by combining them, a spectrum of colours found in nature can be imitated and – using an appropriate hook size – insects ranging from large to small can be replicated.

The pattern listed here has all the basic elements of the Woolly Worm popularised by John Beams. The late John Beams was an enthusiastic promoter of this simple yet effective imitation, and was always willing to give advice on how most effectively to fish it. John had a reputation in KwaZulu-Natal as a catcher of large trout, and evidence of these catches has been well documented in several local books and magazines. The wisdom and wealth of knowledge of this illustrious angler made an enormous impression on me as a neophyte fly-fisherman.

This fly's evolution in South Africa is interesting, particularly as it was first fished as a dry fly. John Beams had been fishing the Smalblaar River, which at the time was running high but clear. He was using a dry fly with a palmered hackle – a Wickham's Fancy – which, because of the heavy water, was unable to stay afloat for long. Despite this it worked well as a wet fly and accounted that day for several rainbows. John subsequently experimented with the colour of the pattern and, when he moved to the former Natal, he tried it in stillwater. Changes to the dressing followed: he tied it

Above *Terry Andrews and the author examine the results of a riffle seining on the Sterkspruit River in the Rhodes/Barkly East area. Seine nets are an invaluable aid for anglers wishing to establish the aquatic and terrestrial insect drift in the current.*

with a hackle with the fibres stripped from one side to ensure a sparsely dressed pattern, and later added a hot-orange butt. Instead of using the conventional chenille popular at the time in American versions, he tied the body with dubbed seal's fur. Eventually the pattern evolved to become the Red Butt Woolly Worm, and is a classic example of the fly-tying philosophy of South Africans such as the late John Beams, Gavin Grapes and Tony Biggs, in that it is tied with a slim body and sparse, palmered hackle.

When fishing rivers, I like to fish the Woolly Worm upstream with a floating line and strike indicator. Unlike many other artificial nymphs that require a drag-free drift to deceive trout, the Woolly Worm will often take fish when it is twitched and tweaked as it drifts downstream. If this fails, allow the pattern to drift past the angler and to sweep across the current at the end of its drift. In stillwater fishing, the Woolly Worm is a useful searching pattern, particularly in larger sizes. I cast it out, allow it to sink to the desired depth, and then retrieve it using either a slow hand-twist or short two-inch strips.

Left *Tom Lewin prospecting the waters of a small Mpumalanga stream. This, and similar-sized streams, provides challenging fishing, but the rewards are well worth the effort.*

RED BUTT WOOLLY WORM

HOOK: Tiemco 3769, 3761, 5262 or 5263, #8 – #14.

THREAD: 6/0 prewaxed, colour to match body.

TAIL: Cock hackle fibres, colour to match body.

RIB: Copper wire.

BUTT: Red floss.

HACKLE: Cock hackle, colour to match body.

BODY: Natural or sparkle-blend dubbing, or seal's fur.
(My favourite colours are olive, brown and black.)

Right Despite some signs of opportunistic feeding, evidenced by a caddis larva and some dance flies (Empididae family), this Sterkspruit River trout was feeding on two main food sources – mayfly nymphs (Baetidae family) and blackfly larvae (Simuliidae family). The vegetation in the top left-hand corner may have contained caddis larvae or may have been eaten accidentally.

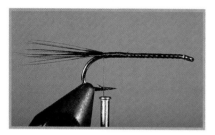

1. For the tail, strip 15 to 20 fibres from a hackle and tie them in above the barb of the hook. The tails should be the same length as the hook shank.

2. Tie in a rib and a length of single strand floss above the barb. Take the thread to a position on the shank just above the hook point.

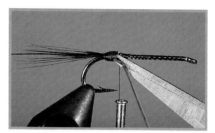

3. Moisten the floss and form a small tag or butt over approximately one-eighth of the hook shank. Tie off and trim the excess.

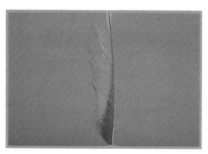

4. Select a hackle with fibres which are one-and-a-half to two times the width of the hook gape. With the concave side of the hackle facing you, strip the fibres off the right-hand side of the feather.

5. Tie the hackle in next to the butt, with the concave side facing away from the fly. Spin a thin noodle of dubbing onto the thread.

6. Wrap the dubbing to form a neatly tapering body.

7. Wind the hackle through the body in four or five evenly spaced turns, tie it off and trim the excess.

8. Wind the rib through the butt, the body and hackle, ensuring that no hackle fibres are trapped by the rib. Tie the rib off and trim the excess.

9. Form a small, neat thread head, half-hitch and trim the thread. Apply head cement to the thread wraps.

Soft Hackle

ANON

ALTHOUGH PATTERNS USING SOFT HACKLES in their construction have been in use for centuries in Britain and Europe, it was the American angler Sylvester Nemes, in his book *The Soft Hackled Fly*, who brought them to the attention of a wider audience. Soft Hackles, known more correctly as 'Spiders' in Britain where they originated, are simple imitations which use feathers of birds such as partridge, grouse, woodcock, snipe, starling and jackdaw. These hackles are usually found on the backs, necks, breasts and the leading edges of the wings and, because of their softness, flexibility and colour, they have a wide variety of fly-tying applications. Many modern dressings have deviated considerably from the traditional British designs and principles, and for this reason I shall use Sylvester Nemes' generic term 'Soft Hackle' instead of the more restrictive and specific 'Spider' designation.

The Soft Hackle flies of which Nemes wrote had their origins in England's northern counties close to the Scottish border, most specifically Yorkshire and Derbyshire. Anglers there developed a wet fly with a short body of silk thread, sometimes sparsely dubbed with fur and hackled with a soft feather. The evolution of this fly design was codified in three books, the first being *The Practical Angler* by WC Stewart, an Edinburgh lawyer, published in 1857. Stewart favoured three simple, non-specific, soft-hackled flies in different colours, which he called Spiders. Stewart's book is noteworthy in that he was the first major angling author to advocate upstream fishing. The second and most important book on the soft-hackled wet fly was published in 1885 by TE Pritt, the angling editor of the *Yorkshire Post*. Called *Yorkshire Trout Flies*, it was significant in that the flies he wrote about were tied to match specific insects and hatches. Although re-published a year later under the title *North Country Flies*, its publication coincided with that of Halford's books on dry fly-fishing on chalk streams. For some reason, Halford's dry fly-fishing techniques were adopted as the socially correct approach to fly-fishing, wet fly-fishing went into decline, and Pritt's book never got the recognition it deserved. The third significant book to deal with soft-hackled flies was *Brook and River Trouting: A Manual of Modern North*

Below *Dusk settles over Waterford in the Drakensberg foothills.*

MIKE SOMERVILLE

Above *Tom Lewin enjoys a well-earned tea break along the shores of Lake Aniwhenua on New Zealand's North Island.*

Country Methods by Edmonds and Lee, published in 1916. This was the most advanced book yet on soft-hackled flies designed to imitate specific insects, and its colour illustrations show not only each fly but also the materials required to tie it. Like Pritt's book, this too was published at an inauspicious time – at the height of World War One – and so did not achieve the impact it deserved. Nemes paid tribute to the works of Pritt, Edmonds and Lee, and his second book, *The Soft Hackled Fly Addict*, published in 1981, reproduces the illustrations and dressings from their books.

Since its simple beginnings several centuries ago, the Soft Hackle has acquired a sizeable and enthusiastic following amongst knowledgeable anglers and fly-tiers, for its fish-catching qualities as well as for its ease of tying. Randall Kaufmann, in his book, *The Fly Tyers' Nymph Manual*, considers the Soft Hackle his standby for fishing back-eddies. Back-eddies are places in a stream where currents flow in a direction opposite to that of the main current, resulting in a whirlpool-type situation where insects are constantly swept in a circular motion. They usually occur near the bank where current velocity is greatly reduced, and are commonly indicated by a froth or scum line drifting slowly in a circular

manner. Although often overlooked by anglers, they may produce spectacular results because large trout are able to hold in the current with minimal effort. Anglers should be careful not to approach a back-eddy from downstream since trout holding or feeding in them are doing so in a direction opposite to that of the main current flow – that is the trout is usually facing downstream. In order for an angler using an upstream approach to successfully fish a back-eddy, the eddy should be skirted and fished from a position upstream of the trout's suspected lie in the current. Some of the largest trout I have taken from South African rivers and streams came from back-eddies on the Mooi and Umzimkulu rivers in KwaZulu-Natal, and the Lunsklip in Mpumalanga.

Although some Soft Hackle flies imitate specific insects, most anglers use them as general imitations of mayfly nymphs and emergers and caddis pupae and emergers. It is one of my favourite patterns when fish are keying onto mayfly nymphs and caddis pupae that are ascending to the water's surface.

These extremely versatile patterns produce fish in both stillwaters and streams. In stillwaters I prefer to fish them on a floating line and long leader to trout feeding visibly in the surface layers. Generally speaking, this coincides with periods of caddisfly emergence at dusk, and takes are usually felt rather than seen. I allow the imitation to sink below the feeding level of the fish and then slowly draw it towards the surface with long, slow pulls which simulate the upward movement of the emerging caddis pupae (see pages 83–85).

In flowing water, a larger Soft Hackle fly is a useful searching pattern, and the slightest current will cause the feather fibres to move and vibrate in the water. It is consequently a very productive fly for prospecting in the slower-moving reaches in rivers such as the Mooi in KwaZulu-Natal.

I fish the Soft Hackle on an upstream dead-drift, but have taken numerous fish by allowing it to swing down and across. Takes will commonly occur as the line starts to tighten downstream, which causes the fly to begin its ascent to the surface.

It is mostly not possible or desirable to incorporate weight in the fly during tying, as the emphasis is on a slender, sparsely dressed pattern. As a result, alternate forms of weighting, such as split-shot, Soft Lead or Twistons, or a heavy fly on the dropper, such as a bead head pattern, are required to sink the pattern deeper.

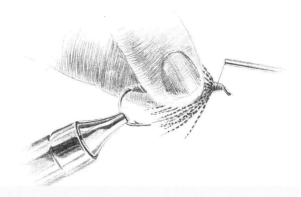

SOFT HACKLE

HOOK: Tiemco 5262, 3761, 3769 or 200R, #10 – #16.

THREAD: 8/0 prewaxed, colour to match body.

RIB: Fine copper wire (optional).

ABDOMEN: Fur dubbing, silk, herl or floss (the most common colours are olives, browns, black, yellow, orange, tan and grey).

THORAX: Hare's ear fur dubbing.

LEGS: Soft body, shoulder or similar hackle from game birds such as grouse, partridge, snipe or woodcock.

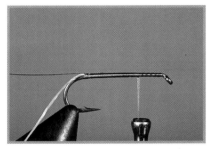

1. Tie in the wire rib and a length of single-strand floss above the barb of the hook. Take the thread to a position approximately one-third of the shank length from the eye of the hook.

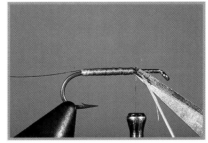

2. Moisten the floss and form a slim abdomen over approximately two-thirds of the shank. Tie off and trim the excess.

3. Wind the rib forward in six or seven evenly spaced turns, tie off and trim the excess. Spin a thin noodle of dubbing onto the thread and form a small thorax.

4. For the legs, strip the webby flue from a partridge feather. Tie the feather in by the tip, directly in front of the thorax, with its concave side facing the hook.

5. Take two to three turns of the feather in front of the thorax, tie the feather off and trim the excess.

6. Form a small, neat thread head, then half-hitch and trim the thread. Apply head cement to the thread wraps.

Cased Caddis

DEAN RIPHAGEN

THE CASED CADDIS IS MY FAVOURITE caddis pattern for South African stillwaters, and yet relatively few fly-fishers know of the insect or the effectiveness of its imitation in taking trout. It is an extremely versatile searching pattern, and anglers wishing to complement their arsenal of imitations should give it some space in their fly-boxes.

Although I have found caddis larvae to be widely distributed in South African waters, it was a day spent at Highmoor in the KwaZulu-Natal Drakensberg that proved to me just how important these insects are to the angler. I had enjoyed a productive day on the upper lake, taking several fish on a damselfly nymph imitation. After a severe afternoon thunderstorm, however, the pattern failed to move any more fish as thousands of minute *Tricorythidae* mayflies began to emerge in the shallows. Within minutes, several trout were feeding on the emerging insects, and the sloshing sounds of the water slapping against their open jaws left me in no doubt that they had switched to feeding on the tiny

mayflies. With so many feeding fish, it was difficult to single out one in particular, but after taking time out from fishing to watch, I soon singled out a big rainbow.

The fish was working along the edge of a weedbed in deep water and from my position it was difficult to cast without lining it. I waited for the trout to move into deeper water further down the weedbed. When it disappeared after a series of slow rises, I selected a tiny #18 Polywing Spinner from a box of dry flies and, with trembling fingers, tied it to the frail 6X tippet. I pitched the tiny fly onto the perimeter of the weedbed along the trout's previous feeding path and waited for it to start rising again. In the half-light of the afternoon it was impossible to make out my artificial amongst the thousands of natural Trico spinners lying trapped in the surface film. When the fish rose near my imitation, I tightened up and the water exploded in a shower of spray. 'Good fish,' I thought as it surged through the water parallel to the bank, but it was only after a nerve-racking battle that I was able to fully appreciate the proportions of this wonderful adversary. At five-and-three-quarter-pounds it was by far the largest trout I had landed on a dry fly, but

Below *Richard Gild with a well-conditioned rainbow from a KwaZulu-Natal lake.*

Above *The sun sets over Waterford, a lake in the KwaZulu-Natal foothills that has produced several fish over the magical double-figure mark.*

in retrospect it was the discovery of abundant caddis larvae in the stomach of the trout that proved to be the most significant event of the day's fishing.

After landing the fish, I noticed several unusual insects, which I later identified as caddis larvae, clambering about on the mesh of the net. When I prised open the trout's jaw I discovered more caddis larvae, along with hundreds of Trico nymphs and spinners. A stomach pumping prior to the release of the trout produced a further forty-seven caddis larvae which I placed in a collection vial for further identification at home. Most caddis larvae are bottom- or weed-dwellers and although many stream-dwelling species are free-living, most stillwater specimens choose to build protective cases of some sort. These have a wide variety of shapes and sizes, ranging from simple, short, tubular segments of grass, reeds or similar aquatic vegetation, to intricately constructed cases of mineral and/or plant matter that are cemented together using silk. The caddis specimens I took that day at Highmoor belonged to the latter variety.

The caddis pattern that I devised for Highmoor has subsequently undergone considerable modification. Initially, I used a simple underbody of seal's fur overwound with soft partridge hackle. However, over several years I was able to reduce my tying time: firstly, by substituting an underbody mixture of Hare-Tron and angora goat dubbing similar to that used in the abdomen of the Kaufmann Lake Dragon (page 24), and, secondly, by using ringneck pheasant body feathers instead of the shorter and softer partridge hackle.

Ringneck pheasant body feathers are longer and stronger and therefore less breakable than partridge feathers and will save fly-tiers a great deal of frustration.

The Cased Caddis is most effective when fished around submerged aquatic weed or on the bottom of the lake bed, and I have developed two methods to fish it properly. The first uses an intermediate line and a leader of six to eight feet. The pattern need not be weighted, but if weight is required, then three to four turns of lead wire around the hook shank will suffice to sink it at the same rate as the line. Fast-sinking fly-lines are inappropriate where imitations are to be fished slowly near the bottom of a lake bed; although such a line will take the pattern down quickly to the feeding level of the trout, it requires a very fast retrieve to prevent the fly from fouling on the bottom. The other technique requires a floating line and a long leader of up to fifteen feet. Again, only a few turns of lead wire on the hook shank are required to take the pattern down to the appropriate feeding level. I prefer this floating-line method when fishing over thick weed into holes or old river channels.

Both techniques require an extremely slow hand-twist retrieve interspersed with lengthy pauses, to simulate the larva as it slowly moves about in search of food. If used with a floating line, it can also be cast out and allowed to drift with the subtle currents found in stillwaters. Because the imitation moves so slowly, takes are often extremely gentle and anglers should be alert and react immediately to the slightest indication of a trout on the line.

CASED CADDIS

HOOK: Tiemco 200R or 5263, #10 – #14.

THREAD: 8/0 prewaxed, colour to match underbody.

HACKLE: Ringneck pheasant rump feathers (these will be palmered through the dubbed underbody and clipped unevenly to resemble the plant material from which the case is made).

UNDERBODY: Medium olive or dark brown Hare-Tron dubbing, or similar, blended with the following colours of Angora goat fur for highlights: blue, purple, green, amber, olive, brown, black and rust.

LARVA: Cream or chartreuse dubbing, tied thin.

LEGS: Five or six brown partridge fibres.

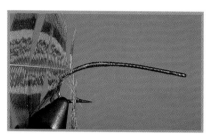

1. Take the thread to a position above the hook barb and tie a pheasant feather in by the tip. Spin a thin noodle of dubbing onto the thread.

2. Cover approximately one-quarter of the shank with the dubbing, ensuring that the underbody is kept thin. Wind the feather tightly through the dubbing, tie it off and trim the excess.

3. Tie another pheasant feather in and spin another noodle of dubbing onto the thread. Form another short section of the underbody and wind the feather through it.

4. Repeat step 3 until approximately three-quarters of the hook shank is covered with the underbody and the pheasant feathers.

5. Spin a thin, short noodle of dubbing for the larva onto the thread directly in front of the underbody and hackle.

6. Form the larva, leaving enough room to tie in legs and to form a small head.

7. Strip five or six fibres from a partridge feather and tie them in beard-style under the hook. These fibres should be approximately one-third the length of the hook shank.

8. Trim the excess partridge fibres, form a small, neat thread head, half-hitch and trim the thread. Apply head cement to the thread wraps.

9. Using a pair of scissors, trim the protruding pheasant fibres into uneven lengths to resemble the sticks and plant matter used to construct the case of the caddis.

The Casemaker

RENÉ HARROP

RENÉ HARROP IS CONSIDERED to be one of the finest fly-tiers in the world. René runs The House of Harrop, a family business producing fine fly patterns. The fly-tiers are René, his wife, Bonnie, and their two children. Their small fly-tying company is located in the town of St. Anthony, near the banks of the famous Henry's Fork of the Snake River, in south-eastern Idaho.

René initially devised this highly productive pattern to imitate stream-dwelling cased caddis larvae, and over several seasons I have come to rely on it to produce trout when more state-of-the-art imitations have failed.

Although many South African rivers and streams teem with free-living caddis larvae, case-making caddis larvae – which are usually overlooked by the angler – are also extremely abundant. Although most case-building caddis larvae spend their time between and under rocks, away from the watchful eyes of trout, many end up drifting with the current. Scientists are still uncertain why large numbers of aquatic insects abandon their stream-bottom dwellings and drift downstream at certain times of the day or night. Gary LaFontaine, in his excellent book, *Caddisflies*, contends that cased caddis larvae do drift freely with the current and may in fact be more important to trout than their non-case-making counterparts. Since they are found in trouts' stomachs, case-building caddis larvae do warrant more time and attention from both the fly-fisher and fly-tier.

René Harrop's Casemaker and George Anderson's Peeking Caddis are excellent imitations of case-making caddis larvae. Harrop's Casemaker has an underbody of gold tinsel chenille, overwound with a sparsely dubbed overbody of hare's ear fur. This allows the tinsel chenille to protrude randomly through the sparse overbody, giving an impressive illusion of life. With newer fly-tying materials like

Above *The spotted tail of a KwaZulu-Natal rainbow trout.*

Crystal Chenille, this pattern can be made to look even more realistic, and fly-tiers should experiment accordingly. I suspect that the Casemaker is an effective fly because the glimpse of the tinsel shining through the fur acts as a trigger which attracts fish that would otherwise ignore a more sombre imitation. The Peeking Caddis is also an extremely effective imitation of the case-building caddisfly and will often produce fish when the brighter Casemaker fails. The angler who carries both patterns will obviously have a choice of options to suit all occasions.

Case-building caddis species cannot swim well and are weak swimmers at best. Consequently, larvae that end up in the current, for whatever reason, are swept downstream. A cast made upstream and allowed to dead-drift downstream is, therefore, the best method with which to imitate these caddis species.

The weight of the sand and tiny pebbles in their protective cases keeps the larvae drifting close to the stream bottom, and imitations should therefore be heavily weighted. In the heavier, faster water so often the home of caddis larvae, additional weight on the leader will occasionally be required to take the imitation down quickly to the feeding level of the trout.

CASE-MAKING CADDIS LARVAE

Case-building caddis larvae construct miniature dwellings both as protection and for camouflage. These cases are constructed of small pieces of debris, the most common materials being tiny rock fragments, sand grains, leaves and twigs, which are cemented together with a sticky substance secreted by the insect. The form and function of cases made by case-making caddisflies are extremely interesting. Portable cases are architecturally well *adapted for specific habitats. In swift currents, for example, the angler is more apt to find cases that are streamlined, relatively resistant to crushing, equipped with ballast stones or with trailing twigs that act as rudders. Because trout cannot extricate the larvae from their cases, they eat both – this is why anglers will often find sticks, stones and plant matter in the trout's stomach. Tiny case-making larvae are important in the diet of the Western Cape trout.*

Anglers who dislike using strike indicators will handicap themselves, particularly in fast pocket-water and riffles. Trout holding in fast water can accept or reject an artificial in an instant, and a leader that moves noticeably in slower water may only twitch slightly in faster water, making strike indicators invaluable – in fact, under these conditions strike indicators will often mean the difference between a good and a mediocre success rate.

THE CASEMAKER

HOOK: Tiemco 200R or 5263, #10 – #16.

THREAD: 8/0 prewaxed, black.

CASE UNDERBODY: Gold tinsel chenille.

CASE OVERBODY: Blended fur from a hare's mask.

LARVA: Natural or synthetic fur dubbing, dyed chartreuse.

LEGS: Five to six brown partridge fibres.

HEAD: Natural fur dubbing, dyed black.

PEEKING CADDIS

HOOK: Tiemco 200R or 5263, #10 – #16.

THREAD: 8/0 prewaxed, black.

CASE: Blended fur from a hare's mask.

RIB: Copper wire.

ABDOMEN: Natural fur dubbing, dyed mustard yellow.

LEGS: Brown partridge hackle, tied full.

HEAD: Black ostrich herl.

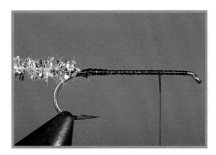

1. Tie in a length of tinsel chenille above the barb and take the thread to a position approximately one-third of the hook shank from the eye of the hook.

2. Form the underbody by winding the tinsel chenille over about two-thirds of the hook shank. Tie off the chenille and trim the excess. Spin a thin noodle of dubbing onto the thread for the overbody.

3. Wind the dubbing over the tinsel chenille, covering most but not all of the tinsel. (These protruding pieces of tinsel will represent bright fragments of rock used in the caddis case.) Bring the thread back to just in front of the overbody.

4. Spin a short, thin noodle of dubbing onto the thread and form the larva, leaving enough room behind the hook eye for a small fur head.

5. Strip five to six fibres from a partridge feather and tie them in beard-style directly in front of the larva. Trim the excess and spin a short, thin section of dubbing onto the thread for the head.

6. Form a small, dubbed head behind the hook eye and then a small, neat thread head, half-hitch and trim. Apply head cement to the thread wraps.

Green Caddis Larva

ANON

THE PATTERN LISTED HERE is a simple one that I have used for many years in South African streams and rivers, and it has also proved to be an effective imitation of the sawfly larvae found in the north-eastern Cape. These larvae are responsible for the defoliation of the crack willow trees growing along the banks of many streams in this area and, according to Ed Herbst who described them in an article in *Flyfishing* magazine, they are to be found there hatching along stream banks from late October to late March.

The larvae hatch in their millions and fall into the water from the willows, providing the trout with a reliable food source for most of the season. The larva is bright green with a dark head and is about the same length as our free-living caddis larvae, so an imitation of the *Hydropsychidae* larva does double duty as an imitation of the sawfly larva. During a day spent on the Kloppershoekspruit during mid-April with Terry Andrews and Bill Sharp, I managed to fool several rainbows and browns using a green caddis larva imitation. One rainbow, a well-conditioned cockfish of eighteen inches, was taken from a fast run; amongst other insects its stomach contained several sawfly larvae, most of these discoloured by the trout's stomach acids.

FREE-LIVING CADDIS LARVAE

*F*ree-living caddis larvae that range freely over river and streambeds are fairly abundant and widely distributed aquatic insects found in running waters in South Africa. While they do build a protective case in which to live, these shelters are not portable, and when the larvae venture from the safety of their cases they are fairly vulnerable to predation by trout. Caddisfly evolution is, in part, determined by the ability of the larva to build a case, and since free-living caddis larvae do not exhibit this trait, it is fairly safe to assume that, in terms of evolution, the free-living type of caddis has not evolved much over the years. Inquisitive anglers who pick up and examine rocks and stones in the faster areas of streams and rivers will notice long, thin tunnels constructed of sand and other fine material on the underside of some of them. The small, dirty-green worm-like insects found in some of these tunnels are free-living caddis larvae. By far the most important family of caddisflies are those free-living specimens that make up the Hydropsychidae family.

The caddisflies that make up the Hydropsychidae family are the most abundant of all caddisfly species found in South Africa and specimens can be found in most of our fast-flowing rivers and streams. They generally prefer cold, clean, fast-flowing and well-oxygenated water, and consequently occur in unpolluted, high-altitude rivers. I have found the greatest concentrations of these ubiquitous aquatic insects in fast headwater streams, and the more alkaline the water, the more abundant they seem to be. Like the cased caddisflies found in our stillwaters, these free-living caddis larvae will be found in trouts' stomachs throughout the angling season, but are particularly abundant during summer.

Hydropsychidae caddis larvae found in South African waters are usually a dull olive, but the colour may vary greatly depending

Above An example of a free-living caddis larva.

NEIL HODGES

on the species. Rhyacophila *caddisflies in many freestone streams in the western United States, in contrast, are an intense bright green and this colour has become known as 'caddis green'. I have noticed that by accentuating the bright green colour of the larval imitation, the catch rate increases correspondingly, even though our* Hydropsychidae *caddisflies are generally much duller. Several excellent dubbings blended specifically to imitate the North American* Rhyacophila *caddis are available locally, but any bright green fur or synthetic dubbing will suffice to tie imitations of our* Hydropsychidae *caddisflies. It is a good idea to blend in some Antron fibres as they add translucence and sparkle to the pattern, thereby greatly increasing its ability to draw strikes from trout that, under similar circumstances, may reject a more sombre pattern.*

Anglers visiting the north-eastern Cape during the fishing season would be well advised to take along an imitation of these insects which, at the height of their hatching activity, fall into the rivers and streams, literally carpeting the stream bottoms.

Free-living caddis larvae imitations are fished in exactly the same manner as the case-making caddis variety (see pages 79–80).

GREEN CADDIS LARVA

HOOK: Tiemco 200R, 5262 or 5263, #12 – #16.

THREAD: 8/0 prewaxed, black.

RIB: Fine copper wire, or 4 lb monofilament.

ABDOMEN: Bright green natural or synthetic fur dubbing.

HEAD: Black or dark brown fur dubbing.

LEGS: Five to six brown partridge fibres.

Above *The stomach contents pumped from an eighteen-inch Kloppershoekspruit rainbow in the north-eastern Cape. This fish was feeding opportunistically on various insects, including (clockwise from top left) a worm-like larva from the* Pyralidae *family, a mature* Baetidae *mayfly nymph and nymphs from the* Tricorythidae *mayfly family, and sawfly larvae (Geometridae family). Usually the sawfly larvae are bright olive, but these specimens have been burnt a pale cream by the trout's stomach acids.*

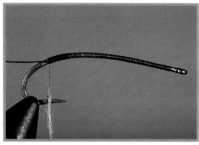

1. Tie in the rib above the barb of the hook and spin a thin noodle of dubbing onto the thread for the abdomen.

2. Form the abdomen, which should be neatly tapered and should cover approximately three-quarters of the hook shank.

3. Wind the rib through the abdomen in six to eight evenly spaced turns, tie it off and trim the excess.

4. Spin a thin noodle of dubbing onto the thread directly in front of the abdomen and form a small fur head.

5. Strip five to six fibres from a partridge feather and tie them in beard-style directly behind the hook eye. Trim the excess. These legs should be one-third the length of the hook shank.

6. Form a small, neat thread head, half-hitch and trim the thread. Apply head cement to the thread wraps.

Sparkle Pupa

GARY LAFONTAINE

THOUGH THE SPARKLE PUPA HAS BEEN in use in the United States for many years now, and despite its effectiveness, I meet few South African fly-fishers who carry this pattern.

A day on the lower Elandspad River in Du Toit's Kloof with two angling companions illustrates the fish-catching qualities of this pattern. We had started at the highway bridge which crosses the river just above its junction with the Smalblaar River. It was a perfect day for fly-fishing, with a gentle upstream breeze to conceal our presence and aid our casting into the tight, holding lies so typical of the stream's lower reaches. This was a time when catches of fifty to sixty fish a day were the rule rather than the exception and it was easy to pick off fish in the faster pocket water. By midday I had released so many rainbows that I had lost count and I was heady with success. But a heavy spinner fall of the Western Cape mayfly, *Choroterpes nigrescens* (darkening dun), brought my success to a standstill as the fish began to concentrate on the females lying spent in the surface.

I tried several patterns, but the trout continued to ignore my offerings. Finally, I tied on a small buff-coloured Sparkle Pupa, greased the wing with silicone paste and pitched the pattern out. I was wading in perhaps two feet of water when a sudden movement at my feet caused me to look down. A sizeable rainbow darted past my legs, crossed the current and intercepted the imitation tight against a vertical cliff

Below *Casting in the late afternoon, when caddis pupae begin to make their way to the surface to emerge.*

face with such speed that I was caught completely off-guard. The fish had cleared at least five to six yards of stream to intercept the fly and, although the tippet returned without the imitation, the incident proved to me just how effective the Sparkle Pupa is at luring trout.

The originator of this fine pattern, Gary LaFontaine, spent many hundreds of hours astream, carefully observing caddisflies in all stages of development. The result was his award-winning book *Caddisflies*, considered to be the definitive reference on caddis biology and associated imitations.

Above *Late afternoon on an Underberg lake.*

In his Sparkle Pupa pattern, LaFontaine brought Sparkle Yarn to the fore and today many patterns use this bright, reflective material. Just prior to emergence, caddis pupae inflate their pupal husks and surround themselves with air. This looks like tiny drops of liquid mercury and Sparkle Yarn is an excellent material for imitating this quicksilver effect.

Antron nylon and Creslan orlon, commonly known as Sparkle Yarn, are triangular in cross-section and consequently reflect light in many directions. Moreover, the fibres do not adhere to one another, even when wet, and attract clinging bubbles of air. As a result, the fly becomes wreathed in a silvery garment of air bubbles in much the same way as the natural emerging caddis.

The Sparkle Pupa can be used either as an exact imitation or, because it can imitate a variety of aquatic insects in the process of emergence, as an attractor pattern. Moreover, it is as effective in streams as it is in lakes, and has proved itself on several occasions during heavy insect emergences on stillwaters throughout the country. Essentially, however, it is an imitation of an emerging caddis pupa and should be fished as a dry fly with a floating line.

Where the pattern is used in rivers or streams, it should be cast directly upstream and fished dead-drift, or quartered upstream. Most caddis pupae emerge relatively quickly at dusk or dark (the emergence is therefore seldom seen by

anglers). Trout feed actively on the emerging pupae as they attempt to break through the film, and much has been written about the wild, slashing rises to emerging caddis pupae and to adult caddisflies. However, anglers should be aware that the speed of a rise is generally a function of current velocity. Trout do indeed slash at the fast-moving emerging pupae and adults in faster water. In stillwaters and the slower sections of rivers, though, the rise forms will usually resemble the gentle, confident rises associated with insects such as emerging mayflies and midge pupae.

In stillwaters, the pattern can be cast individually to rising fish, or it can be used as a searching pattern in the surface film. For this application it has few rivals and will often draw trout from a considerable distance, putting it on a par with Tom Sutcliffe's great searching pattern, the DDD (page 149). Any angler who regularly uses the DDD and similar searching patterns should give the Sparkle Pupa a chance, as it often produces fish when no other pattern will.

Because caddis pupae are fairly active emergers, it may pay to give the fly some movement in the water. When searching stillwaters, the pattern can be cast out and given an occasional twitch. My favourite method of fishing this imitation is to retrieve it with a very slow hand-twist, interspersed with an occasional twitch. Takes vary, but in my experience the trout will usually take the artificial with a slow, porpoising roll, quite similar to that when trout are feeding on midge pupae hanging in the surface film. Striking is unnecessary, and if the angler already has a tight line to the fly, all that is usually required is to tighten the line further by lifting the rod. This is particularly important when light tippets are being used.

An important point to remember when tying the Sparkle Pupa is not to overdress the imitation. Most novices tend to use far too much material, which may reduce its effectiveness. Most Sparkle Yarns come in a weave of four strands and are far too bulky for the range of sizes required. Patterns in #12 to #16 require only two strands of the material, whereas patterns #18 and smaller require only one strand.

SPARKLE PUPA

HOOK: Tiemco 100, 2312 or 200R, #12 – #18.

THREAD: 8/0 prewaxed, brown.

OVERBODY: Antron yarn, colour to match the underbody.

UNDERBODY: Dubbed Antron yarn. The most common colours in use are rust, gold, black, brown, tan and various shades of olive.

WING: Light deer or elk hair.

HEAD: Hare's ear or medium brown fur, or marabou.

1. Pull out two strands from a four-strand section of Antron yarn and, using a fine-toothed comb or dubbing needle, separate the fibres from one another.

2. Take the thread to a position above the barb of the hook and lay the separated Antron fibres around the hook shank.

3. Tie the fibres down, ensuring that they completely encompass the hook shank.

4. Spin a thin noodle of dubbing onto the thread above the hook barb and form a thin, neatly tapering underbody over two-thirds of the hook shank.

5. Pick out the underbody with a dubbing needle or dubbing teaser.

6. Pull the Antron fibres over the underbody and secure them with two to three turns of thread. Do not trim the excess fibres at this stage.

7. Insert a dubbing needle under the Antron fibres and lift them away from the underbody as shown, forming a cocoon of Antron fibres around the underbody. Tie the fibres off and trim the excess.

8. Cut approximately 30 fibres from the hide of a deer or elk and stack them in a hair stacker. (This will ensure that the tips of the fibres are aligned.)

9. Tie in the deer or elk hair directly in front of the overbody. The tips of the hair should extend to, or slightly beyond, the bend of the hook.

10. Spin a thin noodle of dubbing for the head onto the thread directly in front of the hair wing.

11. Form a fur head over approximately one-quarter of the hook shank.

12. Form a small, neat thread head, then half-hitch and trim the thread. Apply head cement to the thread wraps.

Bead Head Nymph

ANON

IF A FLY-TYING TECHNIQUE could be called revolutionary, the addition of metal beads to fly patterns would, in my opinion, certainly qualify. Metal beads have transformed fly-fishing and fly-tying, making effective patterns even more so. The use of metal beads in fly patterns is not new to fly-fishing. Roman Moser, probably Austria's foremost fly-fisherman, has been using them for years on rivers like the Traun, and could even be called the father of bead head flies. Their popularity has now spread worldwide, though they have only really gained acceptance here in South Africa in the last two to three years. These days Orvis even market a special hook, manufactured exclusively for them and designed with a micro barb to accept beads.

It is difficult to say exactly why they are so effective, but I think it may be as a result of two factors: the shine or flash produced by the bead, and the fact that the weight in the bead ensures that the pattern fishes deep along the streambed in the zone where most trout hold for most of the day. Testimony to the effectiveness around the world of bead head patterns abounds: in the February 1992 edition of the *Orvis News* Tom Rosenbauer describes the Bead Head Caddis as a 'magic pattern'. In informal tests, he found that the Bead Head Hare's Ear Nymph outperformed the standard pattern by four to one. The Orvis Company president, Perk Perkins, fishing the Big Hole River in Montana, found that a bead head pattern outproduced a soft hackle imitation, which for many years was considered the most reliable pattern on the river. Malcolm Greenhalgh, writing in the September 1990 issue of *Salmon, Trout and Sea-Trout*, gives some of his tallies for bead head imitations on England's streams: thirty-nine grayling in one day from the Wylye River in 1989 and forty-two grayling from the Wiltshire Avon in December 1989.

Above *The author took this eighteen-inch rainbow from a fast run on the Kloppershoekspruit above Rhodes in the north-eastern Cape. The fish took a Bead Head Nymph fished in conjunction with a smaller nymph pattern on the point.*

Since the capture of my first trout using a bead head pattern in New Zealand more than four years ago, I have used them with great success, both on their own and together with other patterns like small mayfly nymphs, caddis larvae and nondescript patterns like the Hare and Copper (see page 59). I remember clearly the day several years ago spent on the Tekapo River in New Zealand, when I 'discovered' these patterns for myself.

The river was running high but reasonably clear and the fishing had been difficult, with only a few small browns of about three pounds to show for my efforts. Working my way slowly upstream along one of the lower river's several braids, I spotted what I thought was a good fish lying quietly out of

Left *This beautifully marked rainbow cock, taken by the author, took a Bead Head Nymph fished deep through a run on the Kloppershoekspruit above Rhodes in the north-eastern Cape.*

the current in a slick on the side of the river. Because the water was slightly discoloured as a result of some exceptionally heavy rain during the previous week, it was impossible to discern the trout clearly in the current and, in all honesty, I wasn't even sure the shape in the water was a fish at all. (If there is one lesson to be learnt from fishing in New Zealand, it is never to take what you see for granted. Often what appears to be a large boulder in the stream will be a big brown, and I learned through hard experience during my first trip to the islands that it is far better to cast to boulders that look like trout than to assume they are rocks, because often those big 'boulders' would move off into deeper water and disappear when I got too close to them!)

The Tekapo River is an insect-rich one, where mayflies are as abundant as any insect. I tied on a small mayfly imitation, added some split-shot and cast well upstream of the fish, allowing the nymph ample time to get down to the fish in the deep slick. After twenty careful drifts, the shape hadn't moved, so I clipped off the nymph and tied on a Buller Caddis, a pattern that had proved highly effective on other South Island streams. The pattern was heavily weighted so there was no need to add split-shot, but after several casts and no response from the fish, I clipped off the pattern and took out my box of nymphs.

As two flies had failed to interest the trout choosing a new pattern was difficult. Looking at the assortment of nymphs in the fly-box, I couldn't decide what to try next. I had never before fished any of the several simple bead head patterns in the box and had added these unconventional imitations to my nymph collection more as an afterthought than anything else. However, I selected a bead head pattern from my box and, without much confidence, tied it to the tippet.

The bead head fly I had chosen was a bright olive-bodied caddis pattern, with a few lead wraps under the thorax to provide additional weight so that the pattern would get down to the streambed quickly in fast water. The shape I was casting to remained motionless in the water and, as well as questioning the effectiveness of the pattern I was about to use, I wondered whether the 'fish' shape was indeed a trout. I threw the first cast well upstream of the dirty-brown shape. It appeared to be a good cast, the fly landing directly in front of the fish in its drift lane, and the twenty-six-inch hook-jawed brown of six pounds took the pattern on the first drift. Though it gave a disappointing fight in the pool below its lie, it proved to me the effectiveness of these patterns, which have subsequently become my mainstay nymphing patterns for fast water when I need to get the fly to the bottom quickly and keep it there.

While the bead head pattern tied here is a simple one that I fish with great success, almost any standard nymph

Above An angler could mistake this mountain stream for one in New Zealand, so clear are its waters, but it is the fantastic Jan du Toit's River near Goudini in spring. This pristine stream tumbles out of the mountains and offers the fly-fisher some of the most challenging fly-fishing in South Africa. Here Tom Lewin works his way slowly upstream.

pattern can be converted to a bead head imitation with amazing results. I now consider bead head patterns as standard fare in my fly-boxes and rely on them to fish fast, deep water typical of many South African freestone streams.

Several years ago I learned a useful fishing technique from New Zealand guide Frank Schlosser that I now use every time I venture out onto a river or stream. This involves nymphing with two patterns. For many years I was loath to do this as the accepted South African method of fishing two patterns was to tie the dropper pattern to the tag-end of a blood knot. Due to the nature of the nymphing rig, tangles were inevitable and, after the frustration of having to sort out tangled leaders and tippets, I almost always reverted to fishing a single nymph by the day's end. New Zealand anglers have a novel way of fishing two nymph patterns

which seldom results in tangled leaders and tippets: the heavier bead head pattern is tied to the leader or tippet in the conventional manner, and then a smaller nondescript pattern – such as a Hare and Copper – is tied to the bend of the bead head hook with a length of tippet material so that it fishes approximately a foot away from the bead head pattern (see the illustration on page 17). I've successfully used this highly effective technique in rivers and streams throughout South Africa, fishing the nymphs upstream using a floating line, leaders as long as fifteen feet, and a yarn indicator.

One of the advantages of tying on two patterns at once is illustrated by this anecdote. A few years ago, while fishing a quiet stretch of the Bell River just outside Rhodes with Terry Andrews and Fred Steynberg, I hooked a small rainbow which was feeding alongside a steep, undercut bank. While the trout fought in a vain attempt to rid itself of the hook, another fish followed it. When the time arrived to net the small fish, the other fish, also of similar size, was still swimming with the trout I had first hooked, so I decided to try and net them both together. However, there was no

Left *Professional New Zealand fishing guide Frank Schlosser and Mike Somerville pose with a five-and-a-quarter-pound rainbow taken from the Ahuriri River on the South Island. The fish took a small mayfly nymph imitation fished together with a bead head pattern.*
Below *This magnificent twenty-six-inch New Zealand brown took a bright olive bead head caddis pattern.*

TOM LEWIN

need: the first fish had taken the bead head pattern on the dropper, while the other had taken the Hare and Copper on the point! Subsequently, this has happened fairly often.

Mike Somerville and I made a most interesting observation about bead head and standard patterns during a very successful trip to New Zealand a few years ago. Fishing bead head patterns on the dropper and more sombre imitations on the point, we found that the bead head flies were often taken by the rainbows, while the wilier browns took the point fly. Frank Schlosser believes this is because the browns are attracted to the flies as a result of the flash from the bead, but when they intercept the bead head pattern they refuse it because they are shrewd enough to realise that it is a fake. Just as they are about to return to their lie, they spot the smaller pattern drifting by and intercept and eat that fly.

While I fish bead head patterns extensively in rivers and streams, for stillwater fishing I limit the use of beads to Woolly Buggers only, preferring to fish unweighted patterns in our lakes. This is because I believe that beads tied in behind the eyes of stillwater patterns, as well as making the patterns sink quickly, gives them an unnatural diving, jigging action quite unlike that of the live insects they are attempting to imitate. An exception to this rule of mine is, however, a nondescript nymph pattern such as Tom Sutcliffe's Bead Head Zak Nymph (see page 52); this useful pattern serves as a general searching pattern for open waters and around weedbeds, and deserves a place in all stillwater anglers' fly-boxes.

BEAD HEAD NYMPH

HOOK: Tiemco 5262, 5263 or 200R, #8 – #14.
THREAD: 6/0 prewaxed, brown.
HEAD: Gold or copper bead.
TAIL: Partridge fibres.
RIB: Copper wire.
ABDOMEN: Medium to dark brown natural fur dubbing.
HACKLE: Brown partridge.
THORAX: Same as abdomen.

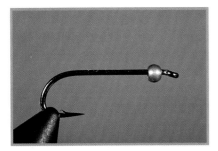

1. Slip a bead onto the hook and fit it snugly against the eye of the hook.

2. Take the thread to a position above the hook barb and tie in 10 to 15 partridge fibres, which should be one-half to two-thirds the length of the hook shank.

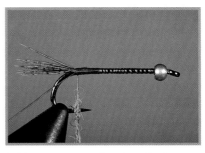

3. Tie in a copper wire rib and spin a thin noodle of dubbing onto the thread.

4. Form a neatly tapering abdomen over two-thirds of the hook shank. Wind the rib forward through the abdomen, tie off, and trim the excess.

5. Tie in a partridge hackle by the tip directly in front of the abdomen with its concave side facing the hook shank. Take two to three turns of the hackle in front of the abdomen, tie off and trim the excess.

6. Spin a thin noodle of dubbing onto the thread and form a small thorax between the hackle and the bead, half-hitch the thread behind the bead, and trim the excess. Apply head cement to the thread wraps.

Rubber Leg Nymph

ANON

Ask most south african anglers if they carry patterns using rubber leg material in their fly-boxes and the chances are that you will receive a negative response. These unusual-looking patterns are popular on the Vaal River where they are used to take yellowfish, yet few South African fly-fishers use them to catch trout. I think the reason for their lack of popularity is due to a lack of publicity and a lack of confidence in the patterns themselves. Little has been written about these flies in local publications and I believe anglers have not given them the time they deserve. Since the day several years ago when a #12 Brown Rubber Leg Nymph, drifted deep through a powerful run on the Hopewell stretch of the Umzimkulu River below

Right *Tom Lewin searching the tumbling currents of the Jan du Toit's River near Goudini. This is the type of water ideally suited to the use of deep-searching nymphs like the Rubber Leg Nymph and Bead Head Nymph.*

Below *Tom Lewin eases an average-sized Witte River brown back into the water. A catch-and-release policy, in force on this stream for many years now, has ensured quality fishing since its introduction.*

Above *Tom Lewin nets a fine brown from the Witte River in Bain's Kloof Pass.*

Underberg, produced a twenty-five-inch rainbow which almost wrenched the rod from my hand and left a painful line burn in my index finger, I have been a convert to these ungainly yet deadly patterns.

Nymphs with rubber legs – and often with rubber tails and antennae – were initially tied to represent stoneflies such as the giant *Pteronarcys californica* found in many of the rivers of the western states of North America (see page 68), and are extremely effective attractor patterns.

Rubber-legged patterns are most effective when fished along the river bottom and should, therefore, be heavily weighted. Additional weight should be added to the tippet where necessary. White rubber legs are extremely effective in deep, fast, discoloured water and will often draw strikes

when smaller, more sombre patterns fail. I fish these artificials on an upstream or upstream-and-across cast, using mending techniques to keep the pattern drifting at the same speed as the current. Strike indicators are essential, particularly for the beginner or intermediate angler, when drifting these heavy nymphs through rough, broken water. When fishing these and other heavily weighted nymphs I use a large yarn indicator, usually half-an-inch in length, well soaked in floatant.

The secret to the pattern's performance is a dead-drift without drag, as this allows the rubber hackle to move freely and to vibrate in the water. If drag is allowed to influence the system, the pattern is pulled along faster than the

Above The author high-sticking a nymph through a run on the Witte River in Bain's Kloof Pass. This is an excellent technique to master when fishing nymphs or dry flies through short, rough pockets and runs.

HIGH-STICKING

It is useful to master a nymphing technique known as 'high-sticking' , particularly when fishing these and other nymphs in fast, pocket water when the nymph must be fished dead-drift without drag. A common problem which occurs when the angler is standing in fast water and casting the fly-line into relatively slower water is that if the fly-line is allowed to float in this faster current it is swept downstream more rapidly than the fly, which then begins to drag.

High-sticking helps to overcome this: the technique involves casting a short line upstream and then holding the rod as high as possible above your body in order to keep as much line off

the water as you can. As casts into pocket water are often so short that only the leader lies on the water the problem of fly-line drag is greatly reduced, and the fly is able to drift along without the negative effect of current drag.

current and the rubber leg material folds flat along the body of the fly, ruining its action. The pattern listed here is one which I have used effectively for many seasons, but fly-tiers should experiment with various patterns until they settle on one which they can fish with confidence. Like beads, rubber leg material will convert almost any established nymph pattern into an enticing and effective probe-and-search nymph. Some already successful patterns (such as the Kaufmann Stone) are now sold tied with rubber legs and a metal bead head – testimony to the effectiveness of these materials.

RUBBER LEG NYMPH

HOOK: Tiemco 200R, 5262 or 5263, #10 – #14.
THREAD: 6/0 prewaxed, colour to match abdomen.
TAIL and ANTENNAE: Rubber leg material, colour of choice.
LEGS: Same as tails.
RIB: Copper wire.
ABDOMEN: Natural or synthetic dubbing, colour of choice.
WINGCASE: White tip turkey tail.
THORAX: Same as abdomen.

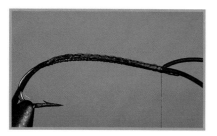

1. Take the thread to above the barb. Tie in two lengths of rubber leg material along the shank, extending past the bend for the tails and forward past the hook eye for the antennae. Divide the antennae on either side of the hook eye.

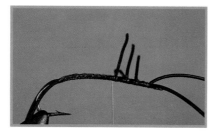

2. To form the legs, tie in three strips of rubber leg material on the front third of the hook, as shown.

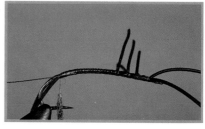

3. Return the thread to a position above the barb of the hook, tie in the rib and spin a noodle of dubbing onto the thread for the abdomen.

4. Form the abdomen over about two-thirds of the shank. Wind the rib through the abdomen in five or six evenly spaced turns, tie off and trim.

5. Tie in a wingcase directly in front of the abdomen and spin a noodle of dubbing onto the thread for the thorax.

6. Form the thorax by wrapping the dubbing forward between the rubber legs. The thorax should be slightly thicker than the abdomen.

7. Pull the wingcase over the top of the thorax, tie off and trim the excess.

8. Form a small thread head. Half-hitch and trim the thread. Apply cement to the thread wraps. Pick out the thorax with a dubbing needle. Trim the legs to about half the length of the shank.

9. The Rubber Leg Nymph seen from above, showing correct proportions.

San Juan Worm

ANUN

THE SAN JUAN WORM was developed to imitate aquatic worms on the San Juan River in New Mexico in the United States; when it was initially introduced several anglers wanted the fly to be banned because it proved so successful on trophy trout!

Most anglers are aware of the ubiquitous midge and may have fished for trout with a pupal imitation (see pages 97–99). Few, however, fish imitations of the larva with any measure of success, although imitations of this stage of the insect's life can, if fished correctly, provide exciting sport during certain times in the season. Midges fall within the huge insect order *Diptera*, which encompasses other well-known insects such as mosquitoes and crane flies. Midges, or 'buzzers' as they are known in Britain, belong to the family *Chironomidae* and have a complete metamorphosis from egg to larva to pupa to adult insect. In terms of its availability to the trout and, consequently, its significance to the angler, the pupa is without question the most important phase of the insect's life cycle. However, this does not mean that the other stages do not also provide sport for

the fly-fisher: trout will often feed both selectively and opportunistically on midge larvae.

Midge larvae, which hatch from eggs, usually attain lengths of approximately one inch and are typically bright red, although other colours, such as yellow and green, occur in certain lakes. The red colouring is due to the presence of haemoglobin in the insect, and this, together with their wormlike appearance, has led to their common name, bloodworms. Haemoglobin is an efficient oxygen carrier and thus the high haemoglobin content in the larvae's bodies enables them to live on the bottom of lakes, where oxygen is in short supply.

They spend most of their lives in tunnels in the mud, where they feed on organic matter and move their bodies in a wave-like motion to bring water over their gills, and are mostly overlooked by anglers as a reliable food source for trout. They occasionally leave their tunnels and journey to

Above *This beautifully marked three-and-three-quarter-pound rainbow fell for a San Juan Worm fished slowly near the surface.*

the surface; entomologists believe these journeys are a search for air (or higher oxygen concentrations). Although the larvae are bottom-dwellers and are well concealed, they are often eaten in great numbers by trout, probably during these excursions to the surface. My detailed analyses over the years of stomach contents indicates that trout eat midge larvae throughout the year, though I have found them in trouts' stomachs in greatest numbers from September through to April when, due to the abundance of the larvae, trout often feed quite selectively on them. Midge larvae are unable to swim effectively and move along the lake bottom or in the weed in a series of active, wriggling thrusts that apparently attract the attention of the trout.

I fish the San Juan Worm (or simply 'Worm', as my angling companions now call it) with a floating line and a leader of about fifteen feet. Much as I do with Flashback Nymphs (see page 55) in stillwater, I fish the Worm either static or with a slow, constant hand-twist retrieve. Often, however, I retrieve the pattern with an erratic hand-twist if

the action is slow. Using these techniques, takes are almost always positive and hook-ups are solid, with fish often hooked deep in the throat. When prospecting deeper water, I resort to intermediate or sinking lines in various densities and almost always use an erratic hand-twist retrieve.

Of the flies that I carry in my fly-box, the San Juan Worm is the easiest to tie, but don't be fooled by this simple pattern: it is one of the most effective imitations that I carry and will outsmart fish in waters that carry a lot of angling traffic. Even when the vernille is hanging onto the hook by a few strands of tying thread after taking numerous fish, this pattern continues to produce the goods. Give it a try.

SAN JUAN WORM
HOOK: Tiemco 2457, 2487 or 3769, #10 – #12.
THREAD: 6/0 prewaxed, red.
BODY: Red vernille (Tuff or Ultra Chenille).

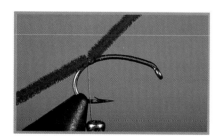

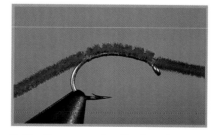

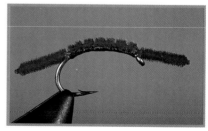

1. Cover the hook with thread from the eye up to a position beyond the barb of the hook. Tie in the vernille, taking several turns of thread around the vernille above the barb of the hook.

2. Continue wrapping the thread over the vernille towards the hook eye in eight to ten evenly spaced turns. Take several wraps of thread around the vernille directly behind the hook eye, half-hitch and trim the thread.

3. Apply head cement to the thread wraps behind the eye, above the barb and along the underside of the shank. Trim the vernille to the length shown and singe the ends over an open flame.

Suspender Midge

JOHN GODDARD/NEIL PATTERSON

IN MANY SOUTH AFRICAN waters, midges *(Chironomidae)* make up a significant proportion of the trout's diet, particularly during winter when they are often the predominant food source. Trout feed very selectively on midge pupae in the surface film during seasonal hatches, and many anglers have had the frustrating experience of being unable to lure a fish with an imitation at these times. An adequate pupa imitation can result in some fine bags of trout and is therefore an essential addition to a fly-box.

In other countries midge patterns provide challenging fishing because fine tippets and limber rods are often needed to fish the diminutive #20 and smaller imitations required to match the size of the naturals. However, in South Africa midges are fairly large, with an average size of about the same as a #12 to #16 hook. In fact, some of our Chironomids have to be imitated by hooks as large as a #8.

In my experience, the best emergences of midge pupae generally occur in the early hours of the morning or at dusk. Midge larvae live in silken tunnels on the lake bottom (see also page 95), and pupate in these tunnels. When the adult is ready to emerge, the pupa wriggles out of the tube and slowly floats to the water's surface, where it splits its pupal skin and emerges as the two-winged adult midge common along lake margins. The pupae are unusual-looking insects, with slender abdomens and pronounced thoraxes. Fine, white, feathery appendages at the base of the abdomen and head are breathing filaments, and I believe that it is important to emulate these features when tying imitations of the pupa.

Midge pupae cover a wide colour spectrum. The most common specimen seen locally is a semi-translucent brownish-black, highlighted with faint tinges of amber and claret. Tom Sutcliffe aptly describes their appearance as having '...a precious stone translucency' – the pupae do indeed have a ruby-like appearance, with a glassy, glowing richness of colour that suggests the pupae have been dipped in varnish.

While midge pupae patterns can be effective fished deep below the surface in the early afternoon before the hatch gets into full swing, anglers will experience the most dependable midge fishing in and just under the surface during calm, flat water conditions when the pupae find it difficult to break through the surface film. Good midge hatches can occur at any time of the year, but I have found that the best surface fishing is to be had from late October until the end of February, with hot, calm, humid evenings providing the best conditions for full-blown emergences and for anglers to take feeding fish on the top. The heaviest

emergences I have seen have taken place at dusk preceded by a relatively windless and hot day. Pupae become trapped beneath the surface film under such conditions, and trout are able to pick off the suspended pupae at their leisure. When trout show themselves at dusk in slow, unhurried rises, it is usually a sign that they are concentrating on the pupae collecting at the surface.

There are several methods of fishing midge pupae imitations, depending on the stage of emergence, but the most successful of all utilise floating lines, long leaders and long, limber fly-rods. At the early stages of an emergence, when many pupae are still to be found deep in the water, the angler may wish to employ a deeply sunken artificial to search blindly for fish. At a later stage, when most of the pupae are to be found in the surface film, it is at the surface that the most exciting and consistent fishing action will occur. During periods of heavy emergence, trout will feed extremely selectively in the uppermost layers of the water on pupae hanging in or just below the surface film. Imitations that are fished even inches below this surface layer will usually be ignored, even if they are the correct shape, size and colour.

Midge pupae rise almost vertically from the bottom to the surface during emergence. When the live pupae become active in the early afternoon and the angler wishes to employ a deeply sunken artificial, the only method to imitate this vertical motion effectively is with a floating line. Intermediate and sinking fly-lines will draw the imitation through the water at an angle to the bottom, quite unlike the

Above *This four-and-three-quarter-pound winter rainbow was patrolling the rocky shore of a lake near Underberg and raced forward to take a Sunken Midge descending through the water. The Underberg area is well known for good midge hatches.*

Above *The stomach contents of a surface-feeding three-pound rainbow taken with a Suspender Midge Pupa show several midge pupae and some empty pupal shucks. It is clear that the Suspender Midge Pupa was the correct choice of pattern to deceive this fish.*

natural motion of the live insect. This blind, searching type of fishing using a deeply sunken pupa requires sharp reflexes and keen eyesight, and the butt of the leader should always be well greased with floatant to provide a marker for strike detection. In addition, when fishing the imitation blind, I like to use the end of the fly-line to relay strikes and so I use the brightest fly-lines I can find. The imitation should be retrieved with a slow but erratic hand-twist, and takes are usually gentle but solid. An alternative method of fishing a deeply sunken pupa is simply to leave it static or to allow it to drift with the wind. The angler should strike at any abnormal movement of the end of the fly-line or the leader, especially if the movement is where the leader enters the water.

For surface-fishing conditions, on the other hand, the Suspender Midge, designed by Neil Patterson and popularised by well-known British anglers such as John Goddard, is the most effective pattern. It makes use of a white polystyrene ball, enclosed in nylon stocking material, attached in front of the thorax to hold the pattern upright in the surface film. This white ball also serves to imitate the breathing filaments of the natural pupa, and makes the pattern easily visible to the angler. The larger the imitation, the larger the polystyrene ball must be. A much larger ball than most anglers would expect is required to fish the imitation in the productive layer in the surface film – this is the key to this pattern's success.

When emergences are heavy and there are many pupae suspended in the surface film, trout cruise slowly below this layer and pick off the pupae at their leisure, either in slow, unhurried, head-and-tail rises or, more commonly, in a series of soft, gulping rises with only the head of the fish appearing. The trout will often feed in a relatively straight feeding path; if the angler sees that this is the case he or she should single out a specific fish and lead the fish by

an appropriate distance. If the cast is too long, simply pull the pattern into the projected feeding path of the fish.

When emergences are not particularly heavy or when light winds create surface waves which scatter the pupae, the trouts' rises will often become random with fish moving in all directions to gulp naturals. This can cause frustrating fishing, as the angler cannot project a feeding path. Under these conditions it is best to cast the pattern out and allow the fish to find it of their own accord. This may sound overly optimistic, given that there are so many naturals with which the fly must compete. However, any angler who has experienced good midge fishing will know that, despite the odds, trout will often take an imitation in preference to the multitude of naturals lying in the water. Suspended midge pupae are normally taken unhurriedly, as the trout seem aware of the fact that their prey is trapped in the film. There is no need for the angler to retrieve the fly, although an occasional twitch will often attract the interest of an otherwise indifferent trout. If the pattern is within the angler's sight and the fish takes it, there is usually a solid hook-up. Trout, however, are able to suck the fly down without any surface disturbance whatsoever, and a greased tippet, although unnecessary to float the fly, will often help in strike detection, particularly in poor light.

For the novice midge fisherman, a rod with limber tip is a must. More experienced anglers can easily handle the hook setting and playing of midge-hooked trout on the faster-actioned graphite rods currently available, but novices should stay with rods that have softer tips as these will protect the delicate tippets often required when using the relatively smaller pupal imitations. I prefer a long, fast-actioned graphite rod of about nine feet, particularly when I am fishing from a float tube or similar low-floating craft. Rod length is, however, not critical, and depends on an angler's personal preferences. Lines in the two to four weight category are best for delicate fishing, and tippets in the 5X and 6X bracket are often required to handle the small imitations required to effectively duplicate some of the smaller varieties of midge pupae. When larger midge specimens are encountered, tippets should be stepped up accordingly, with tippets of 4X often required to handle the #6 to #10 imitations. Well-lubricated reels, with a smooth drag, are extremely important when using pupal imitations, since the fly-line should be able to run off the reel with minimal resistance.

SUSPENDER MIDGE

HOOK: Tiemco 100, 2457 or 2487, #6 – #20.

THREAD: 8/0 prewaxed, colour to match abdomen.

BREATHING FILAMENTS: Polystyrene ball and nylon stocking.

TAIL: White marabou, polypropylene, wool or similar material.

RIB: Flashabou, colour to match abdomen, or fine
   copper wire.

ABDOMEN: Natural fur dubbing (the most common colours
   are black, dark brown, tan, olive and claret).

THORAX: Same as abdomen, or peacock herl.

SUNKEN MIDGE

HOOK: Tiemco 100, 2457 or 2487, #6 – #20.

THREAD: 8/0 prewaxed, colour to match abdomen.

BREATHING FILAMENTS: White marabou, polypropylene, wool
   or similar material.

TAIL: White marabou, polypropylene, wool or similar material.

RIB: Flashabou, colour to match abdomen, or fine copper wire.

ABDOMEN: Natural fur dubbing (the most common colours are
   black, dark brown, tan, olive and claret).

THORAX: Same as abdomen, or peacock herl.

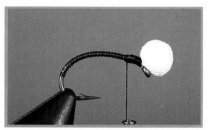

1. Stretch a nylon stocking around the polystyrene ball and tie in the stocking material directly over the eye of the hook.

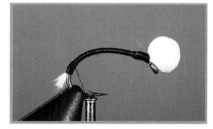

2. Take the thread to a position around the bend of the hook and tie in a few marabou fibres to represent the tail. Break off the fibres to leave behind a short section.

3. Tie in the rib and spin a thin noodle of dubbing onto the thread for the abdomen.

4. Form a thin, neatly tapering abdomen over three-quarters of the hook shank. Wind the rib through the abdomen in six to eight evenly spaced turns, tie it off and trim the excess.

5. Spin a thin noodle of dubbing onto the thread and form the thorax, which should be slightly thicker than the abdomen.

6. Form a small thread head under the polystyrene ball, half-hitch the thread and trim. Apply head cement to the thread wraps. Pick out the underside of the thorax with a dubbing needle.

DRY FLIES

Adams

LEN HALLADAY

THE ADAMS IS TO THE DRY FLY what the Gold Ribbed Hare's Ear is to the nymph: it is the stand-by pattern which, if limited to a single dry fly only, most fly-fishers would select. This pattern is a good imitation of several of our mayflies, particularly the small yet fairly abundant greyish-olive *Baetidae* mayflies encountered in many of our lakes, streams and rivers.

The Adams was first tied in the United States by Leonard Halladay of Mayfield, Michigan, and was named after Charles Adams, who first used it on the Boardman River. When the pattern originated is unknown, but, as it first appeared in the plates drawn by Dr Edgar Burke in Ray Bergman's classic book *Trout*, it apparently predates 1938. Some claim that it was tied to represent a species of adult caddisfly, however I doubt this as the Adams has all the features of a classic Catskill-type mayfly imitation.

That the Adams is a versatile pattern and a fine producer of trout is well known, and it is through the writings of Tom Sutcliffe that the fly has gained the popularity and recognition it so rightly deserves in South Africa. Tom, in his excellent book *My Way with a Trout*, rates the Adams as his most productive dry-fly pattern. I do not believe that any one pattern can cover all aspects of dry-fly fishing, but the Adams fills an important space in any fly-fisher's arsenal of dry flies and as such is one of my favourite dry flies.

I have used this pattern to great effect on many of the fast streams that cut through the mountains of the Western Cape where the diminutive Western Cape *Baetidae* mayflies are common. The Adams has also served me well on the Mooi River below the Kamberg Nature Reserve in KwaZulu-Natal, and it was on this small stream that I experienced the heaviest hatch of *Baetidae* mayflies I have ever seen in South Africa, with swarms of egg-laden females – with bright olive egg sacs – dancing over the surface of the water. On this occasion I used an Adams variation, the Female Adams, and this prevented a potentially frustrating fishing experience.

Simply by varying the amount of fibres in the tail and hackle, the Adams, like most dry flies, can be tied to be fished in either slow or fast water. However, I like to keep the pattern sparse – as it was originally tied – and rely on two variations depending on prevailing conditions. The first variation is the Female Adams, a pattern which is based on the original tying but which makes use of a dubbed chartreuse or yellow fur ball at the base of the abdomen. This pattern is particularly effective during the mating flights of the female *Baetidae* adults, which are easily distinguished from the males by their bright egg sac. The other is the Delaware or Catskill Adams, a fly popularised by Walt and

Below *Fred Steynberg nymphing a quiet stretch of the Bell River just above the town of Rhodes.*

Above *The Bell River at the start of Naude's Neck Pass*

Winnie Dette, two famous fly-tiers from the eastern United States. Of all the Adams variations, and indeed of all dry-fly variations, this is my favourite. It is a pattern that uses a palmered grizzly hackle in its construction and is consequently an excellent floater, particularly in the faster sections of rivers and streams.

Because *Baetidae* mayflies are encountered in both stillwaters, rivers and streams, the extremely versatile Adams has a wide variety of applications. In stillwaters it is at its best when cast to a specific fish either visible in the water or located by its rise sequence. On streams and rivers I prefer to fish the standard and Female Adams in the slower stretches of water and to rely on the Delaware Adams to bring fish to the surface in the faster stretches. The Adams, which is normally tied small, is not a particularly visible or bulky fly and so – generally speaking – I do not use it as a searching pattern. However, if trout are rising the Adams is an excellent choice.

Variation: DELAWARE (CATSKILL) ADAMS
HOOK: Tiemco 100, #10 – #16.
THREAD: 8/0 prewaxed, grey or black.
TAIL: Grizzly and brown hackle fibres, mixed.
WINGS: Grizzly hackle tips, preferably from a hen neck.
ABDOMEN: Medium olive dubbing.
PALMER HACKLE: Grizzly.
HACKLE: Grizzly and brown, mixed.

Variation: FEMALE ADAMS
HOOK: Tiemco 100, #12 – #20.
THREAD: 8/0 prewaxed, grey or black.
TAIL: Grizzly and brown hackle fibres, mixed.
WINGS: Grizzly hackle tips, preferably from a hen neck.
ABDOMEN: Muskrat or similar dark dun fur dubbing.
HACKLE: Grizzly and brown, mixed.
EGG SAC: Chartreuse or bright yellow dubbing.

Anglers should strive to achieve a drag-free drift during the float of the fly. It is only under particularly demanding conditions that a downstream cast will be required, so you should cast the pattern either directly upstream or quarter it upstream and across. When fishing across tricky current flows there are several methods to achieve drag-free floats, including puddle casts, serpentine casts, aerial mends and the like. All fly-fishers who wish to become better anglers should familiarise themselves with these tactics.

ADAMS
HOOK: Tiemco 100, #12 – #20.
THREAD: 8/0 prewaxed, grey or black.
TAIL: Brown and grizzly hackle fibres mixed, or
black moose mane.
WINGS: Grizzly hackle tips, preferably from a hen neck.
ABDOMEN: Muskrat or similar dark dun fur dubbing.
HACKLE: Grizzly and brown, mixed

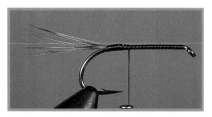

1. Strip approximately 20 fibres from a brown and a grizzly hackle, mix them together and tie them in above the hook barb. The tails should be the same length as the hook shank.

2. Take the thread to one-quarter the shank-length from the eye. Strip the fibres from two hen neck feathers leaving behind only the tips, which should be the length of the shank.

3. For the wings, tie in the hackle tips facing forward over the hook eye and with their concave sides facing away from one another. Trim the excess hackle stems.

4. Pull the wings upright perpendicular to the shank. Secure them with a few turns of thread in front of the wings. Divide the wings with figure-of-eight wraps between the tips.

5. Return the thread to a position above the hook barb and spin a thin noodle of dubbing onto the thread. Form the abdomen over approximately one-half to two-thirds of the hook shank.

6. Select a grizzly and a brown hackle with fibres one-and-a-half times the gape of the hook. Strip the webby flue from the base of the feathers.

7. Tie in the feathers together directly in front of the abdomen, with concave sides facing away from the hook shank. Take the thread to a position behind the hook eye.

8. Wind the first hackle forward, taking two turns of the hackle behind the wings and two turns in front of the wings. Tie the hackle off and trim the excess.

9. Repeat step 8 with the second hackle, ensuring that none of the first hackle's fibres are trapped when winding the second. Form a thread head, half-hitch and trim. Apply head cement to the wraps.

Holsloot Spinner

DEAN RIPHAGEN

WHILE THE FAST-FLOWING freestone rivers and streams of the Western Cape are not renowned for substantial hatches of aquatic insects, the Holsloot River near the small village of Rawsonville has produced some of the heaviest hatches, of a particularly beautiful mayfly, that I have seen in South Africa. It is this mayfly that is responsible for the often frenzied feeding that occurs on this and other streams in that province.

Dr Ferdy de Moor, of the Albany Museum in Grahamstown, suggested from a photograph I sent him that this beautiful insect appeared to be a mayfly of the family *Leptophlebiidae* and, more specifically, of the *Adenophlebia* species, although without examining a specimen of the natural itself he couldn't be certain. While as an amateur entomologist I found this extremely interesting, what interested me more was Dr de Moor's information regarding the wing colour differences between mayfly duns (subimagos) and spinners (imagos). As most fly-fishers know, mayfly duns have dull-coloured wings, while spinners have hyaline or clear wings. According to Dr de Moor, this is because the wings of the dun are covered with fine water-resistant hairs which give them a dull colour. These hairs are usually lost in most mayfly species when the dun moults into the sexually mature spinner. My research into the habits of this mayfly suggests that it is either *Adenophlebia peringueyella* (September brown) or *Adenophlebia dislocans* (summer brown). The September brown is usually encountered from early June to late October, whereas the smaller summer brown hatches from mid-October to mid-January. The two mayflies are almost identical, the only visible distinguishing feature being a difference in size.

The nymphal stage of the *Adenophlebia* species is of limited importance to the fly-fisher because the nymph spends most of its aquatic life on the underside of rocks and stones. Before emergence occurs the nymph migrates along the streambed to the shore and emerges by clambering out of the water at the bank, evidenced by the nymphal shucks which can be found on bank-side boulders. Since emergence takes place at the relative safety of the bank and duns of this species are therefore not forced to ride the currents in order to dry their wings, it is unlikely that the duns are available to trout. Spinners, however, find their way into streams and rivers in great numbers after mating, and it is here that they become vulnerable to trout. One of the most interesting traits of this mayfly is that the spinners often ride the currents for extended periods with their wings in an upright

Top *Looking upstream on the upper Elandspad River in the Western Cape's Du Toit's Kloof Pass.*
Above *The Holsloot Spinner seen from above, tied Arbona spinner-style.*

111

position; this is quite unlike most other mayfly spinners, which lay their eggs in the water and then die with their wings outstretched on the water.

The spinners of this particular mayfly have an elusive, translucent, sooty hue to their bodies that is almost impossible to imitate with either natural or synthetic materials. At the base of the abdomen are two very distinct black bands, an attribute I've attempted to include in my imitation. The wings are clear although heavily marked with distinct black veins and blotches: it is to the fly-tier's advantage to match, as closely as possible, these particular attributes.

As most of the Western Cape's streams are fast-flowing, I initially tied the pattern in the traditional Catskill style with a full hackle, and it has served me adequately during the frenetic feeding activity often sparked off by this mayfly. However, I have experienced refusals in the slower sections of the Holsloot and other rivers such as the Elandspad, mainly in flat-water areas where riffles and runs flatten out into pools, or where flat-water sections speed up as the currents leave the tails of pools. I've solved this hitch by tying the pattern spinner-style, with the wings tied outstretched to resemble the spent adult insect. As I usually fish the pattern through fast water, I've added two turns of hackle on either side of the wings, which I've clipped top and bottom, leaving only a few hackle fibres on either side of the wings. This trick (which I learnt from Fred Arbona's *Mayflies, the Angler and the Trout*) helps to float spinner patterns through fast water.

Because the natural found on the Holsloot and other Western Cape streams is relatively large – imitated on #12 to #14 hooks – the corresponding imitation is also large and heavier tippets are therefore required to turn the pattern over, particularly if downstream winds are a problem. When tying the imitation in sizes smaller than #14, lighter tippets, in the 5X and 6X class, can be used.

Below *Tom Lewin fishing the lower Elandspad River in Du Toit's Kloof Pass on a cold day that produced few fish.*

Most of the hatching and spinner activity of this mayfly occurs at the bank, and gusts of wind and other influencing factors often result in the frail spinners ending up on the water. It pays to drift the fly near the bank, particularly in areas where bankside vegetation overhangs the water: trout accustomed to the presence of the naturals often hold under such overhanging vegetation and will attack a dead-drifted artificial as it passes close to the riverbank.

HOLSLOOT SPINNER

HOOK: Tiemco 100, #12 – #14.
THREAD: 8/0 prewaxed, black.
TAIL: Grizzly hackle fibres.
ABDOMEN: Natural or synthetic sooty dubbing.
RIB: Black floss and black 3/0 monocord.
WINGS: Natural mallard or teal flank feather fibres.
HACKLE: Grizzly.

1. Tie in 20 hackle fibres, which should be the length of the shank, above the barb. Return the thread to a position one-quarter the shank-length from the eye. Tie in 40 teal fibres facing forward.

2. Pull the wings upright, then secure them with a few wraps of thread in front of the wings. Divide the wings with figure-of-eight wraps. The wings should be the length of the hook shank.

3. Return the thread to a position above the barb of the hook, tie in a single strand of floss and spin a short, thin noodle of dubbing onto the thread.

4. Form the rear of the abdomen. Moisten the floss and take two turns of it through the rear end of the abdomen. Tie off and trim the excess floss.

5. Tie in a length of monocord and spin a thin noodle of dubbing onto the thread.

6. Complete the rest of the abdomen, then wind the monocord rib forward in four or five evenly spaced turns, tie off and trim. Tie in two hackles with concave sides facing away from the shank.

7. Take two turns of the first hackle behind the wings and two turns in front of the wings, tie off and trim the excess. The hackle fibres should be equal to one-and-a-half times the hook gape.

8. Repeat step 7 with the second hackle, ensuring that the hackle fibres from the first hackle are not trapped when winding the second hackle through it.

9. Form a small thread head, half-hitch and trim the thread. Apply head cement to the thread wraps.

Royal Wulff

LEE WULFF

THE LATE LEE WULFF IS one of fly-fishing's most famous personalities. He pioneered, developed and publicised the fly-fishing potential of Newfoundland, Canada. He was a proponent of very short 'midge' rods, and was also one of the founders of the exclusive 'Sixteen-Twenty Club', open to those who had landed a salmon of twenty pounds or larger on a fly #16 or smaller. However, perhaps his largest claim to fame arises from his contribution to fly-tying: it was Lee Wulff who, in the 1930s, first used animal hair in the construction of dry flies. From this thinking was born the Wulff series of dry flies, which today are used by anglers throughout the world. The Wulff series includes such popular patterns as the Grey Wulff, the White Wulff, the Green Drake Wulff and the Ausable Wulff, a pattern popularised by the famous Ausable River angler, Fran Betters. Of all the Wulff-style flies, however, the Royal Wulff is arguably the world's most famous attractor dry fly.

Above *This colourful thirteen-inch Witte River brown was taken on a Royal Wulff fished on the upper reaches of the stream.*

The Royal Wulff is a modification of the Fan Wing Royal Coachman. A little-known fly-tier called LC Quackenbush first suggested to Rube Cross that white hair wings and a hair tail would make a more durable substitute for the traditional feather wings and tail. This pattern was initially called the Quack Coachman, but was renamed the Royal Wulff when Lee Wulff included it in his dry-fly series.

Lee Wulff had several requirements in mind when he designed these flies. He wanted a more bug-like, heavier-bodied fly that would provide more flotation than current fly patterns and would better imitate the large grey drakes that hatched out on New York's Ausable River. He considered the tail of the fly to be the most important component of the imitation, as it is the tail that supports the bend of the hook where most of the weight is concentrated. With this in mind, he substituted the more buoyant and durable bucktail for the conventional feather fibre tail. By using bucktail for the wings too on his Wulff patterns the patterns became more buoyant than the traditional dry flies available at that time. In recent years calf tail and calf body hair have replaced the bucktail initially used.

The patterns proved highly effective during their initial trials, and Lee related that during a day he and his good friend Dan Bailey spent fishing with a Grey Wulff on the Salmon River near Malone, New York, he caught fifty-one trout with the same fly without once having to take it off the leader. This was a fantastic feat at the time and proved the durability of the pattern.

What makes the Royal Wulff such an effective pattern? I think its effectiveness is due to a combination of several factors, including its high-floating qualities, good visibility to both fish and fly-fisher, and the use of peacock herl in its construction. Most Royal Wulffs available in fly shops, as well as those being tied by fly-fishers today, make use of black moose body hair for the tail and calf body hair for the wings, and these materials greatly add to the visual appeal and allure of the pattern. The white wings make the fly easy to follow in fast water and because the pattern has a fat, buggy look it will often bring up otherwise disinterested fish from great depths. I am also convinced that the characteristic iridescence of the peacock herl used in the body has a great deal to do with the fly's appeal to the trout.

The Royal Wulff is one of the finest fast-water dry flies available today, which, when tied correctly, will float all day through the roughest waters. For most of my fast-water dry-fly patterns, such as the Royal Wulff, I use three hackles and this adds significantly to their buoyancy. While two hackles are sufficient to float a fast-water dry fly, I prefer the denser barbule count that three hackles provide. Furthermore, I cannot stress enough the importance of using genetic cock hackle capes for tying dry flies, particularly dry flies for fast water. Where the fly-tier's budget allows, avoid the 'Indian' or 'Chinese' hackle necks, as these are inferior to the genetic hackle capes available from sources such as Metz, Hoffman and others.

Recently, there has been growing interest in the use of saddle hackles for hackling dry flies. Previously, saddles were associated with wet flies, streamers and attractor patterns, but such is the exceptional quality of today's genetically engineered saddle capes that they make excellent dry-fly hackles. I have several Hoffman saddle capes bred specifically for dry-fly use which I find myself using more and more for my dry flies. Their barbs are stiffer than other quality-grade hackle capes, they have almost no webby flue,

the fibre density is excellent, and they are usually three to four times longer than conventional dry fly hackles.

I like to tie several Royal Wulffs during a tying session and have developed a neat trick that saves endless frustration at the bench when tying this and other western hair-winged dry flies. Although I tie most of the Royal Wulff using 8/0 thread, I tie in the wings with monocord, which is far stronger and allows much greater pressure to be placed on the winging material, thus preventing frustrating breakages and resulting in a far more durable pattern. I usually tie fifteen to twenty flies during a session, first tying in all the wings with monocord before I complete the process using 8/0 tying thread. I use white monocord when tying in the white calf body hair, as this makes for a neater fly.

Although the Royal Wulff will deceive fish in slower stretches of rivers and streams, it is an ideal pattern for pocket water and fast riffles. The usual dry-fly methods apply when using this pattern, and the nymphing technique known as 'high-sticking' (see page 85) is particularly useful in fast pocket-water stretches of rivers and streams as it allows the angler to keep as much line off the water as possible. Often, casts into pocket water in many of our mountain streams are so short that only the leader lies on the water, reducing the problem of fly-line drag.

Because the Royal Wulff is usually fished in faster water, the trout has only a split second to make up its mind whether to take it or not. As a result takes are fairly fast, and in order not to break off the fly the angler must be aware of the imitation's position on the water and must not over-react when a fish appears unexpectedly. The most appropriate method of hooking fish in these situations, particularly where tippets used are 5X or lighter, is not to strike but simply to tighten on the fish. The speed of the trout will usually be more than sufficient to drive the hook home, particularly if it is taken on a tight line.

ROYAL WULFF

HOOK: Tiemco 100, #10 – #20.

THREAD: Monocord, white, and 8/0 prewaxed, black. (Note that for clarity orange monocord is used in the tying sequence photographs overleaf, but white monocord is normally used.)

WING: White bucktail or white calf body hair.

TAIL: Bucktail or black moose body hair.

BODY: Peacock herl divided by red floss.

HACKLE: Brown.

1. Trim a section of calf body hair from the hide and stack the fibres in a hair stacker. The stacked hairs should be approximately the thickness of a pencil.

2. Take the monocord to a position about a third of the shank-length from the eye. With maximum pressure, tie in the fibres facing forward. Trim excess.

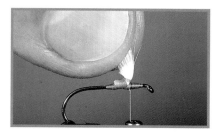

3. Pull the hair fibres into an upright position and secure them with several turns of monocord in front and around the base of the fibres.

4. The wings should be equal in length to the shank. Divide the fibres and separate them with figure-of-eight wraps.

5. Take several turns of monocord around the base of each wing, half-hitch and trim the monocord.

6. Take the 8/0 thread to above the barb and tie in 20 bucktail fibres, which should be equal to the shank-length.

7. Tie in four or five peacock herls by the tips, twist into a rope and form the rear third of the body. Tie off but do not trim the herls. Attach a length of floss. Take the thread to the position shown.

8. Moisten the floss and wind it forward, forming the second of the three sections of the body, tie the floss off and trim the excess. Wind the thread forward to the position shown.

9. Form the third section of the body with the remaining peacock herl, tie off and trim the excess. Note that enough room has been left for two full hackles to be wound.

10. Select and tie in two hackles with concave sides facing away from the shank. For very fast water, three hackles can be used. Trim excess hackle stems, and take the thread to behind the eye.

11. Wind one hackle forward, taking two turns of the hackle behind the wings and two turns in front of the wings. Tie off the feather and trim the excess.

12. Repeat step 11, ensuring that the barbs of the first hackle are not trapped by the second hackle. Form a small thread head, half-hitch and trim the thread. Apply head cement to the wraps.

Humpy

JACK HORNER

THE HUMPY IS CONSIDERED by many anglers to be an indispensable dry fly, particularly on rivers. Both the Humpy and its derivative, the Royal Humpy, are excellent floaters in fast water and can be tied in a variety of colours, making them versatile patterns.

The original version of the Humpy was tied by a San Francisco fly-tier, Jack Horner, in the early 1940s. This simple pattern was called the Little Jack Horner or Horner Deer Hair. It was tied using black thread and a single clump of deer hair for both body and tail on hooks from #10 to #14, but the deer hair tips were not split into wings as they are today. Relatively poor-quality hackle was used and the pattern, unlike its modern-day descendants, was designed to be fished flush with the surface.

Several modifications followed, including Montana guide Keith Kenyon's popular 'goofy deer hair fly' or Goofus Bug, as it became known. It was endorsed by the well-known angler and fly shop owner, Dan Bailey, who called it the Poor Man's Wulff (a name which, however, did not catch on). Soon thereafter he featured the pattern in his catalogue in sizes #10 to #14 and tied with a red, green or yellow floss

Above *This five-and-a-half-pound New Zealand brown fell for a lime-bodied Royal Humpy fished by Mike Somerville.*

underbody, distinctly divided wings and an upper body and tail made of deer or elk hair. In 1967 Jack Dennis improved on the original pattern by substituting white calf tail for the traditional deer hair used in the wings. This made the pattern more visible and easier to track (particularly for anglers with less than 20/20 vision) and created what is today one of the most effective dry flies available, the Royal Humpy. Pat Barnes showed the Poor Man's Wulff to an Orvis representative who was looking for new dry flies, and in 1973 the Orvis catalogue featured a fly called the Humpy – a direct

Below *Terry Andrews fishing a stretch of the Bell River near Rhodes. The scenery around Rhodes is spectacular and there are several quality streams in the area, including the Bell, the Bokspruit, the Sterkspruit and the Kloppershoekspruit.*

Above Mark Yelland and Jimmy Baroutsos fishing the runs and riffles of the Umgeni River in KwaZulu-Natal.

descendant of the Goofus Bug. The 1989 Dan Bailey catalogue featured four distinct Goofus Bug patterns, which gives an indication of its popularity as a contemporary fly pattern.

The Humpy's only drawback is its lack of durability, particularly in the shellback area where the deer hair that forms the tail is pulled back over the top of the body. Once the pattern has been taken by a few fish, the imitation begins to lose its original shape completely. Jack overcame this problem to a certain degree by substituting moose body hair, which is far stiffer yet more durable, for the deer hair in the shellback. However, I have found that a shredded Humpy is as effective as a new one cast onto the water for the first time.

Like the Royal Wulff, the Humpy is an excellent floater in all but the heaviest riffles and pockets. Because the Humpy is heavily hackled it works best in fast riffle or pocket water, such as the headwaters of our rivers and streams, where fish do not have much time to scrutinise a fly (in slower rivers less fully hackled patterns are more effective). The angling techniques recommended for the Royal Wulff (see pages 114–115) apply to the Humpy too.

By varying the body colours of the Humpy, the fly-tier is able to replicate a wide variety of colours found in nature; my favourites are orange, red, lime, yellow and black. While I don't believe that trout become totally selective about the colours used in the body of the pattern, sometimes they appear to show a preference for one colour over another (I have found orange and lime to be particularly effective, especially on the tumbling waters of the Western Cape) and it pays to carry the pattern in several colours.

It is important to match tippet diameters to the size of the imitation used, particularly when fishing bulky western hair-winged dry flies which may strain tippets that are not suited to casting these patterns. This is especially noticeable in strong winds which may cause a light tippet to curl and twist like a corkscrew. Since the Humpy is usually fished in heavier water, the problem of refusals associated with the use of heavy tippets does not play a significant role and anglers can safely step up tippet sizes to 4X, even when #10 and #12 patterns are used. This means that the tippet is placed under less strain during casting, and the leader is better able to turn the fly over when strong downstream winds are encountered.

Variation: ROYAL HUMPY

HOOK: Tiemco 100, #10 – #18.

THREAD: 8/0 prewaxed, colour to match body.

WING: White calf tail or calf body hair.

TAIL AND SHELLBACK: Dark moose hair.

BODY: Red thread or floss. (Colours such as lime, orange and yellow, and fluorescent colours, can be used.)

HACKLE: Brown.

HUMPY

HOOK: Tiemco 100, #10 – #18.

THREAD: 8/0 prewaxed, colour to match body.

WING: Elk hair.

TAIL AND SHELLBACK: Moose or elk hair.

BODY: Floss, elk hair or thread. (My favourite colours, when using floss, are orange, red, lime and yellow.)

SHELLBACK: Moose or elk hair.

HACKLE: The original version called for a few turns of low-grade grizzly hackle: most fly-tiers today, however, use genetic hackle in a mixture of grizzly and brown, or other appropriate colours, such as dun, ginger and the like.

1. Take the thread to a third of the shank-length from the hook eye, stack a pencil-diameter section of elk hair in a stacker and tie it in over the eye.

2. Pull the fibres upright and secure them with a few wraps of thread in front of the wing. The wing should be the length of the hook shank.

3. Divide the fibres and separate them with several figure-of-eight wraps. Take a few turns of thread around the base of each wing to neatly divide the fibres.

4. Take the thread to above the barb, stack 30 moose or elk fibres in a stacker, and tie them in. The tail should be the length of the hook shank.

5. Tie the fibres down along about half the hook shank. Take the thread back to a position above the hook barb.

6. Pull the tail fibres backwards towards the bend of the hook and tie down to form a 'hump'. Tie in a length of floss above the hook barb.

7. Take the thread to a position about halfway along the hook shank, moisten the floss and form the body. Tie off and trim the excess.

8. To form the shellback, pull the moose or elk hair tied back in step 6 over the top of the body, tie off and trim the excess.

9. Tie in two hackles with their concave sides facing away from the fly. Their fibres should be one-and-a-half times the gape of the hook.

10. Wind the first hackle forward, taking two turns of hackle behind the wings and two turns of hackle in front of the wings. Tie off and trim the excess.

11. Wind the second hackle forward, ensuring that none of the fibres of the first hackle become trapped. Tie off and trim the excess.

12. Form a small, neat thread head, half-hitch and trim the thread. Apply head cement to the thread wraps.

RAB

TONY BIGGS

ANY FLY-TIER WHO HAS had the chance to look into Tony Biggs's fly-boxes will have noticed immediately a special trait in all his flies: they are designed to catch fish and not fishermen. Tony considers his approach to fly-tying to be unorthodox and has never followed a technical fly-tying manual. Instead, he has allowed his imagination to lead him – and flies such as the RAB bear testimony to this philosophy. This (together with his acclaimed fishing skills) has earned him a reputation as one of South Africa's most competent fly-fishers. While Tony has been responsible for the development of several flies in South Africa, it is his simple, fast-water RAB that has carved a permanent place for him in our fly-fishing annals.

Born in Britain, Tony cut his teeth on the fine freestone waters of the Western Cape after moving to South Africa in July 1942. He fished a great deal with the late Mark Mackereth, an angler well known for his angling skill, particularly with dry flies, and it was Mackereth, along with

Above *This RAB was tied by Tony Biggs.*

John Beams and Tom Sutcliffe, who influenced Tony's fishing style and fly-tying philosophies. Mackereth's flies were simple palmered patterns and it was after dissecting one of Mackereth's bottle brush-type dry flies that Tony discovered just how simple they really were. This simplicity influenced Tony's tying and is reflected in his RAB.

The easy-to-tie RAB evolved during Tony's early days when he was forced to make ends meet by tying and selling flies. During those years Tony was an avid reader of Negley Farson's *Going Fishing*. Farson strongly advocated the use of red materials in the construction of trout flies, as he maintained that red is highly visible (many fly-tiers and anglers consider red to be highly effective). As a result, Tony used a great deal of red in his patterns, including in the RAB, but was to discover that the colour is not as visible at long range under water as he initially had been led to believe. Nevertheless, the supremely effective RAB retains a red body and ginger or reddish hackle. The white tail was chosen primarily to provide colour balance. The prototype RAB used herls from the glossy green primary wing feather of an Egyptian goose for both the butt and legs (it was these legs that Tony considered the most important aspect of the fly). Unfortunately, Egyptian goose quills are difficult to acquire, even in South Africa, and Tony now uses pheasant tail or blue crane fibres for the body and legs.

The RAB was designed as a fast-water dry fly and it excels in these conditions. While my approach to fast-water dry-fly fishing embraces the use of heavily hackled dry flies such as the Royal Wulff and Humpy, Tony's – as demonstrated by the RAB – is the opposite. The philosophy behind these

NEIL HODGES

Left *Tony Biggs watches as visiting American angler Jim Cassada battles a twenty-inch brown taken from a shallow run on the middle Witte River in Bain's Kloof Pass. Tony is a professional fishing guide, specialising mainly in the streams of the Western Cape.*

patterns is that they should be dressed as lightly as possible and should ride on the very tips of their hackles. What is interesting about the hackles on most of Tony's flies, including the RAB, is that they are extremely long, as are the tails. Some hackles are as long as two inches, which aids in floating the fly through choppy water. The very long tail and hackles ensure that the body remains well above the water and essentially turn the fly into a variant or skater pattern.

Although the pattern is lightly dressed it looks much bulkier than it is and will often bring fish up from deep, fast water. Simply by varying the amount of hackle used in the fly, using more turns of hackle in patterns tied for fast water, Tony has found the RAB equally effective in both fast and slow water. It is also an effective stillwater pattern, and by reducing the amount of hackle in the imitation Tony has used it as a nymph.

The legs are an important component of the pattern. Tony likes to fish patterns with thinner legs as waters begin to thin out towards autumn. In addition, the length of the RAB's legs can be varied to suit specific conditions or water types – Tony often ties his patterns with legs as long as three to four inches, particularly when they are used in certain Mpumalanga streams to entice large fish to the surface. Either the legs can be tied in behind the darker hackle, or the darker hackle can be wound on either side of the legs, effectively supporting them when the pattern is at rest on the water's surface.

The usual fast-water dry-fly techniques apply to fishing the RAB – with one exception. While Tony believes that a correctly tied pattern will not twist tippets, the sheer length of the hackle fibres relative to its hook size will often cause the RAB, with prolonged use, to twist tippets. The problem becomes even more pronounced when the angler has to contend with the strong winds common on many Western Cape streams. The solution is either to step up the tippet size until the problem is eliminated or to use the surgeon's swivel, a knot designed to eliminate twisting caused by large, wind-resistant flies like the RAB. Since the RAB was primarily designed for use in fast water where fish have only a few seconds to decide on the fate of a morsel drifting in the current, the increase in tippet diameter will have a negligible effect on the effectiveness of the fly.

An interesting anecdote relating to this fly is the manner in which it obtained its name. Tony, a friend and Mark Mackereth had spent a day in April 1965 fishing on the lower Smalblaar River with limited success, with only Tony and Mark having anything to show for their efforts. Deciding that a change of venue was in order, they moved

Right Tony Biggs with a Witte River brown just before its release.

to the upper river which, according to Tony, usually fishes better in the afternoon. Tony parted from his companions, and by the time they met up again he had taken five fish ranging from twelve to sixteen inches in length and had returned several others, all of which had fallen victim to the prototype RAB.

Mark and his companion, however, had taken only one small fish between them, and Mark was convinced that it could only have been the pattern that accounted for Tony's success. When Mark examined the fly attached to Tony's tippet he called it a 'Red-Arsed Bastard', and it was from this that the fly took its initials. This name could never have been printed in the hallowed pages of *Piscator*, the journal of the Cape Piscatorial Society, and so the Society's secretary at that time, the legendary AC Harrison, renamed it 'Rough and Buoyant'.

The RAB is one of a handful of truly original South African fly patterns and is a proven taker of trout. Tony's records indicate that the pattern has taken several trophy fish,

including a thin brown, estimated at over seven pounds, from the Witte River in Bain's Kloof Pass; Jan van Huyssteen took eighteen rainbows, the largest a fish of over five pounds, in eighteen casts in Mpumalanga using the RAB; and the editor of *The Complete Fly Fisherman* magazine, PJ Jacobs, took a fish of eight pounds from the Spekboom River in Mpumalanga using the pattern. It is a dry fly that works throughout the country and all anglers who enjoy prospecting the faster water on our rivers and streams should try it.

RAB

HOOK: Tiemco 100, #12 – #18.

THREAD: 8/0 prewaxed, red.

TAIL: White or cream hackle fibres (Tony uses three to twelve, depending on the water to be fished).

BUTT and LEGS: Egyptian goose (dark green primary wing feather), cock pheasant tail or similar feather fibres.

HACKLE: Ginger or red, and white (Tony prefers a white spade hackle).

1. Strip three to twelve fibres from a white hackle and tie them in above the hook barb to form a tail approximately two to three times the length of the hook shank.

2. To form the butt, tie in four Egyptian goose or similar fibres by their butts, and leave the thread just in front of the tie-in point of the tails.

3. Gather the feather fibres together and wind them forward over approximately one-third to one-half of the hook shank. Attach hackle pliers to the fibres and leave them suspended at this point.

4. Wind the thread forward through the feather fibres in open turns. Tie the tips of the feather fibres off but do not trim them.

5. Part the feather fibres so that they stand out in various directions around the hook shank. They should be approximately three times the hook gape, and will form the legs.

6. Taking a ginger or red hackle with fibres about three times the length of the hook gape, tie it in directly in front of the legs, with the concave side facing away from the shank.

7. Take two to four turns of hackle around the shank. Tie off the hackle and trim the excess.

8. Tie in a white hackle with fibres approximately three times the length of the hook gape directly in front of the first hackle, with concave side facing away from the hook shank.

9. Take two or three turns of hackle around the shank, tie off and trim the excess. Form a small thread head, half-hitch and trim the thread. Apply head cement sparingly to the thread wraps.

G and B Low-Floater

GAVIN GRAPES/JIMMY BAROUTSOS

IT WAS A BITTERLY COLD November morning as Jimmy Baroutsos and I clambered down the rubble-strewn path leading to the junction of the Witte and Baviaans rivers. November is normally an extremely warm month in the Western Cape, with temperatures in the kloofs often reaching uncomfortable levels. This day was different, and the low temperature was compounded by a high wind-chill factor caused by an exceptionally strong north-easter. We reached the river in darkness and were forced to huddle behind a collection of large boulders to avoid the biting upstream wind for which we were completely unprepared. The numbing cold did not abate as sunlight began to scythe into the kloof, and rather than sit idly and wait for warmer weather, we decided to move upstream in search of the river's elusive browns.

We fished upstream for an hour before taking a breather alongside a long pool which seemed bleak and lifeless in the low-water conditions. It was not a good day to be on the stream and everything seemed to count against us.

A movement in midstream suddenly caught my attention. Uncertain if I had seen a fish, I brought Jimmy's attention to the movement and pointed out the general location of the midstream disturbance. We were watching the water carefully when suddenly a dimple appeared in the broken water. With polarised sunglasses we eventually were able to make out the vague outline of a trout which appeared to be an average-size brown of about sixteen inches.

With the wind howling upstream a conventional cast was out of the question, so Jimmy waited for a lull in the wind and flicked the fly into the air. With a stroke of luck the fly was blown directly into the feeding path of the brown and, from our position not more than five yards away, we were able to see the fish slowly lift off the bottom to gently intercept it.

When Jimmy set the hook, a commotion broke out on the water's surface, the likes of which I had never before seen on a small Western Cape stream. The fish tore off upstream, turned abruptly and came racing downstream past us in the current.

Above *Mike Harker with a good rainbow from Kimber's 'Old Dam' in the Impendhle highlands.*

I was convinced the frail 5X tippet would shear, but miraculously it held and a battle ensued that is etched indelibly in my memory. On numerous occasions the fish's huge tail slapped against the tippet and its wild thrashings at the surface left us in no doubt that we had completely underestimated its size. How Jimmy ever managed to stay attached to the massive brown will always remain a mystery to me, for she gave a battle equivalent to a fish twice her size. He was indeed relieved when he finally slid the net under the flanks of a magnificent twenty-three-and-a-half-inch brown hen which, after a quick series of photographs, was released so that subsequent anglers could have the chance of going one-on-one with such a wonderful adversary!

The fly that took the brown was a G and B Low-Floater, one of the simplest yet most deadly patterns that I have used locally. If I was forced to choose a handful of dry flies for river and stream fishing in South Africa, the G and B Low-Floater would definitely be included. In fact, the G and B Low-Floater, the RAB, the

Above *A beautiful sixteen-and-a-half-inch Witte River brown, taken on a G and B Low-Floater. It was this particular tagged trout's third capture by the author, testimony to the effectiveness of catch-and-release regulations on this stream.*

Foam Beetle and a hopper pattern would be the only dry flies required to fish effectively the streams of the Western Cape, where trout rely heavily on terrestrial insects.

When I first met Gavin Grapes and Jimmy Baroutsos several years ago, they had been using this pattern for many years and to great effect on the fast streams of the Western Cape. Initially, the pattern resembled the well-known Cooper Bug, or Devil Bug as it is better known in the American states of Maine, New Hampshire and Vermont. The Cooper Bug was first developed in 1937 by Jack Cooper, a professional fly-tier from Salem, New Hampshire, and its popularity quickly spread across the United States where it earned a reputation as an extremely effective pattern on stillwater and stream alike.

The original made use of a single bunch of deer hair for the tail, shellback and head. I modified it somewhat to provide myself with a pattern that would float better on the Cape streams. This entailed tying in additional clumps of deer hair at the head area and flaring them above the hook shank. This flared deer hair was then clipped into an umbrella or parachute shape, which meant that the pattern always landed upright. The large surface area the deer hair provided on the water allowed it to float like a cork through the fastest and roughest waters. Neither Gavin nor Jimmy lay claim to inventing the pattern, although they were using a very similar prototype (hence the name G and B Low-Floater, which soon caught on and became used by several anglers in and around Cape Town). Nevertheless, the modified version of the original has its roots in South Africa and can be considered a truly South African pattern.

What makes this simple fly such an effective pattern? I think the main reason for its effectiveness is that it is a low-floating artificial, and although it does not imitate anything specific, it resembles several food forms in general. I began to take a serious interest in this fly when I discovered, through experience, that – in the majority of cases – a low-floating artificial consistently outperformed standard hackled dry flies, even on fast water. Moreover, the fly is simplicity itself to tie, which means I am able to carry a wide variety of colour and size combinations. In addition, it is a pattern that is seldom, if ever, refused, even by wary fish. I have also discovered that even if the pattern has been shredded by the teeth of several trout it still catches fish; in many cases I have cast to trout with a pattern looking nothing like it did when it left my vice, yet it continues to produce trout when other patterns fail to interest them.

During my university years in Cape Town, this pattern deceived most of the trout I hooked on the Witte River in Bain's Kloof. It was responsible for the downfall of the largest trout I ever took on the Witte, a tagged brown of nineteen inches which, when I landed it for the third time, had gained an inch in length and had fallen for a Swisher/Richards Floating Nymph.

While speaking to Mike Harker a few years ago, he too mentioned that he had devised a pattern along very similar lines, and my research uncovered an article by Peter Sang in the Spring 1987 edition of *Fly Tyer* magazine regarding a pattern of similar design called the Sangster #2. I'm sure that many anglers in other countries have tied similar patterns to this one developed for the Western Cape streams.

I tie the pattern with black, brown, flame orange and chartreuse bodies, but have found the orange-bodied pattern to be most successful. The G and B is best fished on a dead drift, using a tippet diameter slightly larger than normal. (As the large surface area of flared deer hair makes the pattern fairly wind-resistant, the pattern spins in the air and will twist light tippets.) Short leaders of around ten feet will add a degree of control and accuracy to the angler's cast, since wind-resistant flies are particularly affected when long casts are made. Anglers fishing the waters of the Western Cape will find that long leaders are unnecessary because the streams there do not require long casts, particularly waters like the Elandspad in Du Toit's Kloof, the Jan du Toit's River near Goudini, and the Witte River in Bain's Kloof where pocket water fishing prevails in many sections.

G AND B LOW-FLOATER

HOOK: Tiemco 100, #12 – #16.

THREAD: 3/0 prewaxed, colour to match body.

TAIL: Deer or elk hair.

BODY: Synthetic dubbing in colour of choice. (My favourite colours are flame orange, chartreuse, black, brown and olive.)

SHELLBACK: Deer or elk hair.

HEAD: Deer or elk hair.

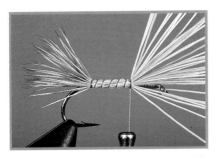

1. Clip 20 to 30 fibres from a deer or elk hide and stack them in a hair stacker. Tie in the fibres above the hook barb along two-thirds of the shank. Do not trim the excess.

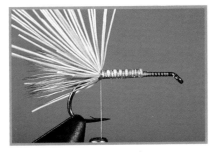

2. Return the thread to a position above the barb and pull the butts of the fibres back over the shank and tie them down. The tail should be the same length as the hook shank. Do not trim the excess.

3. Spin a thin noodle of dubbing onto the thread and form a robust body over two-thirds of the hook shank.

4. Pull the hair fibres over the top of the body and tie them down in front of the body, but do not trim the excess fibres at this stage.

5. Hold a pencil-diameter section of deer or elk hair on top of the hook shank directly in front of the excess hair from the shellback, and take three loose turns of thread around the hair.

6. Holding the underside of the body with the thumb and index fingers of your left hand, pull the thread wraps tight, which will cause the deer hair to flare out above the hook shank.

7. Repeat steps 5 and 6 until the front third of the hook is covered in flared hair. Form a small thread head, half-hitch and trim the thread. Apply head cement to the thread wraps.

8. Remove the hook from the vice and trim the flared hair into an umbrella shape, as shown.

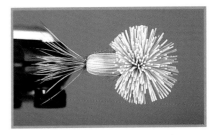

9. The G and B Low-Floater seen from above, showing the large surface area which aids flotation in fast water.

Parachute, Adams

ANON

STORIES OF FISHING SPRING CREEKS, with their selective rainbows, slow, clear water and heavy insect hatches, have always captivated me. I have dreamt of fishing one spring creek in particular, the Harriman State Park water on the Henry's Fork in Idaho. While South Africa is not blessed with spring creeks, the Witte River in Bain's Kloof Pass, although a freestone river, possesses so many spring creek characteristics that it could well be called a freestone spring creek. It lacks the heavy insect hatches that make other spring creeks world famous, but holds trout that, at times, can be infuriatingly selective. Its waters are as clear as any other blue-ribbon stream and it has slow, flatwater sections that will tax an angler's casting and presentation abilities to the fullest.

Some time ago Ed Herbst and I were wading the Witte's quiet waters; by late afternoon we reached a section known to me as 'Guy's Glide'. This slow-water section ends in a deep tailout, which poses presentation and concealment problems. The river's wary browns almost always hold at the tailout in the shadow cast by the bank and, since the glide must be approached at close quarters concealment is always a problem. Coupled with this is the fact that the trout have ample time in which to scrutinise the angler's offering during the fly's drift through the slow water.

On several previous occasions I had presented the imitation from downstream. Everything would run smoothly until the trout turned and began to follow the fly. The current accelerates near the tailout, and the trout would be forced to decide whether or not to chase the fly in a last-minute bid to take it before it tumbled over the lip of the pool. It was at this point, as the trout turned downstream, that the angler in the downstream position would be spotted. The unsuccessful outcome was inevitable, and since I knew good fish called the glide their home, I was always left feeling somewhat frustrated.

With Ed doing the honours with the camera, I had ample time on this occasion to reassess the problem. Clipping off my fly, I tied on a tan-coloured parachute dry fly and made my way carefully upstream. I was convinced that I could deceive the trout in this difficult lie and, keeping low, I was able to manoeuvre into position just below the lip of the tailout. From here I threw a slack line cast upstream, but instead of allowing all the fly-line to land on the water, I threw it onto the bank, allowing only the leader and a small portion of the line to alight on the surface. This, to a large degree, countered the problem of drag, and also ensured that the fly, and not the tippet, reached the fish first.

As if on command, a shape materialised from the dark shadows and quickly transformed into a beautiful golden slab as it passed into the sunlight. From the concealment afforded by the lip of the tailout, I watched as the fish intercepted the fly and slowly followed it downstream. On previous occasions I would have been forced to throw an upstream mend into the fly-line from a standing position just before drag set in, but as drag was not a problem in this instance I could watch from a much lower position and therefore was not forced to betray my presence.

The trout continued to stalk the dry fly, hovering inches from the surface, but was ultimately forced to decide on the imitation's fate when the fly began to speed up as it washed

Left The author battles a good rainbow on the tiny Kloppershoekspruit above Rhodes in the north eastern Cape. This small stream is seldom heard of, yet produces some excellent browns and rainbows.

Above *Bill Sharp fishing the Kloppershoekspruit near Rhodes in the Eastern Cape.*

over the ridge of the glide. Suddenly, there was a boil on the surface and the fly was gone. As I stood up I lifted the rod to take up the slack that lay on the bank in loose coils.

The trout was a hen of seventeen inches, a good fish for the Witte. She put up a tremendous battle on 5X tippet material, using the many obstructions in the glide to her advantage. On several occasions she dragged the tippet across a large submerged rock in mid-stream and I was convinced that the tippet would shear. But, miraculously, it held and I was a very relieved angler as Ed slipped a net under the fish. Her return to the stream meant that she was given the chance to test another angler's skill and to spawn a fresh generation of wild trout.

Parachute dry flies – originally called 'umbrella' flies – are amongst the most underrated of all dry flies, yet they are extremely versatile and effective. Parachutes float low on the water, presenting the trout with a lifelike body silhouette. They are so effective that Ray Bergman touted them in his classic book *Trout* and Doug Swisher and Carl Richards recommended them in their work *Selective Trout*. Not only are they taken for adult mayfly duns, but – as evidenced by the stomach contents of trout caught on Parachute Adams patterns – I'm sure that trout also accept them for emerging nymphs and, at dusk, for mayfly spinners.

Tied with an upright white wing, parachutes are easy to follow on the water, particularly in the evening, and anglers with poor vision or fishing in poor light can take advantage of this. Despite this, few South African anglers use them, probably because they are considered difficult to tie and have been given little publicity. It was during my final year at university that I began to take a serious interest in parachute-hackled dry flies. While I have always enjoyed tying and fishing traditional, fully hackled dry flies, when faced with educated fish on a demanding river like the Witte, one begins to appreciate their limitations, particularly on slower-flowing sections where trout have ample time to scrutinise imitations.

Traditional, fully hackled dry flies will always have their place in fly-fishing, but they are often refused by educated fish, especially in waters that are slow flowing. Why parachute dry flies outperform their higher-floating, fully hackled counterparts is a mystery which I will not attempt to explain. Suffice it to say that these under-used patterns deserve the attention of all fly-tiers and fly-fishers, and will often make the difference between success and failure.

Tying a parachute hackle is not difficult and requires no special tying procedures. Moreover, simply by varying body, tail and hackle colour any mayfly can be imitated, from the largest specimens to the smallest *Tricorythidae*. In addition, the parachute – which has its entire hackle spread in contact with the water thereby supporting its body – will float through all but the roughest waters and is deadly in slower sections.

What makes the parachute dry fly so versatile is that – with a little ingenuity – almost every dry-fly pattern can be tied parachute-style. Patterns such as the Adams convert easily to the parachute style, and are as deadly on stillwaters as they are on rivers and streams. Famous American fly-tier Ed Schroeder has two very effective flies on the market sporting parachute hackles – the Para Hopper and the Para Caddis.

I fish parachutes on all waters, although I prefer to use them on slow water. When cast upstream and allowed to dead-drift downstream, they will often catch selective trout under demanding conditions. On stillwaters, the parachute is best cast to specific fish or it can be cast out and allowed to drift with the wind if fish are not feeding along predetermined paths. I use the parachute most often on stillwaters when the diminutive *Tricorythidae* hatches blanket the water. These tiny mayflies evoke selective feeding by stillwater trout in South Africa, and an imitation that is not the

PARACHUTE, ADAMS
HOOK: Tiemco 100, #12 – #20
THREAD: 8/0 prewaxed, grey or black.
WING/POST: Calf body hair.
TAIL: Grizzly and brown hackle fibres, mixed, or black moose mane.
ABDOMEN: Muskrat or similar dark fur dubbing.
HACKLE: Grizzly and brown, mixed.

correct shape, colour or size usually will be refused. It is at times such as these that a small #18 or #20 parachute will mean the difference between a few fish or no fish at all.

Note: It is impossible to list all the colour combinations available to the fly-tier, as they are endless. However, in order to make a start, I have drawn up a table of basic colour combinations for parachute-style patterns. Tied in a wide range of hook sizes from #12 – #18, they will cover a large variety of adult mayflies found in South Africa.

BASIC COLOUR COMBINATIONS FOR PARACHUTE PATTERNS

	TAIL	BODY	HACKLE
1.	Brown	Brown	Brown/Grizzly
2.	Dark dun	Dark grey	Dark Dun/Grizzly
3.	Cream	Medium grey	Cream/Grizzly
4.	Ginger	Tan	Ginger
5.	Grizzly/Brown	Dark grey	Grizzly/Brown

PARACHUTE (GENERIC)

HOOK: Tiemco 100, #12 – #20.

THREAD: 8/0 prewaxed, colour to match body.

WING/POST: White or grey turkey 'flats' or white calf body hair.

TAIL: Hackle fibres, colour to match hackle.

BODY: Fine-textured natural or synthetic dubbing, colour to match local hatches.

HACKLE: Colour of choice.

1. Stack approximately 30 calf body hair fibres in a hair stacker and tie them in facing forward, approximately one-third of the shank-length from the hook eye.

2. Pull the fibres upright to form the post, and secure them in this position with a few turns of thread in front of the post. Trim the excess.

3. Take several turns of thread around the base of the post and take the thread to above the barb of the hook. The post should be about the shank-length.

4. Tie in 15 moose fibres for the tail, which should be the length of the hook shank. (Another tailing method is to split the tails in the same way as is done in the Floating Nymph [see page 61].)

5. Spin a thin noodle of dubbing onto the thread and form a thin, neatly tapered body, which should be wound tight up against the wing post.

6. Select two hackles with fibres equal to or slightly longer than the hook gape, and tie the hackles in at the post, with concave sides facing towards the hook shank.

7. Spin a thin noodle of dubbing onto the thread directly in front of the post and complete the front section of the body.

8. Wind the hackles clockwise around the post, ensuring that each turn of hackle is wound under the preceding turn. Tie off the hackles and trim the excess.

9. Form a small, neat thread head, half-hitch and trim the thread. Apply head cement to the thread wraps.

Thorax

VINCENT MARINARO

Like parachute-style flies, thorax-style dry flies are vastly underrated and under-used in South Africa, even though they frequently outperform their more established cousin, the Catskill-type dry fly developed by Theodore Gordon in the early 1900s.

Thorax-style dry flies were developed by Vincent Marinaro in the 1950s after he became dissatisfied with the performance of many of the dry flies of the day, such as the Catskill patterns which were used by most anglers fishing his home waters of Pennsylvania. Marinaro felt that there had to be a more productive style of tying dry flies for the slow, clear waters he frequented. His prototype Thorax flies were an attempt to fashion an artificial that would deceive more trout under the often demanding conditions that he faced. These tying developments were described in his classic book *A Modern Dry Fly Code* and to a lesser degree in his subsequent *In the Ring of the Rise*. Like many other patterns, the Thorax dry fly has, through the years, undergone several stages of development and the current Thorax patterns differ considerably from Marinaro's prototype. However, as a pattern type it has endured and deserves the attention of all who enjoy the thrill of taking trout on dries.

Marinaro's original pattern featured split wings of cut-and-shaped hackle points or slivers of flight feathers of birds such as a duck or goose. These split wings were tied in at the centre of the hook shank and had the hackles wound around them. Most Thorax patterns today, however, make use of turkey body (shoulder) feathers, or 'flats' as they are commonly known, which are readily available in a wide range of colours. Hen back feathers and hen body feathers also make excellent thorax-style wings, and fly-tiers and anglers who wish to use these patterns should look for feathers that are wide and webby, with the web extending all the way to the tip. Hen-back feathers also have the advantage that they do not twist light tippets, a problem that is often the result of stiff wing materials.

Originally, the hackles were not wound around the hook shank but around the base of each wing. This hackling system, along with the pattern's split tails, meant that the fly was well balanced and invariably landed upright on every cast. However, although effective, the hackling system made it a rather difficult and time-consuming pattern to tie.

The modern modification of the original Thorax pattern features a single wing tied in approximately one-third of the way along the hook shank. Hackle is wound on either side of the wing and then clipped flush with the shank to give the pattern a low-riding profile. The pattern continues to feature split tails and nearly always lands upright when cast. The clipped hackle and the split tails mean that the Thorax will ride upright through the roughest of waters and, as a result, it is ideally suited to our freestone waters.

The original Thorax patterns tied by Vince Marinaro were developed for the slow Pennsylvania spring creeks and earned themselves a reputation on slow, clear waters where selective trout are often found. In recent years, however, Thorax patterns have come to be regarded as good floaters on fast water, particularly if two hackles are used. As a result, all South African anglers should consider them when building up a supply of dry flies for fast-water applications. They are best fished upstream using a dead drift on rivers and streams, and because they float low in the water they will often fool trout in slow-water situations where higher-riding mayfly imitations may be refused.

In this country their use is not limited to rivers and streams; I use them more and more to imitate several mayflies on our stillwaters. The pattern variations listed here are my own dressings of three common stillwater mayflies which I regularly encounter, namely the tiny *Tricorythidae* mayflies, a greyish-brown mayfly which closely resembles the western American *Callibaetis* mayfly, and a pale

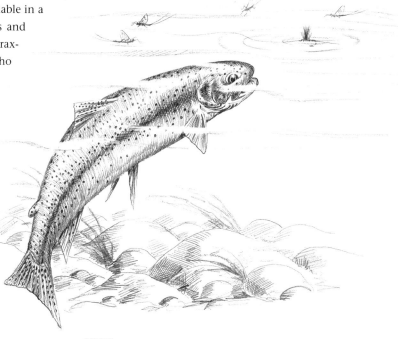

ED HERBST

Above *Jimmy Baroutsos casting to a visible fish in a long pool on the Witte River in Bain's Kloof Pass while the author keeps track of the fish from a large bankside boulder. This river offers anglers excellent opportunities to sight-fish to trout.*

THORAX (GENERIC)

HOOK: Tiemco 100, #12 – #20.

THREAD: 8/0 prewaxed, colour to match body.

WING: Turkey body feather (turkey 'flats'), hen back feather or similar soft, webby feather.

TAIL: Spade hackle fibres or Micro Fibetts, colour to match natural.

BODY/HEAD: Natural or synthetic fur dubbing, colour to match natural.

HACKLE: Genetic hackle, colour to match natural.

Variation: *CALLIBAETIS* MAYFLY

HOOK: Tiemco 100, #14 – #16.

THREAD: 8/0 prewaxed, brown.

WING: Teal or mallard flank fibres

TAIL: Medium or dark dun hackle fibres, or Micro Fibetts.

BODY: Greyish-brown fur dubbing.

HACKLE: Grizzly.

HEAD: Greyish-brown fur dubbing.

Variation: TRICO MAYFLY

HOOK: Tiemco 100, #18 – #20.

THREAD: 8/0 prewaxed, black.

WING: White turkey body feathers.

TAIL: Cream hackle fibres, or Micro Fibetts.

ABDOMEN: Cream fur dubbing.

THORAX: Dark brown fur dubbing.

HACKLE: Cream.

HEAD: Dark brown fur dubbing.

Variation: SULPHUR MAYFLY

HOOK: Tiemco 100, #12 – #16.

THREAD: 8/0 prewaxed, yellow.

WING: Bronze mallard flanks.

TAIL: Ginger hackle fibres, or Micro Fibetts.

BODY: Yellowish-olive fur dubbing.

HACKLE: Ginger.

HEAD: Yellowish-olive fur dubbing.

133

yellowish-olive mayfly that I call a 'sulphur'. However, the thorax-style pattern can be used to duplicate any local hatch on both stillwaters and streams.

On stillwaters, I prefer to fish all these patterns to visible fish, rather than searching the water. In situations where a fish's rise path can be determined, a flush-floating Thorax pattern will seldom be refused.

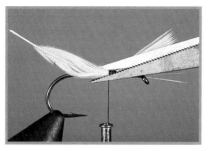

1. Tie in the tips of a turkey body feather approximately one-third of the hook shank from the eye of the hook, facing forward. Trim the excess.

2. Pull the fibres upright and secure them with a few turns of thread in front of the fibres. The wing should be equal in length to the hook shank.

3. Take the thread to a position above the hook barb, spin a short, thin noodle of dubbing onto the thread, and form a small dubbing ball above the hook barb.

4. Tie in approximately ten hackle fibres or Micro Fibetts at the centre of the hook. Dividing the fibres on either side of the ball to form the tails, take the thread down to the dubbing ball.

5. Spin a thin noodle of dubbing onto the thread and form the body over approximately half of the hook shank.

6. Select a hackle with fibres one-and-a-half times the gape of the hook, and tie it in directly in front of the body, with the concave side facing away from the hook shank.

7. Spin a thin noodle of dubbing onto the thread and complete the rest of the body. Wind two turns of hackle behind the wing and two turns in front of it, tie off and trim the excess.

8. Form a small, neat thread head, half-hitch and trim the thread. Apply head cement to the thread wraps. Using a pair of scissors, trim the hackle on the underside of the fly close to but not flush with the body.

9. The Thorax dry fly seen from the front. Note the trimmed hackle which helps the fly to sit up off the water, but still ensures a relatively low-riding pattern.

Trico Spinner

DEAN RIPHAGEN

THE *TRICORYTHIDAE* MAYFLIES are without doubt the most abundant mayfly in our stillwaters and in some areas provide consistent action for several months of the angling season. They often provoke highly selective feeding, and the spinner falls of these minute mayflies offer the angler a unique opportunity to go one-on-one with large trout using small imitations and light tippets.

As a neophyte fly-fisher I was fascinated by British fly-fishing magazine articles on the emergence of *Caenis* mayflies on stillwaters, and the name 'Anglers' Curse' left me in no doubt as to what they did to anglers in the United Kingdom. However, as I became acquainted with *Tricorythidae* mayflies and learnt more about their life cycle and the angling techniques used when fishing appropriate patterns, I came to enjoy the challenges that mayfly emergences

Right and below Tricorythidae *mayflies hovering along bankside vegetation at Mt. Arthur and Loch Rannoch in East Griqualand. The emergences of these tiny mayflies are often so heavy that they appear to be clouds of smoke along the shores of lakes in certain areas of South Africa.*

provide and began to look forward to the dense hatches that came off on many of the stillwaters that I fished.

The mayflies of the *Tricorythidae, Caenidae* and *Baetidae* families are reasonably similar in appearance and size, so from an angler's viewpoint they can be considered as one, and a single artificial will effectively cover them. Small variations occur in their colour, size, tail numbers and tail lengths, but I doubt that trout concern themselves with these minor differences, especially when they are gulping down several insects in one mouthful! For the purposes of this book I have referred to them as Trico mayflies. Should anglers be interested in determining the difference between the mayfly families, however, they should collect

MIKE SOMERVILLE

specimens, preserve them and send them to an aquatic entomologist specialising in mayflies.

The nymphs of the *Tricorythidae* mayfly family are feeble swimmers and prefer to spend their time crawling in weed and bottom detritus, where they feed on diatoms, algae and other plant matter. This behaviour, coupled with their minute size, means that they are relatively unavailable to the trout, and fishing nymphal imitations is a futile exercise during this phase of their lives. However, when the nymphs start making their way to the surface to hatch, trout usually feed highly selectively on them. It is difficult to believe that with the thousands of nymphs emerging, the angler's nymph will stand any chance of success amongst the naturals, but small nymphal imitations (see pages 55–58) will consistently fool trout during emergence periods.

The newly emerged duns are not consumed to any great degree by trout, since they usually fly away from the water immediately after emerging. When the fish begin to concentrate on the adult spinners lying flush in the film, however, and ignore the previously effective artificial nymph, it is time to change to a spinner imitation.

The first sign of the coming spinner fall is the moulting of the sexually immature duns or subimagos (which frequently choose the angler as a site on which to complete their moult from dun to spinner). The duns have smokey-grey wings, while the wings of the spinner are transparent. The dun, folding its wings over its upper abdomen, moults through a split in the skin on the back and emerges as the sexually mature spinner (imago), leaving its flimsy white exoskeleton behind. The spinner then joins the multitude of other spinners in their nuptial dance. Vast swarms of adults hang over bankside vegetation in tall pillars – at a distance these appear to be vertical clouds of smoke wafting up and down in the breeze – a sure sign that a spinner fall will soon take place and demanding fishing will follow.

When conditions are favourable, female spinners return to the water to deposit their eggs and then die; this fall of adult mayflies can bring on frenzied yet selective feeding as trout move to the surface to feed. At such times a skilful angler, armed with the appropriate patterns and tackle, will consistently take trout, while other less-skilled anglers curse their inability to lure the obviously feeding fish.

Because the spinners fall to the water's surface and become trapped there with wings outstretched, trout have ample time in which to ingest them, feeding in a leisurely fashion while cruising in long rise paths. The most prolonged sequence of rises to these spinners that I have seen was a series of fifteen at Hopewell, a large lake in East Griqualand. Other anglers I have spoken to have had similar experiences during hatches of these mayflies. It is easy to understand why American anglers call these fish 'gulpers', since they often gulp down several spinners in one mouthful. Trout do not inspect each insect during these gluttonous feeding sprees, since their window of vision is extremely small at such shallow depths. However, any dry fly that does not resemble the adult in size and shape will usually be rejected outright, particularly if the pattern is a high-floating one.

I am constantly amazed that fish take an artificial despite the competition from hundreds of naturals lying only inches from the fly. Fishing imitations of these mayfly spinners demands skill, light tippets and rods with limber tips. The techniques involved in deceiving trout during a spinner fall are similar to those needed to fish midge pupae suspended in the surface film (see pages 97–99). Naturals generally fall into the #18 to #22 bracket, and tippets in the 5X to 7X class are required to fish the appropriate spinner imitations effectively. Trout often cruise alongside or over weedbeds where they are able to consume hundreds of naturals in a single feeding session. This poses significant problems for the angler once a sizeable fish is hooked, as they usually bolt straight for the protection of weed. Two- to four-weight rods with limber tips will aid anglers unaccustomed to hooking and playing large fish on light tackle, while fifteen-feet leaders will provide a degree of shock absorption when a trout bolts away. Note that when trout are hooked at the surface they are far more skittish and wary than those feeding at greater depths, and bolting is the rule rather than the exception.

Trout will often feed along a fixed path when gulping spinners in the surface film, testing the angler's casting skills to the limit, since casts must be both quick and accurate. There is little margin for error, and failure to place the imitation in the path of the trout will mean that the fly will be missed. When a trout is feeding along a beat, it can gulp several naturals in a single mouthful and it is uncommon for it to deviate from its rise path to intercept an imitation.

During sparse spinner falls trout are forced to cruise around in search of them, which means that they cannot be intercepted in the same way you would catch trout feeding along a beat. If this is the case it is pointless to attempt to intercept a particular fish, and the most effective method is then to cast the pattern out and allow the trout to find the fly in its own time. In these situations, I have found that the number of takes is significantly increased by fishing an imitation that is one size larger than the natural.

Since spinners fall to the surface and become trapped by surface tension, they are unable to escape and, as a result, the fly should not be retrieved at all. However, an occasional twitch will often attract the attention of trout in the vicinity.

Several years ago, when I first began using spinner imitations, the only serviceable and certainly the most popular material for Trico spinner wings was polypropylene yarn which, although effective, was not the best material for the application. Today, however, there are several materials from which to choose, ranging from synthetics like Z-Lon and Antron fibres to natural materials like Cul de Canard feathers and turkey 'flats' feathers. Trico spinner wings, like almost all mayfly spinner wings, are hyaline and there are several modern synthetics to choose from that effectively

duplicate this feature. One that is available locally, manufactured by Orvis, is a material called Sparkle Wing. This excellent material closely imitates the spinner's wings. Whichever material you choose, ensure that it reflects light and, unlike polypropylene yarn, does not absorb water. These wing materials should be tied in as sparsely as possible because, like most flies used for trout, patterns tied sparsely usually outperform those that are overdressed.

TRICO SPINNER

HOOK: Tiemco 101 or 100, #18 – #22.

THREAD: 8/0 prewaxed, brown.

WING: Clear or white Antron yarn, Sparkle Wing material, Z-Lon, Cul de Canard feathers, or similar synthetic or natural winging material.

TAIL: Micro Fibetts or cream hackle fibres.

ABDOMEN: Natural or synthetic dubbing, cream.

THORAX: Natural or synthetic dubbing, medium to dark brown.

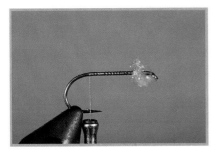

1. Tie in a section of winging material with figure-of-eight wraps at a position approximately one-quarter of the hook shank from the hook eye. Take the thread to a position above the barb of the hook.

2. Tie in three tailing fibres above the barb of the hook. The tails should be one-and-a-half to twice the length of the hook shank.

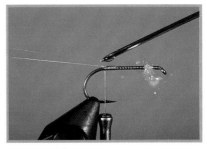

3. Divide the tails by taking one turn of thread under the tail and add a drop of head cement to hold them permanently in this position.

4. Spin a thin noodle of dubbing onto the thread and form a thin, neatly tapering abdomen over two-thirds of the hook shank.

5. Spin a short, thin noodle of dubbing onto the thread and form the thorax by taking figure-of-eight wraps around the wings.

6. Form a small, neat thread head, half-hitch and trim the thread. Apply head cement to the thread wraps. Trim the wings so that they are the same length as the hook shank.

The Stimulator

RANDALL KAUFMANN

THE STIMULATOR IS RANDALL KAUFMANN'S favourite dry-fly pattern, which, coming from someone with vast fishing experience across the globe, says much for its effectiveness. It will take fish under varying conditions and Randall uses it on lakes and streams, but is at its best in fast water. The Stimulator is a combination of several attractor and exciter patterns and imitates caddisflies, stoneflies and, at a pinch, grasshoppers.

What makes the Stimulator so effective? Like many successful dry flies, the Stimulator imitates several food forms in general, yet nothing in particular. By varying tail, hackle, body and wing colours a variety of insects – both terrestrial and aquatic – can be matched. The Stimulator combines the general shape and characteristics of patterns such as the Trude series of flies with the attributes of more established downwing patterns such as the Sofa Pillow, all of which were designed initially to imitate the adult stoneflies found on rivers in the western United States. Kaufmann's Stimulator, however, is not limited to the imitation of stonefly adults: it is used with great success to imitate other aquatic and terrestrial insects, including adult caddisflies and terrestrials such as grasshoppers and cicadas. The Stimulator has all the characteristics of a western-style dry fly designed for fast-flowing freestone waters and consequently is ideally suited to the fast pocket-water stretches of South African rivers and streams.

Below *The upper Bell River valley in Naude's Neck Pass is a place of exceptional beauty, with fishing quality to match. Here Bill Sharp fishes a run during the late afternoon while Terry Andrews looks on.*

It can be tied in large and small sizes as well as in various colour combinations, making it very versatile. Properly tied, the Stimulator is almost unsinkable and will float through the roughest of waters. As with all dry flies, buoyancy is largely dependent on hackle quality – I urge fly-tiers to tie their dry flies using premium-grade, genetic, quality capes wherever possible or the excellent saddle hackles now available. The fly's buoyancy can be enhanced further by selecting hair that is hollow all the way to the tip. With thumb-nail pressure, the hair should flare easily and compress at the tie-in point. Selection of the correct hair can be the key to the successful performance of a fly in fast water, and – where possible – all hair should be tested before being used.

The usual fast-water angling techniques apply when fishing the Stimulator – but with one minor exception. Unlike many other conventional, fully hackled dry flies, I have found that the Stimulator and several other palmered hackle dry flies are often taken when they are allowed to swing across the current into a downstream position from the angler. I have never quite understood why trout take a fly that is dragging across the current, but it happens so often that it certainly pays to try this technique, particularly when trout are refusing patterns that are being fished with a dead-drift technique. Many anglers believe that patterns taken while drifting in this fashion are accepted by

trout as they mistake them for adult caddisflies skittering across the water's surface. Because the Stimulator is such an excellent floater it rides right up on the tips of its hackles and will dance in a most enticing way when allowed to skate across the current, much like an ovipositing caddisfly. Takes, especially if rainbow trout are the quarry, will often be fast and may occur at any point of the fly's drift.

The colour variations of the Stimulator are limited only by the fly-tier's imagination. While I carry the four basic colour combinations listed here, this does not mean that other combinations won't be effective. The many materials available to the fly-tier, such as peacock herl, greatly increase the colour variations an angler can use.

Variation: YELLOW STIMULATOR

HOOK: Tiemco 2312, 200R or 5212, #8 – #16.

THREAD: 8/0 prewaxed, orange.

TAIL: Light elk hair.

RIB: Fine gold wire.

ABDOMEN: Synthetic dubbing, yellow.

HACKLE (ABDOMEN): Light ginger or badger.

WING: Light elk hair.

THORAX: Synthetic dubbing, amber.

HACKLE (THORAX): Grizzly.

Variation: GREEN STIMULATOR

HOOK: Tiemco 2312, 200R or 5212, #8 – #16.

THREAD: 8/0 prewaxed, yellow.

TAIL: Light elk hair.

RIB: Fine copper wire.

ABDOMEN: Synthetic dubbing, green.

HACKLE (ABDOMEN): Brown

WING: Light elk hair.

THORAX: Synthetic dubbing, yellow.

HACKLE (THORAX): Grizzly.

Variation: ORANGE STIMULATOR

HOOK: Tiemco 2312, 200R or 5212, #8 – #16.

THREAD: 8/0 prewaxed, yellow.

TAIL: Light elk hair.

RIB: Fine copper wire.

ABDOMEN: Synthetic dubbing, orange.

HACKLE (ABDOMEN): Brown or badger

WING: Light elk hair.

THORAX: Synthetic dubbing, yellow.

HACKLE (THORAX): Grizzly.

Variation: ROYAL STIMULATOR

HOOK: Tiemco 2312, 200R or 5212, #8 – #16.

THREAD: 8/0 prewaxed, orange.

TAIL: Light elk hair.

RIB: Fine copper wire.

ABDOMEN: Peacock herl divided by red floss.

HACKLE (ABDOMEN): Brown or badger.

WING: Light elk hair.

THORAX: Synthetic dubbing, yellow.

HACKLE (THORAX): Grizzly.

THE STIMULATOR

HOOK: Tiemco 2312, 200R or 5212, #8 – #16.
THREAD: 8/0 prewaxed, colour to match thorax.
TAIL: Elk hair, colour of choice.
RIB: Fine wire.
ABDOMEN: Synthetic dubbing, colour of choice.
HACKLE (ABDOMEN): Colour of choice.

WING: Elk hair, colour of choice.
THORAX: Synthetic dubbing, colour of choice.
HACKLE (THORAX): Colour of choice.

1. Stack 15 to 20 elk hair fibres in a hair stacker and tie them in above the hook barb. The fibres should be half the length of the hook shank.

2. Tie in a length of copper wire and spin a thin noodle of dubbing onto the thread.

3. With the dubbing form a neat, tapering abdomen over two-thirds of the hook shank.

4. Strip the webby flue from a hackle and tie the hackle in with the concave side facing the hook shank. The fibres should be equal to or slightly longer than the gape of the hook.

5. Wind the hackle back towards the tail in six or seven evenly spaced turns, and trap the tip of the hackle with the wire rib.

6. Wind the wire rib forward through the hackle in five or six evenly spaced turns, tie off and trim the excess. Trim the excess hackle at the tail.

7. Stack 20 to 30 elk fibres in a stacker and tie them in directly in front of the abdomen so that the tips of the hair extend to the bend of the hook.

8. Tie in another hackle with the concave side facing away from the hook. Spin a thin noodle of dubbing onto the thread and form the thorax over the front third of the hook shank.

9. Wind the hackle towards the eye in three or four close turns, tie off and trim the excess. Form a small, neat thread head, half-hitch and trim the thread. Apply head cement to the thread wraps.

Elk Hair Caddis

AL TROTH

THE ROCKLEY LODGE SECTION of the Umkomaas River, a challenging stretch of water situated near the small village of Bulwer in the foothills of the KwaZulu-Natal Drakensberg, provided good trout fishing to anglers for many years before the Natal yellowfish established itself in those waters. In particular, one fast-water section of this beautiful river used to captivate me with its dancing riffles and swift pocket water.

Here a large midstream boulder broke the current into two well-defined tongues; one of these was diverted, almost at right angles, towards the bank where it welled up as it struck the side, forming a deep undercut I knew held good fish. On two previous visits to this stretch of water, I had drifted a small rubber-legged Bitch Creek Nymph into the undercut and on both occasions the pattern had produced several yellowfish, some of respectable size. While the yellowfish were always a welcome adversary if the trout were not willing to come to the fly, it was trout that I sought. I was convinced that the undercut held sizeable trout, yet the problem of bypassing the yellowfish remained and I could not figure out a solution. The water was at least six feet deep at the bank and with polarising sunglasses I could easily make out the yellowfish nymphing just above the stream bed. I knew a deeply sunk nymph would find the same quarry it had on previous occasions, so, in the hope that it would go unnoticed by the yellowfish, I decided to drift a dry fly through the undercut.

I removed a box of dry flies from my vest and clinched on the largest Elk Hair Caddis in the box. The pattern had a dark olive body, a dark dun hackle and a bleached elk hair wing. After rubbing in some silicone paste, I cast out the

Below *Dry flies will often account for large trout, such as this magnificent brown taken in New Zealand by Mike Somerville.*

Above *Mike Somerville with a six-and-three-quarter-pound Clinton River brown, which took a small Goddard Caddis.*

imitation using an upstream reach mend to counteract drag. I was forced to throw several upstream mends into the line to avoid the drag associated with an upstream cast quartering a fast stretch of water but, although the fly appeared to drift through the undercut without any drag, it floated downstream unscathed.

After several more drag-free drifts through the undercut I began to question both my tactics and casting, when suddenly a dark shape appeared downstream of the fly. At first glance, I thought it was a large yellowfish, but closer inspection left me in no doubt that the Elk Hair Caddis was about to fall prey to an enormous brown. The trout had risen to the surface in such a leisurely fashion that I expected the rise to be slow and confident, but when it turned, suddenly and showered the bank with spray, I was caught completely off guard and the trout disappeared, taking the fly and a lengthy portion of the tippet with it. I was shaken, but at the same time ecstatic at having fooled such a large opponent at close quarters.

Why the Elk Hair Caddis was able to bring such a large trout to the surface in such deep, heavy water I will never know, but it is a pattern that has proven itself so often in fast water that it has become one of my most trusted imitations. It is an imitation that I used extensively when I first fished the fast mountain streams of the Western Cape.

The Elk Hair Caddis was developed by the famous angler and fly-tier, Al Troth, who guides and ties flies in south-western Montana, and it has become the best-selling pattern in many fly-shops in the United States, particularly the shops located in the western states where fast freestone streams predominate. Its popularity lies in the fact that it is simple to tie, durable when tied properly, and – by changing its body, hackle and wing colours – can imitate any species of caddisfly. Moreover, the Elk Hair Caddis is an excellent pattern on both fast and slow waters, although I reserve it for fast waters, especially the pocket and riffle sections of our rivers and streams. It can, however, be used in stillwaters where its stiff, palmered body hackle ensures that it is able to skitter and skate across the water's surface.

The most effective method of fishing the Elk Hair Caddis is either to cast it directly upstream or to quarter it upstream with a slack line cast which will ensure that a drag-free drift results. However, like Randall Kaufmann's Stimulator (pages 138–140), often the Elk Hair Caddis will be taken if it is allowed to skate across the current as it drifts past the angler, something which happens when the fly reaches a point downstream of the angler as the line tightens. The takes, if they have not come at some point in the drift downstream, will occur as the pattern skates across the current.

ADDITIONAL FAST-WATER CADDIS PATTERNS

PARA CADDIS
HOOK: Tiemco 100 or 5230, #12 – #16.
THREAD: 8/0 prewaxed, tan or brown.
BODY: Blended hare's ear.
WING: Lacquered mottled oak turkey feather, tied tent-style.
POST: Calf body hair.
HACKLE: Grizzly.

NELSON'S CADDIS
HOOK: Tiemco 100 or 5230, #12 – #16.
THREAD: 8/0 prewaxed, colour to match body.
BODY: Natural fur dubbing in shades of olive, brown, tan, grey and black.
WING: Medium-to-dark elk hair.
HACKLE: With body colours of olive, grey or black, I like to use medium to dark dun hackle; with body colours of brown or tan, I like to use either grizzly or brown hackle.
ANTENNAE: Stripped hackle stems.

GODDARD CADDIS
HOOK: Tiemco 100 or 5230, #12 – #16.
THREAD: 8/0 prewaxed, brown.
WING: Spun deer hair, clipped to shape.
HACKLE: Brown.
ANTENNAE: Stripped hackle stems.

Sometimes trout will not take a dead-drifted dry, yet they will attack a pattern that skates across the current, possibly because the skating fly imitates a living natural. Fly-fishers willing to experiment will discover that this happens more often than many anglers realise, and armed with this knowledge they will take trout when others fail to interest them.

ELK HAIR CADDIS

HOOK: Tiemco 100, #10 – #18.

THREAD: 8/0 prewaxed, colour to match body.

RIB: Fine copper wire.

BODY: Fine natural or synthetic dubbing. (My favourite colours are medium olive, dark olive, tan, medium brown, dark brown, dark grey and black.)

HACKLE: There are innumerable possible colour combinations. With body colours of olive, grey or black, I like to use a medium to dark dun hackle; with body colours of tan and brown, I like to use a brown or ginger hackle.

WING: Medium to dark elk hair.

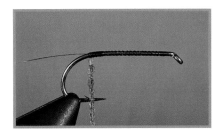

1. Take the thread to a position above the hook barb. Tie in a length of fine wire and spin a thin noodle of dubbing onto the thread.

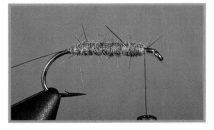

2. Wind the dubbing forward over approximately seven-eighths of the hook shank. Keep the body as thin as possible.

3. Select a hackle and strip the webby flue from the base of the feather. Tie in the feather directly in front of the body with the concave side facing the hook shank.

4. Wind the hackle back along the hook shank in six or seven evenly spaced turns, trap the tip with the wire and wind the rib through the hackle. Tie the wire off and trim the excess wire and the hackle tip.

5. Stack 40 to 50 elk hair fibres in a hair stacker and tie them in directly behind the hook eye, ensuring that the hair does not flare too much. The hair tips should not extend beyond the bend of the hook.

6. Lift the butts of the hair up, form a small, neat thread head, half-hitch and trim the thread. Apply head cement to the thread wraps. Trim the butts of the hair to form a small head above the hook eye.

Xmas Xaddis

ED HERBST

WHEN I THINK OF ANGLERS who have made major contributions to South African fly-fishing, two individuals immediately come to mind – Tom Sutcliffe and Ed Herbst. While Tom needs no introduction, Ed, though he writes for all major fly-fishing magazines and contributes enormously to the sport and certainly puts more back into it than he takes out, prefers to keep a relatively low profile.

I first met Ed many years ago during a fishing trip to the streams of the Western Cape: I had spent a long day on the upper Elandspad River with two friends and was making my way downstream when I happened across two anglers fishing a quiet run on the bend of the river. One waved me a cheerful greeting as I walked behind through the bush, giving them ample berth to continue their upstream angling. These two anglers, it later transpired, were Ed Herbst and Tony Biggs's late son, Damon. Though we did not meet officially that day on the Elandspad River, I followed Ed's writings with interest. His experiments with artificial flies interested me because he was forever importing unusual fly-tying materials to try in his patterns. To me, Ed is the Gary LaFontaine of South African fly-tying, and I believe that in the Xmas Xaddis he has developed a pattern that will come to be regarded as a reliable dry fly by all South African fly-fishers.

Above *Ed Herbst with a fine Witte River brown taken on a dry fly. This was one of twenty such fish taken by Ed and the author during a fantastic day's fishing on the lower river.*

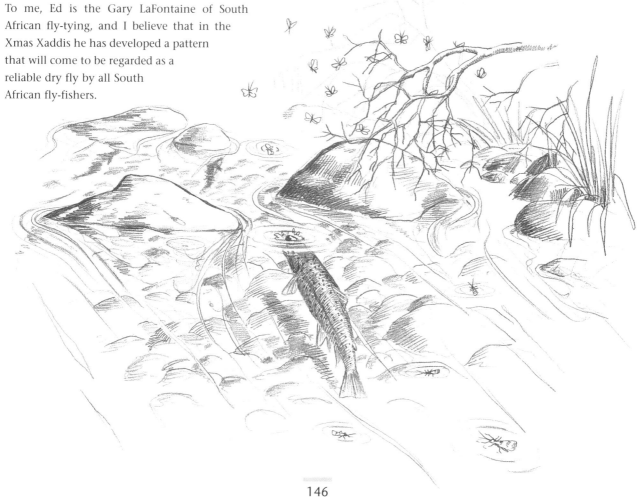

The Xmas Xaddis, like many successful South African dry flies, evolved on the fast, tumbling mountain streams of the Western Cape. Ed says the pattern is a combination of existing facets of fly design and two new materials – Cactus Chenille and nylon organza – which, when incorporated into a dry fly, significantly enhance its appeal.

The Xmas Xaddis had its origins in a *Fly Fisherman* magazine article entitled 'The New Synthetics' by American angling author, Gary Borger. For many years Gary used a snail pattern reminiscent of the effective Renegade, a simple dry fly with a hackle at either end of a peacock herl body. By replacing the peacock herl with Cactus Chenille, he found that his snail pattern was greatly improved. Cactus Chenille consists of a material trapped between two twisted threads, but in this case the material is Flashabou.

Ed tied up a single pattern for a trip to the Barkly East area, but for one reason or another did not make the trip and the fly was not put through its paces. It was relegated to his fly box until a trip to the Holsloot River near Rawsonville in December. The day was cold and blustery, promising little and initially delivering little. He knew that the previous weekend Tom Sutcliffe and his son had taken several fish from the Smalblaar River in the adjoining Du Toit's Kloof valley and had found beetles among the stomach contents of several of these trout. Ed had only one beetle pattern in his box, and after a fishless hour lost the fly. The only other pattern he had which looked like a beetle was Borger's Cactus Chenille Snail, tied on a heavy wire hook. Without much hope of success, he tied it on and cast it into the next run. Despite the heavy hook, the fly floated surprisingly well, and a fish vaulted out of the water to take it. Missing the fish, Ed put another cast into the run and again the fish repeated its performance – Ed once again failed to connect with the fish. Unbelievably, a third cast produced a third rise, albeit a conventional one, and again Ed missed the trout. A fourth cast into the same run induced a much larger trout to rise to the fly, but after a brief connection the fish was gone.

Feeling rather disconsolate, Ed made his way up to the Stettynskloof dam wall further up the valley. After a break for lunch, he fished the spillway pool below the wall of the lake. Despite the strongly flowing water, the fly had drifted no more than a few inches before it was taken by a fish much larger than that considered the norm for the river. Despite being broken off, the pattern had raised five fish in five casts, while other patterns had failed to interest the trout at all.

Ed concluded that the pattern's success lay in the strands of Flashabou in the Cactus Chenille which reflected many points of light, creating the impression of movement in the same way a series of still images, when projected onto a screen, create the illusion of movement. Ed had also used

Above *Ed Herbst fishing the lower Witte River with a nymph, using a dry fly as a strike indicator.*

another material mentioned in Borger's article – nylon organza (also known as Twinkle, Crystal or Sparkle Organza) which, according to Borger, '...has filaments that twinkle and shine with a pearlescent glow'. These filaments not only glow but also have a crimp in them, not unlike miniature Krystal Flash, and have been used with great success by Borger for wings in spinner patterns. Ed incorporated these filaments into the pattern using Lee Wulff's loop-wing technique, giving the pattern a moth- or caddis-like appearance.

The Xmas Xaddis floats reasonably well because the broad base of the wings provides a stable platform on which the pattern can ride, and there is plenty of material to soak up floatant. The pattern is also easy for the angler to see because the material used in it reflects light, making it twinkle as it floats downstream (Ed believes it is this effect under the water that attracts fish).

Those who are curious may be wondering how the pattern got its name: the Cactus Chenille is reminiscent of the tinsel draped over Christmas trees, and the Lee Wulff loop-style wing and Krystal Flash antennae give the fly a caddis-like appearance, hence the name 'Xmas Xaddis'.

Many anglers who have fished this pattern have had a dramatic change in their fishing fortunes, finding that the fly will draw trout from considerable distances, even from undercut banks. Trout seem to take the fly aggressively, which Ed believes is a result of the sparkle the fly emits, creating the key impression of frantic movement. Ed fishes it upstream, using a dead drift, and says there is no reason to impart movement to the fly since the materials used in its construction do this already. Tom Sutcliffe says that the Xmas Xaddis could supplant the DDD as South Africa's most successful stillwater dry fly, and all who have tried it have been impressed by the distance trout will move to take it and the aggression with which they do so.

Above *The Xmas Xaddis tied by Ed Herbst.*

XMAS XADDIS

HOOK: Tiemco 100, #8 – #18.

THREAD: 8/0 prewaxed, colour to match underbody.

WING: Krystal Flash or Orvis Holographic tinsel and organza filaments. (Ed prefers grey or pearl Krystal Flash.)

UNDERBODY: Mixture of Lite-Brite dubbing material and seal's fur, or SLF substitute, blended.

OVERBODY: Cactus Chenille. (Ed's favourite colour is brown.)

RIB: DMC metallic thread (preferably #4270), Anchor Lamé embroidery thread (preferably shade 322) or fine copper wire. (DMC or Anchor Lamé threads are available from embroidery or wool shops.)

HEAD: Peacock herl.

ANTENNAE: Krystal Flash.

HACKLE: Brown or grizzly.

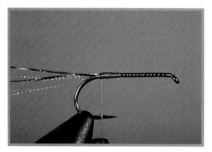

1. Tie in approximately 10 to 12 organza filaments and a length of Holographic Tinsel above the barb of the hook, on each side of the hook shank.

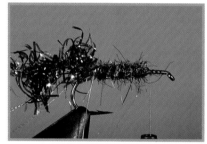

2. Tie in the rib and Cactus Chenille above the hook barb. Spin a thin noodle of dubbing onto the thread and form the underbody over two-thirds of the hook shank.

3. Pick out the underbody, making it as loose as possible, then wind the Cactus Chenille forward, covering the underbody, and tie off. Wind the rib forward through this overbody, tie off and trim the excess.

4. On either side of the hook shank, wrap the organza filaments around the Krystal Flash and then fold them forward and tie off in front of the body, forming a heart-shaped silhouette if the pattern is looked at from above.

5. Tie in two or three peacock herls and a hackle in front of the overbody, with the concave side of the hackle facing away from the shank. Tie in two lengths of Krystal Flash vertically to form the antennae.

6. Form the head with the herls and tie off. Take two or three turns of the hackle through the herls, tie off and trim the excess. Form a neat thread head, half-hitch and trim the thread. Apply head cement to the wraps.

DDD

TOM SUTCLIFFE

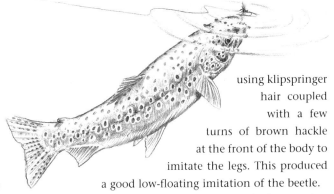

THE UNPARALLELED DDD is without question the most famous dry fly in use on South African stillwaters today. The DDD was created by the now legendary South African fly-fisherman Tom Sutcliffe, a person who has channelled all his free time and energy into the pursuit of trout and all activities allied to fly-fishing. Tom graduated with a medical degree from the University of Stellenbosch, and it was on the streams surrounding Stellenbosch that he was taught the skills of fly-fishing by the late Mark Mackereth, an angler well known for his abilities to deceive trout with a fly. Tom's occupation later took him to KwaZulu-Natal, a province renowned for its lake fishing, and it was on the lakes in the Impendhle and Dargle areas that the DDD quickly established its reputation.

While the DDD could be said to represent several types of food, I, like Tom, firmly believe that the pattern, with its bulky shape and low-floating appearance, represents a terrestrial of some sort. The fact that the fly is very effective on windy, gusty days when terrestrials are easily blown into the water bears testimony to this, and it heads my list as the 'number one' searching dry-fly pattern on stillwaters throughout the country.

The fly was designed originally to imitate a terrestrial beetle discovered by Tom on the Umgeni River in KwaZulu-Natal in November 1976. On that day Tom had nothing with which to imitate the fall of beetles and so, with Mackereth's suggestive Caribou Spider still fresh in his memory, he tied up a rather bulky imitation of the beetle using klipspringer hair coupled with a few turns of brown hackle at the front of the body to imitate the legs. This produced a good low-floating imitation of the beetle.

The DDD was, however, named after another KwaZulu-Natal angler, Bill Duckworth. Bill and Tony Biggs spent a day fishing at Roldan, the middle lake at Nhluzane in the Dargle area. The fish were rising in rough, choppy water, and these rises went unnoticed by Bill's somewhat inexperienced eyes. Tony, on the other hand, was having considerable success with a certain large, bushy dry-fly pattern. After Bill was given some of these patterns by Tony, he succeeded in duping a few fish. By the end of the day, the fly had accounted for numerous fish. Later that evening he asked Tom Sutcliffe to copy the pattern. The copy was fashioned on the beetle Tom had found on the Umgeni River, the only difference being the addition of a tail. Bill, new to fly-angling at the time, soon convinced himself that no other pattern would take trout. Bill's success with the fly was incredible. He began to catch as many, and sometimes more, trout than his more experienced colleagues. In his honour Tom named the fly Duckworth's Dargle Delight, or DDD.

Interestingly, while Tom Sutcliffe has always believed that the untidier the pattern, the more effective it will be, DDD

Below This magnificent hook-jawed six-and-three-quarter-pound rainbow cockfish took a DDD fished along the wall of a private Underberg lake. It was this rainbow's third capture in less than a year: proof of the effectiveness of catch-and-release regulations.

Below Tom Sutcliffe with a magnificent seventeen-pound steelhead taken from the Bulkly River in British Columbia.

Above *A DDD tied by Tom Sutcliffe, showing the use of a spun hair collar rather than the conventional hackle collar.*

patterns tied by Bill were even more untidy than Tom's, but he believes this adds to the fly's effectiveness and claims they often work better than Tom's 'neater' versions. I, on the other hand, am a fly-tier who prefers to carry neatly tied imitations, regardless of the pattern type, in my fly-boxes, but this is not to say that one style is more effective than the other. Certainly, some patterns such as the DDD seem to perform better the more they are chewed by trout. (I have caught trout on DDD patterns that look nothing like my original, but I am still unable to live with a fly that comes off my vice looking as though it has already been through the jaws of a few fish! I prefer to let the trout themselves turn my tidy, well-trimmed patterns into almost unrecognisable, tattered objects.)

Such large, untidy flies are often very effective: the largest fish taken from the Nhluzane waters a few seasons ago was a nine-and-a-half-pound brown taken by Andrew Fowler fishing a large DDD. While it earned its reputation on the KwaZulu-Natal lakes and thus is commonly regarded as a stillwater pattern, the DDD is unusual in that it is extremely versatile and fishes well on both lakes and streams.

Despite the fact that there are many other similar artificials tied with spun deer (or klipspringer) hair bodies, I believe the effectiveness of the DDD results from a combination of factors, some of the more obvious being: its size, which aids in attracting trout from a great depth or distance; its low-riding profile in the water, which will often produce fish when high-floating patterns will be ignored; and, when it is tied with spun klipspringer hair, its light colour, which makes it highly visible to both fish and fisherman. It is certainly a pattern deserving of space in every stillwater angler's fly-box and it will often produce trout when the normally more effective sub-surface nymph and attractor patterns fail to interest them.

The DDD is probably the most widely used dry fly in South Africa and has accounted for many of the largest trout taken on dry flies from our stillwaters. Coupled with its versatility and effectiveness is the fact that it requires no specialised angling techniques, making it an easy pattern for novices to fish. As a prospecting pattern, it has few rivals and can be simply cast out and allowed to ride the chop. The DDD is at its most effective on windy days when a surprising number of trout will move into the upper water in search of wind-blown aquatic and terrestrial insects. In these conditions trout seem to feel safe cruising below the veil of broken, choppy water in search of food. When terrestrial insects are blown onto the water most become trapped by the water's surface tension; trout seem to realise their predicament, often showing themselves in quiet dimples and lazy, slow rises in the waves and surface chop. In order to notice a rise in these weather conditions it is necessary for the angler to study the water carefully before casting.

One of the best areas to prospect with a DDD in our stillwaters is along weedbeds that reach to the surface. Trout often cruise along these weedbeds in search of aquatic and terrestrial fare, and weedbeds that grow in deep water and which reach to the surface are favoured, since they provide food as well as the protection afforded by deep water. The imitation should simply be cast out alongside the weedbed for the trout to find of their own accord. If the surface action is slow, it pays to give the pattern an occasional twitch with a single, short strip of the line.

Another excellent area to prospect with the DDD is along the windward shore of lakes, where terrestrial and other wind-blown insects are found during and after windy weather. Strong winds stir up the bottom silt close to the bank, making the area even more inviting for trout to feed in as they can go largely undetected. My favourite tactic is to anchor my float tube some distance offshore and to cast directly downwind into the area of turbulence. Because the quarry is largely unseen, be aware that a trout can appear most unexpectedly and is often able to suck in an imitation with only the slightest surface disturbance. In this situation, the angler must allow the trout ample time to turn down before tightening on it.

The DDD is fairly wind-resistant and consequently anglers must step up their tippet sizes to prevent the fly from twisting the leader during casting. I usually step up my tippets by a factor of one 'X': where a certain hook size might normally require a 5X tippet, I use 4X to prevent the coiling associated with bulky, wind-resistant patterns. Since the fly is usually used in windy weather and broken water, increasing the tippet diameter makes little if any difference to the effectiveness of the imitation.

DDD

HOOK: Tiemco 100, #6 – #12.

THREAD: 3/0 monocord, brown or black.

TAIL: Klipspringer or deer hair.

BODY: Klipspringer or deer hair.

HACKLE: Brown or dun spade hackle.

LEGS (OPTIONAL): Single strand of Krystal Flash.

Note: Hugh Huntley's variation of the DDD does not have a hackle. He 'spins' a collar of klipspringer hair in front of the body. Both Tom Sutcliffe and Hugh Huntley tie in a single strand of Krystal Flash to project out at the neck as a pair of 'legs'.

1. Tie in approximately 20 to 30 klipspringer hair fibres above the barb (do not first stack them in a stacker). The tail should be approximately the length of the hook shank.

2. Trim a clump of klipspringer hair from the hide; the hair section should be approximately the diameter of a pencil. Hold the fibres over the hook shank and take three loose turns of thread around them.

3. Pull the thread tight so that the fibres spin and flare out around the hook shank.

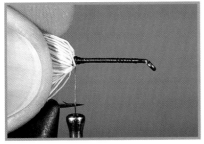

4. Using the fingers of your left hand, pull the fibres back and take a few turns of thread in front of them.

5. Repeat steps 2 to 4 until seven-eighths of the hook shank is covered in spun klipspringer hair. Half-hitch and trim the thread.

6. Remove the hook from the vice and trim the hair into the shape shown, making sure the tails are not accidentally cut. Note that the underside has been trimmed close to the hook shank.

7. Replace the hook in the vice and re-attach the thread directly in front of the body. Tie in a soft spade hackle in front of the body with the concave side facing the hook shank.

8. Take two or three turns of the hackle in front of the body, tie off the feather and trim the excess. The hackle should be one-and-a-half to two times the gape of the hook.

9. Form a small neat thread head, half-hitch and trim the thread. Apply head cement to the thread wraps.

Dave's Hopper

DAVE WHITLOCK

'HOPPERTUNITY TIME', as well-known angler, author and entomologist Dave Whitlock calls it, is a unique time of the year when anglers are able to deceive some of the largest fish of the season on dry flies. As summer advances, grasshoppers become increasingly active in streamside vegetation and may end up in the water as a result of strong winds, rain, annual crop harvests, grassfires, predation or severe cold. Once they become trapped in the surface tension, they are relished by observant trout on the lookout for an easy meal, and may afford the angler some of the most spectacular sight-fishing of the year.

Grasshoppers thrive in areas with over sixty days of sunshine a year, and with daytime temperatures that average fifteen degrees Celsius, and so do exceptionally well in South Africa. Hopper activity increases as temperatures begin to climb above fifteen degrees Celsius; to most South African anglers this translates into mid-spring to late-autumn fishing, with peak hopper fishing occurring during the heat of summer. Hoppers are welcomed by fly-fishers as they become active along river and stream banks at a time when the more significant hatches are on the wane. Consequently they are of great importance, particularly to anglers who enjoy the sight of trout feeding actively at the surface.

As summer approaches, more and more terrestrial insects take up residence in bankside vegetation and stay there until the weather becomes so consistently cold that they cannot move about. The best grasshopper habitat is sunlit, grassy fields bordering streams and rivers, and anglers in areas such as KwaZulu-Natal and the Eastern Cape can look forward to excellent hopper fishing, especially during harvesting when terrestrials are forced to leave the lands.

While other adult insect species, such as mayflies and caddisflies, are able to float completely above the water, hoppers lie with a good deal of their bodies partly submerged and, once trapped by surface tension, they are seldom able to escape. The usual reaction from a hopper which finds itself on the water surface is to kick and thrash furiously in an attempt to free itself, but once drained of energy it rides the current with only an occasional twitch or kick. All anglers should remember this behaviour when fishing these robust imitations.

Many of the older, more established hopper patterns – such as Joe's Hopper – are fully hackled, high-floating imitations which in no way duplicate the natural insect. I have found them unsuccessful and have turned to Dave Whitlock's very effective, low-floating imitation, Dave's

Hopper. This is a pattern that, unlike earlier hopper imitations, rides in rather than on the water's surface. Its clipped, deer hair head rides in the surface film, while the body lies in or slightly below the surface, much like a natural. Moreover, the deer hair head means it floats well, despite riding low in the water, and is therefore ideally suited to South Africa's fast-flowing freestone streams.

Controversy will always rage as to whether legs are an important feature of a grasshopper imitation, but I firmly believe that the more closely the features of an insect are imitated, the better. Furthermore the legs of the imitation lie, together with much of the body, beneath the water's surface and are thus clearly visible to the trout. I have much greater confidence in imitations with legs than in those without. Body colour, size and the general outline of the imitation are also important features. I keep hoppers in colours ranging from olive to tan and yellow, and in sizes ranging from #8 to #12. While I prefer the patterns with buoyant spun deer hair heads, 'bullet-head' hoppers are also popular with anglers, particularly those from North America who fish slow-flowing spring creek waters where trout have ample time to scrutinise flies. However, for South Africa's fast, bouncing riffles and runs, and for dry-fly fishing in pocket water, more buoyant patterns tied with spun deer hair (such as Dave's Hopper) are more appropriate.

While anglers from all over the world have written about the wild manner in which trout rise to hopper patterns, this is largely a generalization. The speed and ferocity of a rise is, to a great degree, dependent on current velocity, and trout holding in slow water will often sip a hopper pattern as gently as if they were taking a mayfly dun or emerger held in the film. In fact, trout seem to realise that a hopper lying in the surface film cannot escape. Since I have been fortunate enough to spend considerable time on the clear streams of the Western Cape observing trout eating natural grasshoppers and their imitations, I can vouch for the validity of my line of thought. The largest hopper-caught trout that I ever landed, an eighteen-inch brown henfish from the lower Witte River in Bain's Kloof Pass, sipped down a rubber-legged hopper pattern as confidently and gently as if the pattern had been a midge pupa suspended in the surface film of a lake.

During hopper feeding sprees trout usually lie in the shallow water close to the edges. This makes them more vulnerable to predation than at other times and, as a result, they are skittish and far more alert to abnormal disturbances. It therefore pays to adopt a careful approach at all times and to keep as low a profile as possible, avoiding wading whenever possible and quick movements.

Since the best hopper fishing usually occurs during windy conditions, and since the patterns are usually large, bulky

Above *Tom Lewin drifts a dry fly past a rock on the Witte River in Bain's Kloof Pass. This lie held a tagged brown of sixteen inches that had been caught and released over a dozen times by the author and other angling companions.*

and wind-resistant, rods that generate high line-speeds will greatly aid the angler in his efforts to cast hopper imitations. In the steep-sided kloofs of the Western Cape winds usually blow upstream during the day, which makes fishing hopper patterns that much easier. On rivers and streams of a lower gradient, such as many of those in KwaZulu-Natal and the north-eastern Cape, winds can blow from any direction, making casting the wind-resistant hopper patterns a real chore. Fast-actioned four- or five-weight rods, in lengths from eight to nine feet, are ideal for this type of fishing in

South Africa and will greatly aid the angler casting hopper imitations, as will short, stout leaders and tippets. I like to keep my leader and tippet under twelve feet, as this improves casting control and accuracy enormously, particularly when placing the fly under overhanging bankside vegetation and into undercut banks. (Trout feeding on grasshoppers will usually feed at the bank where most naturals can be found before they are swept into the main current.)

Tight, accurate casts (enhanced by short leaders) into the difficult lies adopted by trout feeding at the bank are required. I always place my first cast short of the target to avoid the possibility of lining a visible fish; this is also a good tactic when searching the water. Begin your casts somewhat short of the area where you suspect a trout will be lying, and then slowly increase their length. If I can see a trout feeding I 'splat' the pattern down just inches behind it on the first cast – this often causes the trout to turn and take the fly. If this tactic does not work, gradually increase the length of each subsequent cast and dead-drift the pattern over the fish, giving it an occasional twitch to simulate the struggling movements of the natural trapped in the film. A trout will seldom pass up the opportunity to attack a fly twitched this way, and it pays to be alert so that you are not taken off-guard by a sudden, quick rise to the surface.

Stillwater anglers too can use grasshopper patterns to fool trout, especially on the on-shore shallows of a lake during hot, windy days. These patterns will also draw fish up from the depths of a lake, and Tom Sutcliffe reports that he has had some of his most enjoyable hopper fishing in water ranging from six inches to six feet deep. In stillwaters trout take hoppers with slow, deliberate rises or with splashy rises.

Indeed, I have often had trout leap clear of the water, taking the imitation on the return to the water. Many anglers associate hopper fishing with hot, dry and windy conditions, when grasshoppers are most active. However, when fishing rivers and streams, anglers should remember that hopper patterns will move trout on cooler days too.

DAVE'S HOPPER

HOOK: Tiemco 5212, #8 – #12.
THREAD: 3/0 monocord, yellow.
LEGS: Yellow-dyed grizzly hackles, clipped and knotted.
OVERWING: Speckled oak turkey wing quill coated with Dave's Flexament.
TAIL: Red deer hair.
BODY: Yellow polypropylene.
RIB: Brown hackle, clipped.
UNDERWING: Pale yellow or gold dyed deer hair.
COLLAR: Deer hair.
HEAD: Deer hair.

1. To prepare the legs stick two hackles to two lengths of sticky tape. Trim the hackle fibres along each side of the hackle stems as shown (the sticky tape allows you to trim the fibres very neatly).

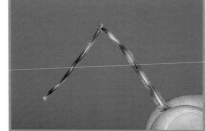

2. Strip the remaining sticky tape off the trimmed hackle stems. Tie an overhand knot in both trimmed hackle stems to form the 'knee' of the leg.

3. Heat a dubbing needle and bend the tip of each hackle stem around the heated needle to form the 'feet'. The distance between the 'knee' and the 'foot' should be approximately two-thirds of an inch.

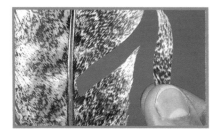

4. Form the wing by coating a speckled oak turkey wing quill with Dave's Flexament. Trim a sliver approximately one-fifth of an inch wide from the feather.

5. Fold the feather sliver in half lengthways and trim the end so that when the sliver is opened up the end is 'V'-shaped.

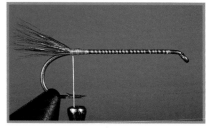

6. Take the thread to a position above the barb of the hook and tie in 10 to 15 deer hair fibres. The tail should be approximately one-third of the hook shank.

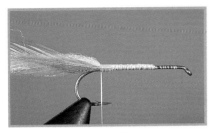

7. Tie in a length of polypropylene on top of the hook shank and a hackle, with the concave side of the hackle facing away from the hook shank.

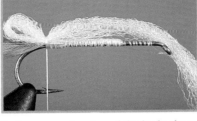

8. Form an extension of the body above the tail by making a small loop, one-quarter of the shank-length; tie this extension down above the hook barb.

9. Take the thread to about one-third of the shank-length from the eye and wind the rest of the polypropylene towards the thread. Tie off and trim excess.

10. Wind the hackle forward in six evenly spaced turns, tie off and trim. Trim the hackle flush on top and so that elsewhere they are approximately equal to the hook gape.

11. Stack 10 to 15 deer fibres in a stacker and tie them in above the body; they should not extend beyond the tips of the tails. These fibres will form the underwing.

12. Tie in the wing, which should cover the underwing and should extend beyond the tips of the tails.

13. Tie in the legs on either side of the wing. The 'knees' of the legs should fall between the hook barb and the hook bend.

14. Trim a section of hair from the hide of a deer and, holding the hair above the hook shank, take three loose turns of thread around the hair directly in front of the wing.

15. Pull the thread tight, which will cause the hair to spin and flare out. This initial hair spinning will form the collar and a small portion of the head.

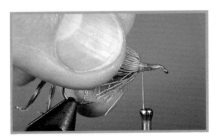

16. Pull the hair backwards with the fingers of your left hand and take a few turns of thread in front of it.

17. Spin further clumps of deer hair onto the shank until the shank is completely covered in spun hair. Half-hitch and trim the thread. Apply head cement to the thread wraps.

18. Remove the fly from the vice and trim the deer hair to the shape shown. Trim the hair close to the hook shank on the underside of the fly, leaving a collar around the wing.

Para Ant

GARY BORGER

ANTS, WHICH PLAY an important part in the diet of trout, occur in every terrestrial ecosystem except in Antarctica. Because they forage for food in bankside vegetation they are easily blown into the water where they form an abundant food source for trout. When falls of flying ants occur on streams and lakes (this is not common) trout will usually feed selectively on them to the exclusion of all else, making for particularly frustrating fishing. While most anglers encounter ants at some point while fishing, and despite the fact that ant imitations often fool wary fish that may shun better-known and more widely used flies, almost all fly-fishers neglect the role of the ant in fly-fishing. Fly-fishers will find that it pays to carry a selection of both

winged and non-winged ant varieties. These tiny imitations may save the day when fish begin to take ants that are trapped helplessly in the film. The best falls of the winged ants occur on hot, humid days, either during or after a spell of rain, whereas the terrestrial ants encountered along streambanks can be found on the water during any warm month of the year, especially when strong winds are blowing.

Several years ago while fishing a stretch of water in the Mpumalanga highlands I encountered a good example of the selectivity displayed by trout during a hatch of flying ants. This stream is renowned for its easy rainbows, and the trout will usually take almost any well-presented offering. However, in the late afternoon on the day of our arrival, a cold front moved over the river valley and a steady drizzle set in for the weekend. We had deceived numerous fish on various offerings when suddenly a hatch of small flying ants began to come off. Despite the fact that we were presenting our dries to

Below *A tagged Witte River brown earns its release.*

Above *A Para Flying Ant seen from above, showing the delta-style hackle point wings. This pattern is best fished with a dead-drift to trout holding in the current, or should be cast into back-eddies and left there to drift without the angler imparting significant movement to it. Despite their diminutive size, ant patterns will often account for some good trout during the season.*

Above *The stomach contents of a Spekboom river trout show its dependence on both aquatic and terrestrial insects. The insects (clockwise from top left) are a beefly (*Bombylidae *family), a horsefly larva (*Tabanidae *family), mayfly nymphs and shucks (*Tricorythidae *family), a wasp (*Vespidae *family), a cranefly larva (*Tipulidae *family) and caddisfly larvae (*Hydropsychidae *family).*

the trout without drag, the fish steadfastly refused them, although they continued to work the surface film. While it appeared as though the trout were feeding on emerging nymphs, we knew they were feeding on the flying ants.

After discovering that the hooks had rusted I had thrown out all my ant patterns only weeks before, and I was left in a situation where I could not match the fall of ants. What saved the day for me was a tan-coloured mayfly spinner with split wings. After trimming off the tail, clipping the hackle on the bottom flush with the hook shank, and bending the wings to a fully spent position, I was able to use this mocked-up flying ant imitation to deceive trout still feeding wantonly on the ants.

There are several ant imitations from which to choose, ranging from elaborate ones such as the balsa-bodied McMurray Ant patterns to extremely simple imitations tied with dubbed fur and a few turns of hackle. Over the years, however, I have fallen in love with a pattern developed by Gary Borger, an angler who visited South Africa in 1989 and who is well known to most South African fly-fishers through his books and magazine articles. The Para Ant was developed by Gary in 1971 and was perfected in 1981 after the introduction of a special tying technique championed by Idaho fly-tier, René Harrop. This technique involves spinning a ball of dubbing onto the tying thread and then tying it in above the hook shank (in the same way that a ball of dubbing is tied in on a Floating Nymph to represent the

unfolding wings of an emerging mayfly dun [see page 67]). Gary's initial attempts at a Para Ant made use of a post in the middle of the hook shank to support the parachute hackle. However, as this tying technique partially obscured the thin waist required in an ant imitation, it was dispensed with. Today the pattern is tied with a hackle wound around a dubbing ball situated at the front of the hook shank. An advantage of tying in a dubbing ball above the hook shank is that, unlike most ant patterns which use a dubbed ball at the rear of the imitation, the hook gape is not occluded.

When most South Africans think of flying ants, they think of the large brown termites that emerge during or after rainfall. While these do occur along stillwaters and streams, it is the small black ants that are encountered on a more regular basis. These are best imitated on hooks ranging from #12 to #16 and should be black or dark tan in colour.

Back-eddies near stream and river banks are favourite places to fish ant patterns, especially when falls of the winged variety occur, since trout will often lie in these eddies and casually feed in a circular motion, leisurely sipping ants that collect in these areas. When the small black ants fall to the water, they are unable to escape. Initially they struggle to free themselves from the surface tension, but these efforts soon diminish, leaving them to drift helplessly at the mercy of the current. Accordingly, patterns should be fished dead-drift, with an occasional twitch, particularly as they come close to a visible trout.

PARA ANT

HOOK: Tiemco 100, #14 – #20.

THREAD: 8/0 prewaxed, colour to match body.

ABDOMEN (GASTOR): Polypropylene or similar synthetic dubbing in black, cinnamon or dark tan colours.

WAIST: Tying thread, colour to match body.

HEAD: Polypropylene or similar synthetic dubbing in black, cinnamon or dark tan colours.

LEGS: Hackle, colour to match body.

WINGS (OPTIONAL): Hackle points or synthetic winging material. I use brown or grizzly hackle points for the cinnamon and dark tan ants, and white or grizzly hackle points for the black ant.

Note: The original Para Ant did not make use of wings and was a simple pattern tied with two dubbing balls and a hackle. The instructions below for the tying of the Para Ant include two hackle tip wings, which makes for an extremely effective Para Flying Ant.

1. Spin a short, thick, relatively loose noodle of dubbing onto the thread. Lift the dubbing noodle vertically above the hook shank. Push the dubbing down upon the thread to form a ball above the hook barb for the abdomen. Wrap the thread to secure the abdomen in this position. (See also Floating Nymph, page 67, steps 8 and 9.)

2. Take the thread about halfway along the shank towards the eye, covering approximately half the shank with thread.

3. Strip the fibres from two hackles, leaving only the tips behind. Tie in these tips on either side of the hook shank in the style of a delta wing. The wings should be the length of the hook shank.

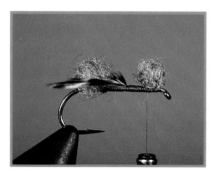

4. Cover the front half of the hook shank with thread, taking the thread to behind the eye of the hook. Spin a noodle of dubbing onto the thread for the head. Form a dubbing ball for the head using the technique described in step 1.

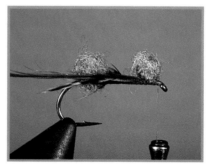

5. Strip the webby flue from a hackle with fibres the length of the hook gape. Tie in the hackle in front of the head, with the concave side facing down.

6. Wind the hackle parachute-style around the base of the head, tie off and trim excess. Form a thread head, half-hitch and trim the thread. Apply head cement to the thread wraps at the head and along the hook shank.

Foam Beetle

ANON

Above *A beautifully marked Witte River brown which fell for a Foam Beetle. Tom Lewin was the angler.*

LIKE ANTS AND GRASSHOPPERS, beetles are terrestrial insects that do not willingly enter the water. When they do, however, they are usually eaten by observant trout on the lookout for an easy meal, and consequently deserve the attention of all fly-fishers. Fishing terrestrial beetle imitations was perfected by anglers such as Vince Marinaro, Ed Koch, Joe Brooks and others who frequented the fertile spring creeks of the Cumberland valley in Pennsylvania. These creeks are home to large, shy, selective brown trout that often ignore hatch-matching patterns, yet frequently succumb to terrestrial insect imitations such as the Crowe Beetle and Letort Hopper.

My research indicates that anglers fishing the Pennsylvania spring creeks were using foam beetles as early as 1960. Vince Marinaro used a beetle consisting of a coffee bean glued to the hook shank, while Don Dubois used a pattern called a 'Flure' – a combination of a fly and a lure. The Flure was made by tying a section of oval foam to the top of the hook shank, but many anglers refused to use it because it wasn't made of the traditional fur and feather materials. Today, almost every fly-shop sells foam body material.

Because South African rivers and streams do not support the often profuse aquatic insect life that occurs in many foreign countries, our trout are forced to augment their diet with terrestrial insects, which during the warmer months of the year can provide a significant percentage of their fare. Most anglers know that, for example, the mountain streams of the Western Cape are fairly acidic and consequently lack heavy populations of aquatic insects. Trout can and do reach respectable proportions in these streams, however, and this is as a result of a diet which consists largely of terrestrial insects such as ants, beetles, grasshoppers, bees and the like. When I have pumped the stomachs of fish caught on streams such as the Jan du Toit's, Elandspad, Witels, Witte and so on, the stomach contents have often revealed a predominance of terrestrial insects, with beetles featuring prominently. Rivers and streams throughout South Africa have the potential to produce good 'terrestrial' fishing, and because beetle imitations can be tied in a reasonably bulky

Above *Terrestrial beetles are an important food source for trout on many of South Africa's rivers and streams, particularly acidic waters such as the streams of the Western Cape where aquatic food is relatively scarce. Here Tom Lewin poses with a Witte River brown which took a Foam Beetle.*

fashion they are useful as both searching patterns and specific imitations that can be cast to visible fish. Such is the effectiveness of beetle patterns that were I forced to choose one pattern for all my dry-fly fishing in the Western Cape, it would, without a second's hesitation, be a Foam Beetle.

Several beetle patterns are available today, and, in most situations, they do an adequate job of deceiving trout. The first beetle imitations that I used were based on the lines of the popular Crowe Beetle which is tied entirely of deer hair. While this pattern produces fish, it is not a particularly good floater nor is it durable. After it has taken a few trout its

hair body becomes shredded by the trouts' teeth, it loses its beetle-shaped outline, and is no longer buoyant.

My answer is the Foam Beetle, a pattern that is simple to tie and which floats like a cork through the roughest of waters. It should be borne in mind when tying imitations that beetles are low-floating insects. This is a very important feature of most terrestrial insects, and low-floating imitations will consistently outperform patterns that are tied to float higher in the water. Although the Foam Beetle is tied with closed-cell foam, this foam is pulled over the back of the pattern, allowing the lower half of the fly to ride in and not on the water. The pattern is also far more durable than those tied with deer or elk hair, and I have taken as many as twenty trout with the same fly.

The low silhouette of beetle patterns makes them difficult to follow on the water. This minor hitch is easily overcome by tying in a small section of easily visible bright nylon yarn or similar bright water-repellent material (my favourite colour is orange); as this material is tied in on top of the fly it in no way diminishes the fly's effectiveness. Or use an excellent beetle body material, marketed by Orvis, called Quick-Sight Beetle Bodies; this has a chartreuse or orange dot of varnish painted on the top of the foam material.

Beetles range in colour from black to brown or bright green, but I doubt that trout become selective to colour – certainly not in South Africa. The iridescent peacock herl used in the body of the pattern imitates effectively the bright green beetles often found by anglers on lakes and streams; if you allow peacock herl to stand in the sun for a few days, it quickly changes colour to an iridescent brown – effective for imitating the bronze beetles often found in the stomachs of trout.

The same principles that apply to fishing other terrestrial imitations apply to fishing the Foam Beetle: the pattern should be dead-drifted downstream and occasionally twitched to simulate the struggles of the natural insect. It is an excellent pattern on both stillwater and stream, and when tied with a bright section of yarn at the head, it is highly visible and can be followed under most light conditions. The Foam Beetle, if tied in a rather buglike way, makes a very effective search-and-probe pattern and will often bring fish to the surface in deep, rough water, especially when it is 'splatted' down in the vicinity of a trout's lie.

FOAM BEETLE
HOOK: Tiemco 100, #10 – #16.
THREAD: 8/0 prewaxed, black.
LEGS: Orvis Flexi Floss, or similar legging material.
SHELLBACK and HEAD: Black closed-cell foam (Polycelon).
BODY: Peacock herl.
INDICATOR: Orange or chartreuse Glo-Bug yarn, or similar.

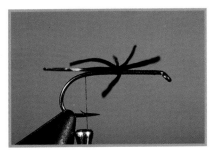

1. Take the thread to a position half to a third of the length of the hook shank from the eye, and tie in three strands of leg material. Take the thread to a position above the barb of the hook.

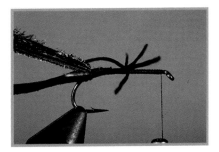

2. Tie in a strip of closed-cell foam and four or five peacock herls. Return the thread to a position behind the eye of the hook.

3. Twist the herls into a rope and wind them forward towards the hook eye, dividing the legs with the herls as you go. Tie the herls off and trim the excess.

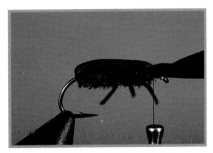

4. Pull the foam over the top of the body and tie it down securely with a few tight turns of thread.

5. Tie in a length of yarn above the shellback. Pull the remainder of the foam back with your left hand, form a small thread head, half-hitch and trim. Apply head cement to the thread wraps.

6. Trim the remainder of the foam to form a head above the hook eye, and trim the indicator into a small ball. Trim the legs so that they are each equal in length to the hook shank.

Para Damsel

ANON

MOST SOUTH AFRICAN stillwater fly-fishers have fished damselfly nymph imitations, and patterns such as Hugh Huntley's Red-Eyed Damsel are firm favourites in many fly-boxes. However, few anglers use the adult form of this abundant insect even though it can produce some spectacular action, particularly on days when the weather may seem too hot for enjoyable fishing.

Adult damselflies are easily distinguished from dragonflies by the attitude of their wings when they are at rest. Damselflies hold their wings folded together over the top of their abdomens, while dragonflies hold their wings at right angles to their abdomens. In addition, damselflies are not as large and robust as dragonflies, and are more likely to find themselves on the water, particularly during strong winds. Once on the water, they are unable to escape and are easy prey for an opportunistic trout on the lookout for a high-calorie meal. This usually occurs during the warmer months of the year when adults can be seen flitting over the water's surface as they deposit their eggs. Interestingly, certain damselfly species display a little-known phenomenon rarely witnessed by anglers: these species actually crawl completely below the water's surface onto submerged weedbeds or other vegetation to lay their eggs. Once they have completed their egg-laying, they drift back to the surface and are consumed by trout patrolling the fringes of the weed or reeds.

Though it doesn't happen often, anglers armed with an appropriate adult damselfly imitation can look forward to some exciting action when trout are feeding on the egg-laying or spent adults. It is not uncommon to hear anglers tell of trout taking an artificial before it lands on the water, and anglers who see trout leaping clear of the water during the height of summer should immediately take note of the insect activity above the water surface. In my experience, the only aquatic insects to regularly induce explosive rises similar to those that occur during the flight of adult damselflies are caddisflies and hatching midge pupae. Midge and caddisfly hatching activity generally occurs at dusk or under the cover of darkness, so explosive rises during the daytime considerably narrow down the angler's choice of imitation, making the fishing of an adult damselfly a good choice.

I have found that the best tactic when fish are leaping clear of the water during hot, midday spells is to cast the pattern out and simply to allow it to drift. Rises vary from a

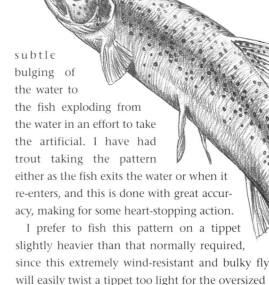

subtle bulging of the water to the fish exploding from the water in an effort to take the artificial. I have had trout taking the pattern either as the fish exits the water or when it re-enters, and this is done with great accuracy, making for some heart-stopping action.

I prefer to fish this pattern on a tippet slightly heavier than that normally required, since this extremely wind-resistant and bulky fly will easily twist a tippet too light for the oversized fly. It is best fished over and around submerged weed and reedbeds, particularly when the naturals can be seen dipping their abdomens into the water or crawling beneath the water's surface.

Top right *The Para Damsel seen from above.*

Right *A Lakensvlei rainbow in the net.*

Damselflies are found in a variety of colours, but the most common colour, found on our high-altitude stillwaters, is an iridescent blue which is difficult to imitate. While many damselfly imitations on the market make use of synthetics such as polypropylene, I use a damselfly constructed almost entirely of dyed blue deer hair and find this more than adequate to imitate the spent adults encountered during egg-laying periods.

PARA DAMSEL
HOOK: Tiemco 5212 or 5263, #10 – #12.
THREAD: 3/0 monocord, black.
THORAX, POST and ABDOMEN: Bright blue deer hair.
WING: Medium dun hackle.
HEAD: Bright blue deer hair.

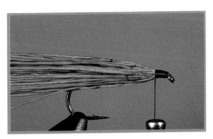

1. Cut a section of deer hair, the diameter of a pencil, from the hide and tie the fibres in directly behind the hook eye. Ensure that the fibres completely encompass the hook shank.

2. Form the thorax by taking three or four tight turns around the deer fibres so that the thread is positioned half way along the hook shank. Separate the top third of the deer fibres; lift this section up away from the hook shank.

3. Take two tight turns behind the upright deer fibres to secure them in this position. Continue to wind the thread around the remaining deer fibres until the thread is positioned above the hook barb.

4. Continue to wrap the thread around the deer fibres in close turns, forming an extended abdomen, until this extended abdomen is approximately the length of the hook shank.

5. Take a few tight wraps around the end of the deer hair where the abdomen ends, then wrap the thread back along the abdomen until the upright post is reached.

6. Strip the webby flue from a hackle with fibres twice the length of the hook gape. Tie in the hackle at the post with its concave side facing down. Trim the excess hackle stem.

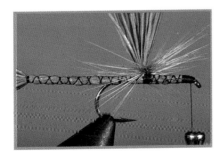

7. Parachute-style, take two to three turns of the hackle around the base of the deer hair post, tie off and trim the excess. Return the thread to a position just behind the hook eye.

8. Pull down the deer hair post over the top of the thorax, tie down the fibres, half-hitch and trim the thread. Apply head cement to the thread wraps at the head and at the end of the abdomen.

9. Trim the deer hair above the thread head, leaving a short section of hair to represent the head, and at the end of the abdomen.

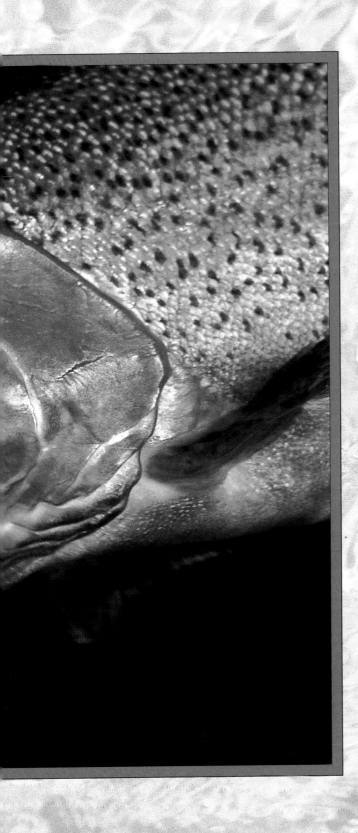

STREAMER
AND
ATTRACTOR
PATTERNS

Woolly Bugger

ANON

EAST GRIQUALAND IS RENOWNED for producing over-sized trout, and Stiggs Cathcart's beautiful lake, Belmont, is no exception. When anglers first began fishing this lake several seasons ago it was producing wild, powerful rainbow trout which averaged over eight pounds. The evening before I tested the waters, one of my companions, Roland Walker, landed the smallest-ever fish from the lake, a trout of four pounds which cartwheeled over the water just as the last rays of sunlight left the valley; the largest fish ever taken, almost twelve pounds, had fallen to the rod of well-known angler Mark Yelland. I shivered with anticipation as I paddled out into the clear, winter water of the lake, that tested a frigid seven degrees Celsius on my thermometer. The lake was heavily weeded in its shallower margins, making them almost impossible to fish with a fly. A broad channel snaked through the weed in lazy bends, a reminder of the old riverbed that had once cut through the now

flooded valley floor. It was in this channel that the majority of the fish had been taken, and as I finned towards this wide passage in the weed, I considered my chances of landing one of the lake's leviathans.

It took a few minutes to reach the mouth of the channel. Once there I took a box of Woolly Buggers from my vest. I decided on a pattern with an olive body and black tail; after clinching it to a strong tippet, I systematically began to cover the channel with a fan-like series of casts. After an hour's fishing, I hadn't seen or felt a fish (I later discovered that this was the norm for the lake at that time) and decided to move further into the channel. My companions, Mark Yelland and Roland Walker, had had similar luck and decided to scout out a lake rumoured to be situated further up the valley. Alone, I settled down to some serious, concentrated fishing.

After a further hour in the channel, I decided a colour change was in order and replaced the olive and black Woolly Bugger with a brown and black pattern with a few strands of Flashabou in the tail. I cast out the fly and once again systematically began to work the open channel, using a slow but erratic retrieve interspersed with short pauses.

It was during the retrieve of a cast I had laid out tight along the weed on the side of the channel that the intermediate fly-line slowly tightened, and I immediately lifted the rod in response to the resistance. When the line suddenly went slack I thought I had fouled some weed, but it tightened again and I knew I had hooked into one of Belmont's rainbows. I let out a shout of joy as the fish turned slowly in the open water of the channel, taking slack line off the stripping apron of my tube.

As the fish took line, a knot formed and I briefly contemplated trying to free it as it passed through the guides. My better judgement told me to concentrate on the fight at hand, and I watched anxiously as the knot passed slowly through the eyes of the rod to slip away into the clear, icy water. I was easily able to turn the fish before it could run the entire fly-line off the reel, and became convinced that I had hooked one of the lake's smaller inhabitants. But when the fish buried itself in a thick clump of floating weed drifting in the channel and I was forced to pressure it for the first time, the realisation that I was attached to a truly enormous fish made my heart pound in my ears. For the first time in many years I became conscious of the bitter disappointment

Top left *The author with an average-size rainbow from Waterford near Underberg. The trout have managed to attain such proportions through a strict catch-and-release rule laid down by the club managing the lake: only fish over ten pounds may be removed.*
Left *This tagged Waterford rainbow, taken by the author using a Bead Head Woolly Bugger, is about to be released.*

I would feel if I lost it. I held the trout as hard as I could under the circumstances. By carefully pumping the rod I was able to bring the fish slowly to the surface. Thick weed covered both the leader and fish, but I could see clearly that the trout was of trophy proportions. I gradually drew it towards the tube, wondering how I was going to land it with a hopelessly small net.

With the release of the trout in mind, slipping my fingers through its gills was out of the question and I knew the fish would not give me too many chances should I bungle the netting. I slipped the net into the water and slowly drew the enormous cockfish over the frame. He was a magnificent specimen, easily better than thirty inches, with a huge hooked jaw that seemed to grimace at me. Strangely, he was a bright silver colour, unusual for a cockfish in the middle of winter. Large black spots reached to the very tip of his upper jaw and I thought I would never again see such a beautiful trout. I guessed his weight to be between eleven and twelve pounds.

The fish reached the end of the net meshes, but more than half its length still hung from the frame. When I tried to lift it onto the stripping apron of my float tube, it fell back into the water and slowly swam away. I managed to stop it before it could move more than two or three yards from my position but, although the fish was beaten, I could not move it nearer to the tube. I watched as its paddle-sized tail wafted slowly back and forth in the water.

The stalemate ended abruptly when the tippet suddenly parted, and the fish – which until then I had thought was completely beaten – disappeared into the weed in a flash. Ultimately, the trout would have earned its freedom after a quick photographic session, but the fact that I will never quite know its exact weight haunts me whenever I think of that wonderful morning.

I consider the Woolly Bugger and its derivative, the Bead Head Woolly Bugger, in their various colour combinations to be invaluable for fishing stillwaters across the country. These are suggestive patterns that represent nothing in particular, yet, most importantly, have movement. There are not many flies with the fish-catching properties of the Woolly Bugger. The list of large fish that have taken this pattern – a small percentage of which I have landed – seems endless: a huge, double-figure rainbow hen from the Fly Fishers' Association's tiny lake, Surprise Pool, on the Fort Nottingham road, which struggled to clear its massive bulk from the water before falling on a light 5X tippet; a fish of incredible strength from Des Joyner's beautiful lake near Swartberg in East Griqualand, that took fifty yards of backing off the reel before throwing the hook, this just after I had released a fish of seven pounds on the previous cast; a fish in Reggie's Lake on the Ivanhoe estate in the Impendhle area that straightened a Kamasan B800 heavy-wire hook on its fourth jump; and a ten pound hen from the lake at Waterford, that picked up a Bead Head Woolly Bugger as I fished it over shallow weed during the early morning. With this fly on their tippets, all anglers will be assured of catching an oversize fish sooner or later.

The Woolly Bugger has its origins in the eastern United States and is said to be a derivative of the popular Woolly Worm, a pattern well known to most South African anglers. This makes good sense, since the Woolly Bugger is essentially a Woolly Worm with the addition of a marabou tail. Russell Blessing, an American fly-fisherman, tied the original Woolly Bugger in 1967 to imitate the hellgrammite larvae that he discovered on the Susquehanna River. His pattern featured a body of variegated chenille and a palmered hackle trimmed to a stubble. After reading a magazine article about a pattern, known as a Blossom Fly, tied with a chenille body and marabou tail, Blessing adapted his pattern by winding a palmered hackle through the body, arriving at what is today known as the Woolly Bugger.

The Woolly Bugger was slow to catch on in the eastern United States, but through the writings and fishing schools of angling author Doug Swisher its reputation quickly spread over the western half of the continent. Today it is considered indispensable by most anglers visiting the rivers and lakes of the western states such as Montana, Idaho and Wyoming.

167

Most South African anglers consider the Woolly Bugger to be a stillwater pattern. My confidence in this pattern as a producer of trout in stillwaters is such that I reserve an entire fly-box exclusively for Woolly Buggers in various colour and size combinations. While I suspect that the Woolly Bugger is also capable of producing some very large trout from the slower-moving pools on the lower sections of many of our rivers, I prefer fishing in the riffles, glides and runs and so cannot testify to the pattern's effectiveness in these waters.

The Woolly Bugger is extremely versatile and can be used as both a suggestive and an attractor pattern. I fish it as a suggestive imitation in subdued tones during most of the year (alongside other great producers such as dragonfly and damselfly nymph imitations) and as a streamer pattern tied in bright colours during the winter months' spawning season, when trout often aggressively attack the pattern. In the warmer months of the year, from September to mid-April, I fish the Woolly Bugger in various shades of olive, brown and black, and prefer to keep my retrieves slow but erratic. Although I add a few turns of lead wire around the front of the hook shank, it sometimes pays to add a small split-shot an inch or two above the fly in order to spice up the action with a distinctive jigging motion in the water.

I don't believe that any one colour combination is more effective than another although, interestingly, an angler may have more success fishing a certain colour pattern than his companions have with the same pattern in another colour, even though they are using the same line and retrieve. This simply may be due to the unsuccessful angler losing confidence in his pattern, but it's easy enough to remove that variable by carrying standard and bead head Woolly Buggers in various colours.

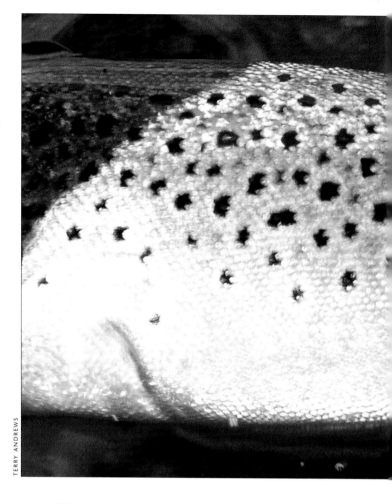

TERRY ANDREWS

Above *This Sailor's Gift brown, taken by Chris Jones, fell for a Woolly Bugger tied with bead chain eyes.*
Below *The clearly visible channel snaking through the weed in the lake at Belmont, East Griqualand is the remains of the old riverbed which once cut through this now flooded valley.*

A small, thinly dressed olive pattern works extremely well over and around submerged weed during the height of summer, possibly because it is a reasonable imitation of the damselfly nymphs which are freely available to trout during these hot summer months. Many anglers like to tie these lightly dressed patterns with a hackle from one side of which the fibres have been stripped; as the hackle fibres do not mat together, this ensures a sparser imitation.

During winter the Woolly Bugger, tied in subdued hues, will continue to produce trout consistently, but it pays to keep a few patterns dressed in vivid, bright colours should other colours fail. I particularly like to fish orange and yellow Woolly Buggers during the winter months; at this time of year the angler should experiment with retrieves ranging from extremely slow to fairly fast.

With the recent revolution in fly-tying caused by metal beads, it was inevitable that a bead would be added to the Woolly Bugger. The beads add sparkle as well as the jigging action I consider to be crucial to this pattern's effectiveness – in fact, I and my fishing companions find ourselves fishing the Bead Head Woolly Bugger more now than we do the original pattern. Most American fly-shop catalogues sell Woolly Bugger variations, many of these incorporating Crystal or Cactus Chenille for the body. This makes for a highly effective variant which is particularly successful during winter.

Patterns should be fished over and around weed, log falls, reed beds and other obstructions which harbour trout food and are patrolled by fish on the lookout for a meal. The Woolly Bugger is my favourite pattern for prospecting in old river channels (in which I have hooked my largest trout).

Retrieves should be varied to determine which is the most effective on the day, though in a lake slow retrieves will almost always deceive the largest trout. Most anglers retrieve stillwater patterns far too quickly, which serves only to alert wary trout. By slowing down your retrieve and thinking about what you are doing, you will become more successful. I usually use a slow but erratic hand-twist retrieve, or a few two- to three-inch-long strips followed by a pause.

Different trout inhabiting the same lake may take the fly either very gently or with a ferocity that will leave the angler with a flyless tippet and trembling hands: it pays to be prepared for the worst scenario. Irrespective of the time of the year, tippets should match the fly size and the size of the fish expected, so I usually use 3X or 4X tippets.

Above *Terry Andrews took this seven-pound rainbow cock from a private lake in the Bushman's Nek area using a Bead Head Woolly Bugger. This fish made no less than nine runs into the backing.*

Above *Another victim of the Woolly Bugger. This Mt. Arthur rainbow, taken by Tom Lewin, took the fly fished on an intermediate line in shallow water.*

WOOLLY BUGGER

HOOK: Tiemco 300 or 5263, #2 – #14.

THREAD: 6/0 prewaxed, colour to match body.

TAIL: Marabou. (I often like to add a few strands of Flashabou or Krystal Flash to the tail.)

BODY: Chenille, or dubbing blend. (My favourite dubbing blend is the one used for the abdomen and thorax of the Kaufmann Lake Dragon: medium olive, dark olive or brown Hare-Tron dubbing [a mixture of hare's fur and Antron], or similar, blended with the following colours of Angora goat dubbing for highlights: blue, purple, green, amber, olive, brown and rust.)

RIB: Copper wire.

HACKLE: Webby saddle hackle.

HEAD (OPTIONAL): Metal bead.

USEFUL COLOUR COMBINATIONS

	TAIL	BODY	HACKLE
1.	*Olive	Olive	Olive
2.	*Black	Olive	Black
3.	*Brown	Brown	Brown
4.	*Black	Brown	Black
5.	*Black	Black	Black
6.	*Black	Peacock	Black
7.	Orange	Orange	Orange
8.	Yellow	Yellow	Yellow
9.	Red	Red	Red
10.	Purple	Purple	Black

NOTE: This list of colour combinations will serve the angler throughout the year. Those marked with an asterisk (*) are the most popular colours in use around the world today.

1. Strip a thick clump of marabou from a plume and tie it in above the barb. The tail should be the length of the hook shank. Note that the marabou is fluffy all the way to its tips.

2. Tie in a length of chenille and a length of copper wire, and take the thread to a position behind the eye of the hook. Wind the chenille forward around the hook shank, tie it off and trim the excess.

3. Select a soft, webby saddle hackle and tie the feather in with its concave side facing the hook shank. The fibres should be approximately one-and-a-half times the width of the hook gape.

4. Wind the hackle towards the tail in six to eight evenly spaced turns, trap the hackle tip with the wire and wind the wire through the hackle up to the hook eye. Tie off and trim the excess wire and the feather tip.

5. Form a small, neat thread head, half-hitch and trim the thread. Apply head cement to the thread wraps.

6. This shows a Woolly Bugger variation which uses a dubbing blend to replace the chenille body, a metal bead and Flashabou tied in with the marabou tail.

Zonker

DAN BYFORD

THE ZONKER, A BAITFISH IMITATION, is one of my favourite streamer patterns and has accounted for some of my largest stillwater trout. When trout begin to concentrate on small baitfish in the shallows, the action can be fast and furious, with strikes that leave the angler shaking with excitement. The Zonker is a superb searching pattern, especially during winter when trout aggressively hit streamer and attractor patterns, and it is also a good fly to choose when trout are visibly chasing minnows.

The Zonker was invented by Dan Byford of Steamboat Springs, Colorado, and is one of the most realistic yet suggestive baitfish imitations available. It demands a fair deal of patience during tying and can prove a tricky pattern

Right and below *Lake inlets, such as these at Loch Rannoch and Little Kariba, are good places to prospect for large trout during winter when fish that are attempting to spawn will aggressively hit streamer and attractor patterns.*

to tie properly, particularly for novices. As with all patterns, the only way the fly can be mastered is to tie several, until all the problems associated with its tying are overcome.

I began to take an interest in the Zonker as an effective baitfish imitation after an experience many years ago on a lake controlled by the Natal Fly Fishers Club. Rondebosch is a large expanse of water just off the National Road not far from Mooi River in the KwaZulu-Natal Midlands. Like many

of KwaZulu-Natal's prime trout waters, it is now infested with largemouth black bass which have caused a decline in trout numbers in the lake, once rated as one of the Club's finest trout-fishing venues.

I had been wading the shallows, fishing a small mayfly nymph over the submerged weed that lined the shore, when I heard a loud splashing sound from an area along the bank, obscured from my vision by a row of thick bush. When I finally reached the area, the only evidence of a fish was the spreading rings of a rise which sent ripples running onto the bank nearest the commotion. As I gazed at the ebbing ripples, another fish slashed at the surface fifty yards along the bank, and I was just in time to see several small minnows leaping from the water. I watched, fascinated, as the minnows fled in panic – so intent were they on escaping the predator that several landed on the shoreline at the water's edge, not far from my position.

Frantically, I stripped in the floating line and cut back the tippet. I attached a large Zonker which I had tied only days earlier as an experiment and waited along the bank for further action. Sure enough, a school of minnows again took to the air not far from my position, and I worked furiously to get the Zonker into the area of the disturbance before the trout moved back into deeper water. The fly landed with a loud splat close to a huge boil on the perimeter of the commotion, and I barely had time to take in the slack before the line was ripped from my hands. The trout took fifty yards of backing before showing itself in a graceful, arching jump that carried it several feet through the air. Even at that range I could make out its massive form quite distinctly, but the fight was not destined to go the full distance. The fish fell heavily on the 2X tippet, breaking it instantly.

It was the only Zonker that I had in my collection of baitfish imitations, and even though I tried every other baitfish pattern in my possession, nothing seemed to work, so I vowed to tie up a selection of Zonkers in various colours and sizes on my return home.

It is well known that during certain periods in the stillwater angling season trout will feed heavily on small minnows in certain lakes, and anglers who lack the appropriate imitation will find themselves missing out on some of the most spectacular action of the season. While some lakes have fish that concentrate heavily on small baitfish, others have no minnow feeding activity whatsoever, and it pays to listen to anglers' stories about the incidence of minnow activity. Local knowledge is an important factor in being adequately prepared for minnow feeding action, should it occur. I have never seen or heard of trout feeding on minnows at Highmoor in KwaZulu-Natal, for example, but Gubu, that famous stillwater in the Eastern Cape, is

Above *Streamers and attractor patterns will account for some of the biggest fish of the season. Terry Andrews took this hefty eight-pound rainbow hen from The Potts in East Griqualand just prior to a huge electric storm.*

renowned for its minnows. Another lake I fish in the Bushman's Nek area has huge minnow populations upon which the trout feed extensively; trout caught there often regurgitate minnows, some as long as three inches.

Trout that feed extensively on minnows will almost always be very deep, well-conditioned fish. They frequently work in schools, herding large shoals of minnows into shallow water or shallow bays before tearing into them, often devouring several small fish in these feeding sprees. This feeding phenomenon is particularly noticeable during the colder months of the year when other food forms are scarce. When anglers see small fish leaping out of the water, or several large trout moving at high speed at the surface, it is a good indication that trout are chasing schools of minnows, and a Zonker will produce spectacular fishing.

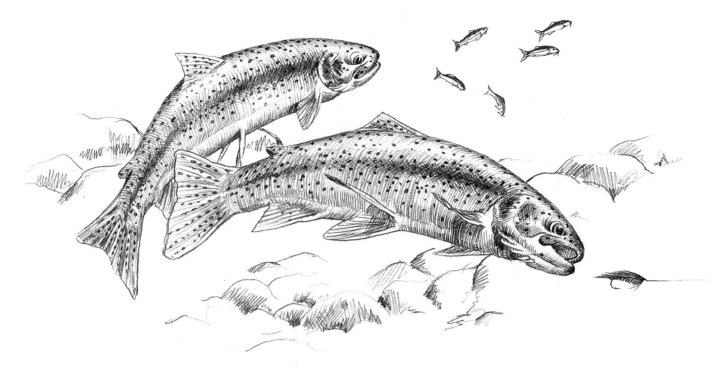

The Zonker is a time-consuming and elaborate pattern to tie and requires a fair deal of practice before its proportions are correctly mastered. The underbody, which gives it its underslung shape, is normally formed with aluminium or lead tape, which is bent around the hook shank and then cut to shape. If a translucent mylar is used as an overbody, I like to colour the underbody with floss or waterproof marking pens. When tying several Zonkers I have found that it is most time-efficient to shape and colour the underbody tape before starting. Because of its mylar body construction, the fly is quickly shredded by the trout's teeth, so I now coat all my Zonker bodies in epoxy.

As small baitfish will often be found along the shallows of our stillwaters, it is here that the fly-fisher should concentrate his efforts. My technique is to wait for a disturbance to erupt and then cast the Zonker as quickly as possible into the area of feeding activity. This requires a powerful, fast-actioned rod. My previous favourite was a nine-foot rod designed for a seven-weight line; however, with the graphite fly-rods on the market today, a five-weight outfit is more than capable of handling these patterns. A stiff, fast-actioned rod is required to cast the Zonker, because once its rabbit strip 'wing' has soaked up water it is difficult to cast the pattern efficiently with a light-line rod.

If fish are targeting minnows in shallow water or at the surface, I use either floating or intermediate lines which will ensure that the pattern does not sink below the level of the feeding trout. I like to give the fly a second or two to sink and then begin a fast, erratic retrieve to keep the pattern from sinking too deeply. An erratic retrieve of a few strips of two to three inches, followed by a pause, is just the ticket to imitate an injured or crippled minnow – quickly recognisable to trout as easy prey.

A fast-moving pattern will usually induce savage strikes from trout, and this savageness seems to be exaggerated when streamer and attractor patterns are used. Tippets should thus be strong – I prefer to use tippets from 1X to 3X. Even with these tippets, there are often occasions when the angler will be smashed up, but this is what makes this form of fly-fishing so exciting!

ZONKER

HOOK: Tiemco 300, #2 – #8.

THREAD: 3/0 monocord, red and black.

UNDERBODY: Metallic tape, cut to shape.

UNDERBODY COLORATION (OPTIONAL): White or olive fluorescent floss wrapped over the back two-thirds of the underbody, and red floss over the front third of the underbody (to represent gills). Waterproof colour pens or paint can also be used to give coloration to the underbody.

OVERBODY: Mylar tubing, colour of choice, with core removed.

WING: Tanned rabbit hide with fur attached (my favourite colours are grizzly, olive and brown).

HACKLE: Grizzly saddle.

COATING (OPTIONAL): Clear epoxy cement. (If using, this should be applied to the mylar overbody after step 5 and allowed to dry before the subsequent tying steps are completed.)

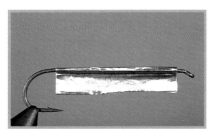

1. Bend a strip of metallic tape around the hook shank as shown. Colour the underbody if required (optional).

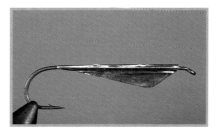

2. Cut the tape to the shape shown. This metallic tape will form the underbody of the pattern.

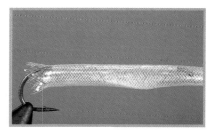

3. Wrap the red tying thread around the shank behind the underbody and above the barb. Push the mylar tubing over the underbody as shown.

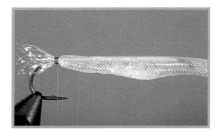

4. Tie the mylar down with the red tying thread, but do not trim the thread. Trim the end of the mylar so that it protrudes behind the bend of the hook and beyond the barb by about one-quarter of the hook shank.

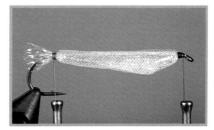

5. Attach the black tying thread to the hook shank behind the eye; trap the mylar with a few tight turns of the thread. Trim the excess mylar.

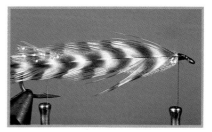

6. Strip the webby flue from a hackle with fibres about one-third to half the length of the hook shank. Tie in the hackle with the concave side facing the shank.

7. Take two or three turns of the hackle in front of the body, tie off and trim the excess.

8. Stroke the uppermost hackle fibres down around the sides of the body and secure them in this position with a few wraps of thread.

9. Trim the end of a strip of tanned rabbit hide as shown.

10. Tie in the trimmed point of the strip of rabbit hide behind the eye, and trim the excess. Form a neat thread head, half-hitch and trim the thread.

11. Stretch the hide over the top of the body and part the fibres above the barb of the hook. The hide strip should extend just beyond the tips of the trimmed mylar.

12. Tie down the hide strip with the red thread, half-hitch and trim the thread. Apply head cement to the thread wraps above the barb of the hook and to the head.

White Death

ROBIN FICK

THE RISE I COULD SEE from my position some ten yards off the bank was the kind associated with a trout sipping midge pupae at the surface. Dusk had settled over the lake several minutes earlier, and although fish were moving at the surface it became increasingly difficult to see them in the fading light. Just before dusk, however, I had spotted a small dimple along a weedbed and had managed to manoeuvre myself so that I had the last minutes of fading sunlight on the far side of the rising fish. Even using the light to my advantage, it was difficult to make out the rise in the flat, oily water, and I found myself relying on my sense of hearing to calculate the casting distance required to cover the rise.

I unhitched a small White Death from the hook keeper, stripped off a length of line and waited for the trout to move again in its position on the far side of the floating mat of weed. It was several minutes before a faint dimple appeared, and the longer I waited, the more difficult it became to detect the rise in the enclosing cloak of darkness. The trout was moving approximately twenty-five yards from me and, since I could wade no further, it was impossible to close the distance between myself and my unseen quarry.

The first cast pitched perfectly over the weedbed, and the pattern settled quietly into the surface film inches off the weed. I gave it several seconds to sink and then began an erratic retrieve using short, sharp strips. On the second strip, the floating line was suddenly wrenched taut. As I tightened up, the fish exploded from the surface in a shower of spray. I was convincingly broken on 4X tippet material and quickly clinched on another White Death of similar size.

The following cast landed in almost the same position as the first one, and I again gave the fly time to settle in the water before beginning an erratic retrieve. Unbelievably, the line was again wrenched taut as the water exploded. I watched in amazement as a large rainbow cartwheeled over the weedbed, breaking the tippet as it crashed back into the water. When I had finally stopped shaking and had retrieved the broken tippet, darkness had enveloped the lake. Although on previous occasions I had enjoyed success under the cover of darkness with this deadly pattern, I no longer felt the inclination to continue fishing and – still shaking – I waded back to the bank with mud sucking at my wader boots.

The White Death is yet another very effective fly from Robin Fick's vice. It was originally tied to imitate certain species of adult caddisflies which re-enter the water to lay their eggs. (This diving re-entry is well documented in Gary

Above *Mike Somerville watches as a Waterford rainbow earns a well-deserved release. The fish took a White Death.*

LaFontaine's *Caddisflies*.) However, in addition to its intended purpose, I have discovered a use for the White Death for which I have found few equals: this is during the emergence and spinner fall of the tiny *Tricorythidae* mayflies which are found in many stillwaters across South Africa.

During emergences of these *Tricorythidae* mayflies trout become extremely selective to the naturals, both in the nymphal and spinner form. I usually rely on a small nymph imitation during the emergence of the mayflies and a simple spinner imitation during the spinner falls in order to fool trout which gulp the naturals in the surface film. This is exciting fishing, but for the neophyte fly-fisher unaccustomed to fishing small nymphs and spinner imitations in the surface film, both the emergences and the spinner falls can lead to great frustration.

Prior to the spinner fall of these tiny mayflies, however, trout feed selectively on the emerging nymphs both in the intermediate water layers, as the nymphs make their way to the surface, and at the surface. This is often when trout can be seen bulging just below the surface, ignoring traditional patterns. Small nymphal imitations from #16 to #18 can be extremely effective but are not infallible. When the visibly

bulging trout are gulping nymphs or spinners in the surface film yet still refuse suitable imitations, the White Death alone will, for some inexplicable reason, still take trout.

It is not only during *Tricorythidae* mayfly emergences that the White Death is effective: I have had success with this pattern, in small sizes, throughout the day and have even taken trout at midday during the heat of summer. One experience in particular will always remind me of the pattern's effectiveness.

Many years ago, Robin Fick and I spent an afternoon at the two lakes at Highmoor. The hours after midday produced one of the heaviest *Tricorythidae* hatches I had ever seen, and from our float tubes we each managed to release a dozen trout in the flat, glassy smooth conditions. By the late afternoon, we had had our share of fishing, yet despite the frenzied rises which had begun at about two o'clock, I saw no other anglers taking fish. Walking back along the wall of the upper lake, with our tubes slung over our shoulders, we stopped to enquire about the luck of an NFFC member who was casting a long line off the wall. He, like the other anglers, had had an unsuccessful day. Robin offered him a small White Death and explained that it represented an adult caddis returning to the water in order to lay its eggs; the angler gave it a sceptical glance but tied it on nonetheless. His first cast produced a brown of three pounds – the only fish taken that evening by any of the anglers fishing off the wall!

I find myself using the White Death more and more, predominantly during the emergence and spinner fall of Trico mayflies, but also as a versatile searching pattern. Despite the fact that the White Death was designed originally to imitate diving caddisfly adults, I am sceptical that trout take it for this reason as, with its all-white colour, the pattern imitates nothing in particular. I rely on a trout's aggression and curiosity to induce takes, and as a pure attractor pattern, the White Death is deadly.

During Trico emergences, I fish it in reasonably small sizes (#12 to #16) on a long leader of up to fifteen feet coupled with a floating line. Since trout are usually found in the upper water layers during the emergence of these mayflies, it usually pays to fish fine and far off to avoid spooking them, and light tippets geared to the small fly sizes should be used. Anglers who retrieve their flies with long, fast strips will find that they spend most of their fishing time tying on fresh patterns. I prefer either a hand-twist retrieve or an erratic retrieve using short, one-inch-long strips. Takes are almost always positive and anglers should bear in mind the size of the fish it is possible to encounter as well as the light tippets being used. Once hooked, it pays to allow the trout to bolt away and expend its energy before applying pressure and beginning the fight in earnest.

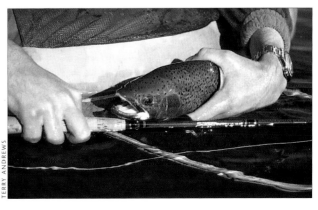

Top right *This well-conditioned four-and-three-quarter-pound rainbow fell for a White Death fished in shallow water.*
Right *This rainbow attacked a White Death during a hatch of* Tricorythidae *mayflies at a small lake in the Balgowan area.*

TERRY ANDREWS

When using the White Death as a searching pattern in the late afternoon and evening when caddisflies often emerge and later return to lay their eggs, I like to prospect with a slightly larger pattern size; tippet sizes can be stepped up accordingly. It is also an effective streamer pattern in smaller sizes, and can be used to imitate small, young-of-the-year minnows. In this case retrieves can be speeded up somewhat, and I prefer a retrieve of several strips of three to four inches, interspersed with long pauses. Takes can occur at any time and are sometimes savage, even from small fish.

Above Mike Somerville caught this six-and-a-half-pound rainbow with a White Death fished just below the surface at last light.

WHITE DEATH
HOOK: Tiemco 3769, 3761 or 5262, #10 – #16.
THREAD: 6/0 prewaxed, white.
BODY: White chenille.
UNDERWING (OPTIONAL): Pearlescent Krystal Flash.
OVERWING: White marabou.

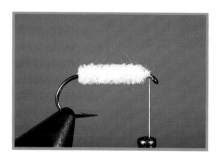

1. Tie in a length of fine chenille above the barb of the hook and return the thread to a position behind the hook eye. Wrap the chenille to form the body, tie off and trim the excess.

2. Tie in four or five strands of Krystal Flash above the body and trim the excess. The strands should extend to or slightly beyond the hook bend.

3. Tie in a clump of marabou above the Krystal Flash strands. The marabou fibres should not extend beyond the hook bend. Form a small thread head, half-hitch and trim. Apply head cement to the thread wraps.

Soft Hackle Streamer

JACK GARTSIDE

THE NAMES PHEASANT HOPPER, Sparrow and Evening Star may not mean much to most South African fly-tiers and fly-fishers, but these patterns are well known in the United States. Created by Jack Gartside, an angler whose reputation as an innovative fly-tier has spread, not because he has published any books or magazine articles but simply by word of mouth, the patterns are all extremely effective and, most importantly, are very easy to tie, making use of materials which are cheap and freely available.

Jack Gartside is a Boston-based fly-tier who has probably the most unusual job of any fly-tier: he is a part-time cab driver in Boston during winter, tying flies during any free time. His summers are spent in Montana, where he ties flies and fishes. He gave up a stable career in Boston as an English school teacher to pursue a life that would afford him more free time to do the things he loves best – fishing and tying flies. Born in Boston in 1942, Jack learned to tie flies before

Above *This view down to the lake at Belmont shows the extensive weed in the shallows and the weed-free channels, always good areas to prospect for trout, snaking through them.*

he learned to cast them, starting at the age of eight. His attitude is simple, as are his patterns: he believes that as long as he is able to tie and sell enough flies to keep him on the saltwater flats or the stream, he will be happy. The fact that to this day he is able to pursue this lifestyle bears testimony to the success of his approach.

Initially unable to afford expensive materials, he relied on inexpensive pheasant plumage for most of his flies, and today many of his most popular patterns still make abundant use of this material. The defining characteristic of all his patterns is simplicity in both form and design; in addition, he believes that there is no such thing as an exact imitation. As he firmly believes that form follows function,

Above *The author took this six-and-three-quarter-pound rainbow fishing a streamer pattern in Scott's Lake in East Griqualand. The fish was regurgitating small minnows when it was landed, proving that a streamer pattern was the correct choice.*

his patterns effectively suggest but do not overstate the essence of the living prey. They are also simple to tie and easy to fish, making them good choices for neophyte anglers.

Gartside's best creation to date is probably a pattern known as the Soft Hackle Streamer, a fly that has earned itself a reputation as a deceiver of large trout and one that fulfills every element of his fly-tying philosophy. The pattern is simplicity itself to tie and makes use of marabou, a material widely used by fly-tiers throughout the world, including South Africa.

After reading about it in *Fly Fisherman* magazine I began using this simple yet deadly pattern several years ago, and it has accounted for some heavy trout from our stillwaters. The pattern takes only a few minutes to tie and, by using different colours of marabou, can be dressed in a wide assortment of colours and in an almost endless variety of colour combi-

nations. A fly that a novice can master within minutes, it has no body and consists of only a hook, a few strands of tinsel and two feathers – simplicity itself!

Because the Soft Hackle Streamer is tied with marabou (marabou 'bloods' or 'shorts' are the best materials for the pattern's application) it pulsates in the water – something which anglers should use to their advantage. Gartside believes that the best retrieve for this pattern is a series of three-feet pulls interspersed with pauses of a few seconds, as he believes that a retrieve using short strips pulls the fly out of the fish's mouth.

The beauty of the Soft Hackle Streamer is that it uses no weight, yet the pattern will sink quickly once the marabou has soaked up water. It was originally tied on a Mustad O'Shaughnessy 3406 hook, a heavy, wire, ring-eye hook ideally suited to the application of the Soft Hackle Streamer since it is strong, short-shanked and has a wide gape. It is not available locally, but an excellent substitute is the Kamasan B200 Deep Water Nymph Hook.

The Soft Hackle Streamer has become one of my favourites for searching the water during the winter months when trout are often reluctant to take usually successful flies. Depending on where the fish are to be found, I fish it at any depth on fly-lines ranging from floaters to fast sinkers. Tippets should be on the strong side and, as is often the case, 3X tippet material simply may not be enough to handle the savage, jolting strikes associated with these patterns.

One of the country's most fervent advocates of the Soft Hackle Streamer is Darrel Holton, who has good reason to believe in its effectiveness. Several years ago the fly accounted for two trout from Platorand in Mpumalanga, a lake notorious for its difficult rainbows. The two trout in question both took Darrel's scale to over seven pounds, and such specimens would make a convert of any angler who is prepared to give this simple pattern the fishing time it deserves. Darrel ties his patterns on a #6 hook, and his favourite colours are brown, white, black and chartreuse with a brown collar.

SOFT HACKLE STREAMER

HOOK: Tiemco 3769, 3761, or 5262, #2 – #8 (the Kamasan B200 is almost identical to the 5262 but does not have the same heavy-gauge wire).

THREAD: 6/0 prewaxed, colour of choice, or to match body.

TINSEL: Flashabou, or gold or silver mylar.

WING: Pheasant or other marabou plume.

COLLAR: Barred mallard flank, pheasant rump, guinea, or other long, soft hackle feather.

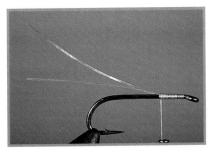

1. Tie in two uneven strands of Flashabou halfway along the hook shank. The longer of the strands should be at least the length of the hook shank.

2. Select a marabou plume and tie it in by the butt, halfway along the hook shank.

3. Wind the plume forward in open turns, tie it off and trim the excess.

4. Tie a mallard flank or similar feather in by the butt directly in front of the marabou plume. The concave side of the feather should face the hook shank.

5. Take two or three turns of the feather around the hook shank in front of the marabou, tie off the feather and trim the excess.

6. Form a small, neat thread head, half-hitch and trim the thread. Apply head cement to the thread wraps.

Marabou Muddler

DAN BAILEY

THE MUDDLER MINNOW, or 'Muddler' as it is usually called, is justifiably famous and is used throughout the world with great success. It has its origins on the Nipigon River – famous for its large brook trout – in Canada, where it was developed during a fishing trip by the late Don Gapen, a well-known Canadian angler whose ambition it was to catch a world-record brook trout. After clamping his vice to a boat beached on the banks of the river, Gapen set about tying flies for the following day's fishing. Little did he know that the pattern he was about to tie would become legendary.

The fly was known as Gapen's Special Fly or simply Gapen's Fly. Gapen tied these flies by the dozen and sold them at his fishing lodge (called the Chateau Bungalow). Because of the pattern's incredible popularity, his friends urged him to give it a name. He decided to call the pattern the Muddler Minnow in memory of the small sculpin minnows that lived in the Wisconsin streams and rivers he fished in his boyhood. These small fish were commonly called muddler sculpins or muddler minnows by the locals, and they produced large brown trout when fished as bait.

Gapen once wrote that he fished it not only as a minnow imitation but, in smaller sizes, as a nymph, as a grasshopper during the grasshopper season, and even as a mayfly. While I do know of anglers who have fished the Muddler Minnow as a dry fly during grasshopper season in South Africa, it is without question at its best when fished as a streamer.

Although originally designed as a minnow imitation, the Muddler can catch fish where minnows are not prevalent. Over the years, such versatility was bound to lead to hybrids, which are now so popular that they overshadow the original pattern. The most popular of the hybrids is the Marabou Muddler, invented and popularised by the late Dan Bailey, the famous fly-shop owner from Montana. Dan Bailey made the Marabou Muddler internationally famous by substituting marabou for the turkey quill wing, silver tinsel chenille for the body, and adding a red tail. He then topped the marabou wing with strands of peacock herl, inventing what is today one of the finest producers of large, trophy trout.

The Marabou Muddler's two greatest assets are its bulky head and marabou wing, which give it the appearance of a food-form worth consuming. When retrieved erratically, the marabou wing pulsates enticingly (a factor completely lacking in the original Muddler Minnow). Tied in a variety of colours, the Marabou Muddler is a pattern that can be worked slowly during most of the season, but during winter it can be fished with a somewhat faster retrieve which will often take some of the largest fish of the season.

I have used the Marabou Muddler with great success throughout the season but, as with most streamer patterns, they are most effective in winter when large, aggressive cockfish will attack them. Because I prefer to fish these patterns in large sizes, such as #4 and #6, they require a fairly powerful rod to throw them the long distances required on some of our stillwaters. I use a stiff-actioned five-weight rod, since the saturated deer hair head and wet marabou wing can make casting a chore, particularly if faced with the raw winter winds of late July and most of August.

I usually fish this pattern in shallow water with an intermediate line, but when the fishing is slow I use fast-sinking lines to take the pattern into deep water. Retrieves should be varied to ascertain the trouts' preferences on the day, and tippets should be suitable for the conditions and

Left *The author hoists a six-pound rainbow in the net. The fish fell for an attractor pattern.*

TERRY ANDREWS

Above Dusk settles over Belmont, one of East Griqualand's most picturesque lakes.

the size of the fish likely to be encountered. Even reasonably small fish moving at speed will pop tippets in the 2X to 4X class if the angler's retrieve is fast and erratic, so it pays at all times to be prepared.

The Marabou Muddler is one of my favourite streamer patterns; I fish a comprehensive range of this pattern which, tied in a wide variety of colours and sizes, makes a superbly versatile and effective fly.

MARABOU MUDDLER

HOOK: Tiemco 300, #2 – #8.

THREAD: 3/0 monocord, cream or light tan.

TAIL: Red hackle fibres.

BODY: Tinsel Chenille or Crystal Chenille, colour of choice. (My favourite basic colour is silver, but any colour can be used to complement the underwing.)

UNDERWING: Marabou, colour of choice. (The most common colours in use today are yellow, orange, red, white, olive, brown and black.)

OVERWING: Peacock herl and Krystal Flash.

COLLAR and HEAD: Spun deer hair.

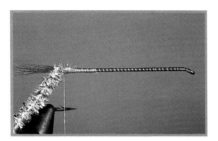

1. Above the barb, tie in 15 hackle fibres for the tail and a length of tinsel chenille. The tail should be one-third the length of the hook shank.

2. Return the thread to a position about a quarter of the shank-length from the eye, wind the chenille forward to the thread, tie off and trim excess chenille.

3. To form the underwing, strip a thick clump of marabou fibres from a plume and tie it in above the body so that it extends to the tip of the tail.

4. Tie in four to six strands of Krystal Flash above the underwing. These Krystal Flash strands should be equal in length to the marabou underwing.

5. Tie in four to six peacock herls above the strands of Krystal Flash. These too should be the length of the marabou underwing and should be tied with their concave sides facing downward.

6. Clip a thick section of deer hair and stack it in a hair stacker. Once stacked, hold the fibres over the hook shank as shown and take three loose turns of thread around them.

7. Slowly draw the thread wraps tight, allowing the hair to spin and flare out around the hook. This will form the collar as well as a portion of the head. The collar should be one-quarter to one-third the length of the hook shank.

8. Spin further clumps of deer hair around the front quarter of the shank, so that the shank is covered up to the hook eye, half-hitch and trim thread. Apply head cement to the half-hitched knots.

9. Remove the fly from the vice and trim the head into the shape shown. Ensure that the collar fibres are not accidentally clipped.

Surface Muddler

DEAN RIPHAGEN

IN THE DYING RAYS of the afternoon sun, I watched as trout porpoised softly on the surface. A Suspender Midge had produced several fish up to two pounds in size, and earlier a large fish had stitched my leader through a thick mat of floating weed, forcing me to paddle over to the growth to retrieve it. The fish had been working a hatch of tiny midge pupae in the surface film, providing several hours of exciting fishing.

As it began to get dark, a warm, gusting wind started to blow, effectively ending a superb afternoon's fishing. My three companions, all of them from the Cape, had failed to capitalise on the frenzied surface action and between them had released only a few of the lake's residents. It had been a learning experience for them, as the lakes of the Western Cape do not provide anything like the consistent surface action of those in KwaZulu-Natal.

When the wind began to blow consistently and my companions in their float tubes displayed their obvious intention to head for the bank and call it a day, I realised that the midge fishing was truly over. Scanning the lake from my central position on the water, I could see no further movement. Suddenly a fish boiled some fifty yards away and, galvanised into action, I hastily hitched the midge pupa imitation to the hook keeper of my rod. Placing the rod at the rear of my float tube, I selected another heavier, stiffer-actioned rod equipped with a floating line. Clipping off the dragonfly nymph imitation which I had used to great effect that morning, I replaced it with a large, black, mylar-bodied Surface Muddler pattern. Once the pattern was securely tied to the stout 2X tippet, I coated it liberally with silicone paste and began to scan the choppy water.

Several minutes passed. Having seen no further surface action, I decided to prospect the water rather than wait for a fish to show itself at the surface. The large, wind-resistant pattern was difficult to cast into the strong wind, but I was satisfied with the twenty yards I was attaining. Once the fly settled in the water, I allowed it a few seconds to float around in the chop before starting a fast, erratic retrieve of a few rapid, short strips, interspersed with pauses of a few seconds. The pattern created a considerable disturbance on the water – in the same way that a popping bug does for bass

– and the sounds it made were clearly audible. Several casts produced no surface action, but I had great confidence in the fish-producing qualities of the pattern and continued to pitch it out into the strengthening wind.

Midway through the retrieve on a long cast, during one of several lengthy pauses, the water suddenly erupted behind the fly and a huge rainbow cleared the surface in a graceful, vaulting arc. Even in the inky gloom I could make out its massive bulk as it crashed down on the Surface Muddler, taking the fly as it re-entered the water. The disturbance caused by the trout sent ripples lapping onto the bank closest to me, and I knew I had hooked a very good fish.

The trout did not bolt frantically in a bid to escape but took line with powerful determination, jarring the rod as it peeled line off the reel. The rod bucked and bounced in my hand, but just as I settled down to do battle with the trout, the line suddenly went slack for no discernible reason.

Retrieving the fly-line, I discovered that the fly was missing. A closer examination of the end of the tippet revealed a tiny series of corkscrews in the nylon, the result of a knot tied in haste. Disgusted with my neglect, I reeled in the fly-line and made my way slowly towards the bank where my companions patiently waited.

Right *Richard Gild, a relative newcomer to the sport of fly-fishing, managed to land and release this hefty seven-and-a-half-pound Waterford rainbow while fishing in the vicinity of the inlet into the lake. He was broken up on the very next cast by a much larger fish.*

Exciting surface takes such as these are often experienced by anglers who have discovered the secrets of fishing large, buoyant attractor patterns on the surface. Often, when no other patterns will produce trout, I clinch on a large Surface Muddler and work it back erratically on the surface. The action is some of the most exciting of the season, as these patterns frequently entice trout to the surface that would otherwise not be prepared to rise.

I first discovered this exciting fishing technique over a decade ago during a particularly warm summer day on a lake in the Impendhle highlands. The lake was one of a series set on the terraces of a gently rolling hill. When we started prospecting the water in the late afternoon, the surface water was a warm twenty-four degrees Celsius. We managed a few trout on small damselfly nymph imitations fished slowly along the weed, but when small minnows started taking to the air along a weedbed on the fringes of the lake, my companion handed me a small but bushy Muddler Minnow pattern and advised me to try it. It saved the day, and despite the rain from a squall line which passed over the lake and provided some relief from the hot weather, we continued to take trout at the surface. An autopsy of a small trout proved my companion correct: it was crammed with small minnows, several of which I was able to return to the water.

I use the Surface Muddler in situations such as these when trout can be seen feeding on small minnows near or at the surface. This exciting form of fly-rod angling, that provides opportunities to take large trout at the surface, occurs far more often than most anglers suspect. Trout often herd minnows into the shallows where they attack the trapped prey. Minnows leaping wildly into the air are a sure sign that trout are in the vicinity, even though the trout may not be visible at the surface. A Surface Muddler pitched into the area of disturbance will often draw savage strikes from the feeding trout, and it pays to be armed with the correct tackle, as large fish can be hooked using these patterns.

The Surface Muddler is not effective only when trout are feeding on small minnows; it can also be used effectively to search the water when a lake appears devoid of fish. I have found that the best time to fish this pattern is during windy weather when the ruffled surface conceals the fly-line. A stripped fly-line can cause a reasonable disturbance on the surface, and choppy water helps to conceal this. Moreover, trout are often inclined to move to the surface during rainy, windy days because the upper layers become well oxygenated as a result of the disturbance caused by these elements.

I prefer to gear my tackle to the pattern being fished and almost always use the Surface Muddler on a stiff-actioned five-weight outfit, which makes the task of throwing these large, wind-resistant patterns much easier. The fly, the tippet and the leader should be well greased with a silicone floatant to ensure that it fishes on the surface and stays there throughout the retrieve. A floating line in conjunction with a reasonably long leader of twelve feet will ensure that the trout is not able to connect the fly to the disturbance caused by the stripped fly-line.

I cast the pattern out, wait a few seconds for it to settle in the water, then retrieve it with short, erratic strips, interspersed with long pauses of up to five seconds. This causes the pattern to move a lot of water, creating a surface disturbance in the same way a bass bug does, thereby attracting trout. This particular method of retrieval gives the impression of an injured minnow, and trout can attack the pattern at any point in the retrieve. I use 2X to 4X tippets, depending on the prevailing conditions, but even with these heavy tippets trout still may manage to break off the fly.

SURFACE MUDDLER

HOOK: Tiemco 300 or 5263, #6 – #10.

THREAD: 3/0 monocord, cream, light tan, black or red.
  (I like to use red thread on the butt.)

UNDERBODY (OPTIONAL): White or black foam.
  (This provides additional flotation for the pattern.)

OVERBODY: Mylar piping, colour of choice (my two standard
  colours are pearlescent and black).

WING: Black moose mane or deer hair.

COLLAR: Spun deer hair, natural or dyed black.

HEAD: Spun deer hair, natural or dyed black, clipped to shape.

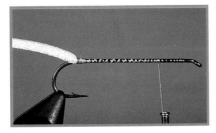

1. Take the thread to a position above the barb of the hook and tie in a flat section of foam. Return the thread to a position approximately one-third of the shank length from the eye of the hook.

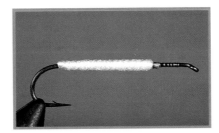

2. To form the underbody, wind the foam in overlapping turns towards the eye until the thread is reached, tie off the foam, half-hitch and trim the thread.

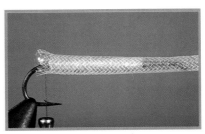

3. Attach the red thread above the barb of the hook. Remove the core from a section of mylar piping and push the mylar piping over the foam underbody.

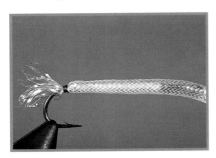

4. Tie down the mylar above the barb of the hook with the red thread, half-hitch and trim the thread. Trim the mylar so that the butts of the mylar are about equal to one-quarter of the hook shank.

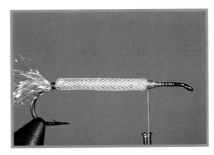

5. Re-attach the thread directly in front of the underbody, tie down the mylar overbody, and trim the excess.

6. Stack a thick clump of moose hair in a stacker and tie in the hair directly in front of the mylar overbody. The tips of the hair should extend up to the bend of the hook.

7. Stack a thick clump of deer hair in a hair stacker and, holding the stacked deer hair as shown, take three loose turns of thread around the hair.

8. Slowly pull the thread tight, allowing the hair to spin and flare out. Repeat steps 7 and 8 until the front third of the hook shank is covered in flared hair. Half-hitch and trim the thread.

9. Apply head cement to the thread wraps and to the wraps at the butt of the fly. Clip the flared deer hair into the shape shown; the larger the head and collar, the better the pattern will float.

Glossary

Attractor A general fly that does not represent a specific food form. This term is also used to denote patterns tied to represent baitfish or minnows.

Barb The small section of raised steel directly behind the hook point which serves to increase the fish-holding ability of a hook.

Dead-drift To allow the fly to drift without drag on or in the water at the same speed as the current.

Drag The downstream pull of water currents on a fly-line and leader which results in the fly being drawn downstream faster than the current on or in which it is drifting.

Dropper An additional fly tied to the leader or tippet above the point (lower) fly.

Dry fly A fly tied to represent the adult form of an insect and designed to float on the surface or, in certain cases (depending on the pattern), in the surface film.

Dubbing 1. The spinning of fur or other fibres onto the tying thread so that it can be wound around the hook shank to form the body, thorax and/or abdomen of a fly;
2. The natural fur or synthetic fibres used to form the body, thorax and/or abdomen of a fly.

Dun/subimago The first adult stage of a mayfly; at this stage it is sexually immature, usually has grey wings and is unable to feed as the mouthparts are atrophied.

Emerger 1. A term to describe an insect that moves up towards the water's surface before hatching into the adult stage, or, more specifically, the transitional stage between the aquatic nymph or pupa and the adult;
2. A fly fished in the surface film to represent this transitional stage.

Eye The small loop at the end of the hook shank, to which the leader or tippet is attached.

Floatant A chemical which may be applied to a dry fly or emerger pattern to ensure its buoyancy on the water. (Natural CDC oils from the preen glands of ducks also may be used as floatants.)

Gape/gap The space between the hook point and the shank.

Leader The solid or braided length of monofilament attached to the end of the fly-line.

Mend The repositioning of a fly-line after the cast has been made. This can be done after the cast is complete but before the line lands on the water (an in-the-air mend) or after the line has landed on the water (an on-the-water mend). Mends usually are associated with rivers and streams, but also can be used on stillwaters.

Nymph 1. A stage in the metamorphosis of an insect that comes after the egg but before the adult;
2. A fly fished as an imitation of a nymph, larva or pupa.

Opportunistic feeding A trait displayed by trout marked by a low to high availability of mixed food items upon which trout feed without discrimination.

Palmer To wind a hackle in a spiral through the body, thorax and/or abdomen of a fly.

Ribbing A strip of material wound in a spiral through the body, thorax and/or abdomen of a fly for a segmented effect.

Rise The upward movement of a trout through the water to the surface to intercept aquatic or terrestrial insects floating on the surface or in the surface film.

Selectivity A trait displayed by trout whereby they are able to select specific insects in preference to others – this often results in frustration for the fly-fisher when artificials are refused as a result of this behaviour.

Shank The section of a hook from directly behind the eye to above the barb.

Shuck The nymphal or pupal case or exoskeleton from which the adult insect emerges.

Spinner/imago The final, sexually mature adult stage of a mayfly. The wings are usually clear and, like the dun, it is unable to feed due to atrophied mouthparts.

Streamer A fly that is tied to represent baitfish and minnows – usually brightly coloured, flashy patterns.

Tippet The usually fine length of monofilament tied to the end of the leader, and to which the fly is tied.

Index

The page numbers set in **bold** type refer to photographs.

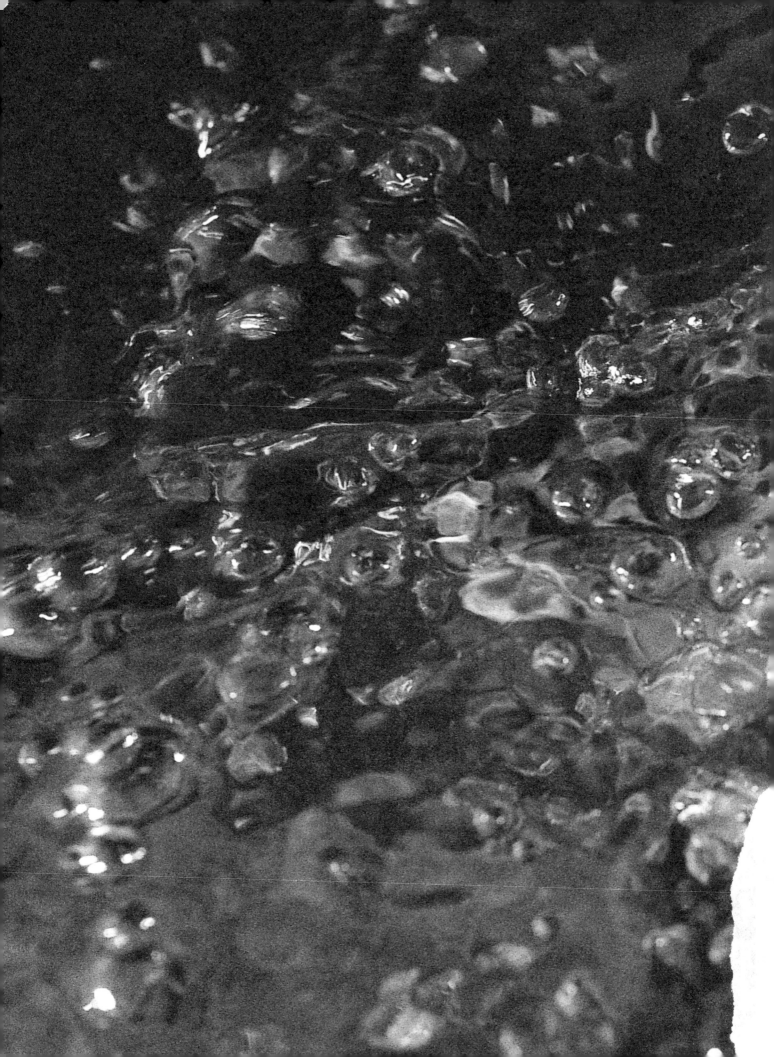